Sarawak

A geographical survey of a developing state

James C. Jackson, M.A., Ph.D.

Leverhulme Fellow in Commonwealth Studies,
University of Hull

UNIVERSITY OF LONDON PRESS LTD

GB SBN 340 09383 8

Copyright. ©1968 James C. Jackson
Illustrations copyright. ©1968 University of London Press Ltd

University of London Press Ltd
St Paul's House, Warwick Lane, London EC4

Printed and bound in Great Britain by
T. and A. Constable Ltd, Edinburgh

Contents

Maps and diagrams

Plates

Tables

Preface

Located on the north-west coast of Borneo in the centre of South-East Asia, Sarawak, with an area of 48,250 square miles, is almost as large as Malaya and nearly twice the size of Ceylon; it comprises 38 per cent of the total area of the Federation of Malaysia, of which it forms the largest constituent State, but it contains only one-tenth of the total population. For long, the name of this large, sparsely-peopled, jungle-clad State evoked only a romantic image as the domain of the White Rajahs and the land of the *Orang-utan*. During the 1960's, however, Sarawak featured prominently in the world press, bearing the brunt of Indonesian 'confrontation' and experiencing active internal Communist agitation.

The history of modern Sarawak began with the first visit of James Brooke to Kuching in 1839. At that time the area lay under the control of the Brunei Sultanate; antimony mining had begun over a decade earlier inland of Kuching and in the late 1830's the miners were in revolt against their Brunei overlords. Brooke returned to Kuching in 1840 and, in return for his help in suppressing this revolt, he was offered as his personal domain an area roughly equivalent to the present First Division; he was installed as the first White Rajah in 1841. Further territory was acquired from Brunei in 1853 and 1861 and in 1864 Britain recognized Sarawak as an independent State. James Brooke was succeeded as Rajah by his nephew Charles Brooke in 1868. During the reign of the second Rajah, which ended in 1917, large additions were made to the Sarawak Raj and with the transfer of Lawas in 1905 the State had extended to its present boundaries (Fig. 14); in the meantime, Sarawak was accorded British protection in 1888. Sarawak remained the personal domain of the Brookes until 1941. In that year the third Rajah, Sir Charles Vyner Brooke, introduced a new constitution ending this period of absolute power and giving responsibility to a new Council Negri, or State Council. Before the end of 1941, however, the whole of Sarawak was occupied by the Japanese

A*

who surrendered in September 1945. The third Rajah returned to Sarawak the following year; despite some local opposition, he decided that Sarawak should come under the British Crown and in July 1946 it became a Crown Colony. Sarawak remained a Crown Colony until 1963, when it joined the new Federation of Malaysia.

Much was written on this State in the nineteenth century but, apart from detailed studies of the Chinese, Iban, Land Dyak and Melanau communities undertaken in the late 1940's and early 1950's under the auspices of the Colonial Social Science Research Council, there is little available for the more recent period except various government annual reports, and for most departments these have not appeared since 1962. There is a complete lack of a comprehensive survey of the State on which students can rely as a guide. In connection with my interest in the history of agriculture in the area, the University of Hull kindly provided a grant for me to visit Borneo in March 1966. This enabled me to tour several parts of Sarawak and to acquire as up-to-date an impression as was possible in the time available. Subsequently, material collected from a variety of sources was combined with field observations to produce the text that follows. Many readers will recognize that the basic organization owes much to *Burmese Economic Life* by J. Russell Andrus and to *Land and People in Nigeria* by K. M. Buchanan and J. C. Pugh;[1] others may feel that I have adopted a mixture of the approaches of the German and the Frenchman in the late Professor Debenham's story, and that the result warrants condemnation on this score.[2] The basic purpose of this book, however, is to present a comprehensive up-to-date survey of the geography of Sarawak to fill the gap in the material readily available to undergraduates, teacher-training college students and others interested in this Bornean State.

I have endeavoured to avoid the pointlessness that sometimes characterizes geographic studies of this type by taking social and economic development as a theme around which to weave the text. In a newly-independent, developing state this is clearly a safe approach because social and economic progress is the over-riding interest of politicians and laymen alike, but it also permits the logical introduction

---

[1] J. Russell Andrus, *Burmese Economic Life*, Stanford, Stanford University Press, 1948, and K. M. Buchanan and J. C. Pugh, *Land and People in Nigeria*, London, University of London Press, 1955.
[2] See F. Debenham, *The Use of Geography*, London, English Universities Press, 1957, pp. 15-17.

of much historical information essential to an understanding of both the patterns and processes of development. Moreover, any study of this type must consider past and present government policy, because, to a large extent, land use is determined by tradition on the one hand and official social and economic development policies on the other. Finally, timing suggests the desirability of such a theme for in so far as is possible the text presents a survey of the situation in 1965 and outlines the major geographical impediments to further development; it will, therefore, provide a benchmark against which to measure the success of the First Malaysia Plan, scheduled to run from 1966 to 1970.

During my stay in Sarawak I received unstinted help from very many people and my sincere thanks are extended to all; in particular, however, I wish to record my thanks to Mr J. R. D. Wall, formerly Soil Surveyor with the Department of Agriculture, and his wife for their very generous hospitality and to Mr P. L. Leonard, Agricultural Economist, Department of Agriculture, Mr J. S. Tupholme, Assistant Rubber Director, Department of Agriculture, and Mr G. K. Nair, Chief Statistician, for their ready willingness to devote their valuable time to discussion. Of my former colleagues at the University of Malaya Prof. D. W. Fryer was always ready to provide advice and information; Dr J. G. Lockwood and Mr R. J. Eyles kindly suggested amendments to Chapter 1; for their aid I am grateful. Finally, this book is dedicated to the two people who made the effort worthwhile: to my wife, for her patience and encouragement and for her painstaking and sometimes ruthless criticism of points of style and interpretation, and to our daughter, as a future reminder of her Malaysian background. For all errors of fact or of judgment I accept full responsibility.

J.C.J.

Petaling Jaya,
Selangor   June, 1966

Note.—Throughout the text values are quoted in Malaysian dollars. M$1=2s. 4d. sterling.

To Suk-Han and Karen Anne-Marie

1 The Environmental Setting

The under-developed countries of the world are embarking on programmes of rapid development aimed at providing for their peoples
the economic and social standards already attained by the developed
countries. In these states the selection of suitable means of accelerating
the pace of development depends ultimately on their human and
physical assets and potentialities. Yet it is precisely in under-developed
areas such as Sarawak that least is known about the environmental
setting; there is no fund of acquired knowledge on which to draw and
reconnaissance investigations proceed hand in hand with planning. In
Sarawak detailed geological mapping is primarily a post-1950 development and soil surveying to a large extent a post-1960 development.
Initial topographic mapping is still in progress and, indeed, some parts
of Sarawak remain largely unexplored. Only four climatological
stations exist, together with thirty-seven rainfall stations. These are
concentrated heavily in western Sarawak or along the coast and twenty-
four of them were first established between 1948 and 1954; only
eleven began recording prior to 1930. The following pages seek merely
to paint a broad picture of the environmental setting within which
the social and economic development of Sarawak is proceeding and to
highlight, where possible, the developmental problems it poses.

Geology and Geomorphology

The first geological survey of western Sarawak was made by Hiram
Williams in 1845. Thereafter during the nineteenth century several
travellers made geological observations, notably A. R. Wallace and
Odoardo Beccari, and later employees of the Borneo Company Limited
published accounts of prospecting activities in this area which were
supplemented by the geological work of others in the 1920's and 1930's.
Elsewhere in Sarawak geological exploration began on a large scale

after the opening of the Miri oilfield in 1910, but from the 1920's to the 1940's this proceeded irregularly and mostly on a limited scale. Since the Second World War, however, the oil companies have intensified their geological exploration work very considerably.

In 1949 a Government Geological Survey Department was established for the British Territories in Borneo. This has been extremely active in field investigation, photo-geological interpretation and the publication of its findings, and there has been close co-operation between government and oil company geologists. During the 1950's a series of geological memoirs based on reconnaissance surveys appeared covering the whole of Sarawak and culminating in the publication of *The Geology of Sarawak, Brunei and the Western Part of North Borneo* in 1960.[1] When Dr. Posewitz published his 'Geological Sketch Map of Borneo' in 1892 the whole of Sarawak was geologically either 'but slightly known' or 'unknown';[2] by 1960 a map of the geology of Sarawak at a scale of 1:500,000 had appeared. Nevertheless detailed investigation continues and new discoveries may modify current interpretations.

The greater part of Sarawak is geologically very young, and well over four-fifths of the State comprises Tertiary and Quaternary sediments (Fig. 2). Indeed, Sarawak contains one of the fullest successions of Tertiary deposits in the world and these have attained tremendous composite thicknesses in the case of one formation of 35,000-50,000 feet. Lithologically these sedimentaries show very considerable internal variation and often dip steeply, if not almost vertically, particularly in central Sarawak; in consequence, sandstones, greywackes, shales and siltstones frequently outcrop in quick succession producing a marked series of ridges and valleys. These geological features are largely the result of geosynclinal conditions and it seems most appropriate to summarize the geological evolution of the State rather than to present a simplified descriptive regional geology.

Geological evolution
Borneo forms part of an extension of continental Asia known as

---

[1] P. Liechti *et al.*, *The Geology of Sarawak, Brunei and the Western Part of North Borneo*, Kuching, Government Printer, 1960, Geological Survey Department British Territories in Borneo, Bulletin 3.
[2] T. Posewitz, *Borneo: Its Geology and Mineral Resources*, London, Edward Stanford, 1892.

Figure 1   Administrative boundaries.

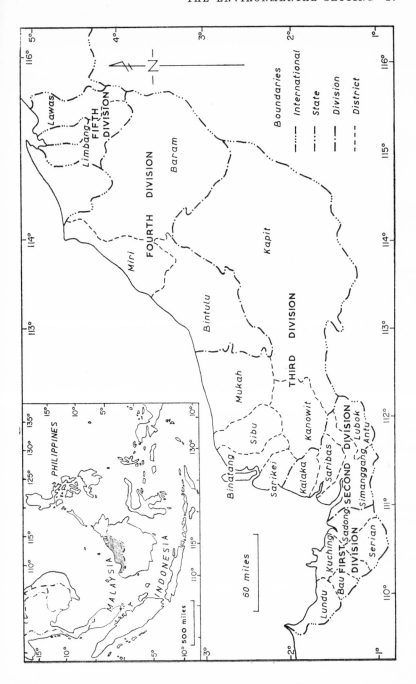

Sundaland or the Sunda Shield.[3] The core of this continental mass remains exposed in western Kalimantan and in Sarawak west of the Batang Lupar and comprises mainly Palaeozoic schists and meta-morphosed volcanic rocks largely concealed by a thick cover of later Mesozoic and Tertiary sediments in west Sarawak. Nevertheless, this is the only part of the State where rocks of pre-Cretaceous age outcrop (Fig. 2).

Tectonically active throughout Palaeozoic and Mesozoic times, the Sunda Shield has since been a relatively stable area. The oldest rocks in west Sarawak are schistose sedimentaries of pre-Upper Carboniferous age. Subsequently limestones, cherts and shales were laid down in Upper Carboniferous and Lower Permian times and, after fairly intense folding, shales, sandstones and conglomerates were deposited during the Upper Triassic; concurrently, volcanic rocks were extruded in the Serian area. Local subsidence to the south and south-west of Kuching resulted in the deposition of limestone in late Jurassic times and, at the beginning of the Cretaceous, this was succeeded by the deposition of shale, sandstone and conglomerate. Intrusive igneous activity was widespread in west Sarawak during the Upper Cretaceous and at the same time marine deposition gave way to predominantly deltaic sedimentation. This continued into the early Eocene in the Kuching-Lundu area and, spreading eastwards, deltaic sediments accumulated during late Eocene and Oligocene times along the Indonesian border in the Silantek area. A considerable number of stocks, sills and dykes were intruded into these various marine and deltaic sediments, possibly in the mid-Miocene. These are of considerable significance because most of the important metallic deposits in west Sarawak are associated with them, particularly where they are intruded into limestone as in the Bau area. The youngest igneous rock in west Sarawak is an andesite lava at Sematan, possibly of early Quaternary age, and important as a source of bauxite.

---

[3] Liechti *et al.*, op. cit., pp. 2-5 and 291-302; R. A. M. Wilson, *Annual Report of the Geological Survey, Borneo Region Malaysia, 1964*, Kuching, Government Printer, 1965, pp. 76-82.

Figure 2(A) Northwest Borneo Geosyncline. (After Liechti *et. al.*, op. cit., Fig 1.) (B) Geology. Based on 'Mineral Resources of Sarawak and Sabah, Malaysia', (1:2,000,000), 3rd edition, 1965, with the permission of the Acting Director, Geological Survey, Borneo Region, Malaysia.)

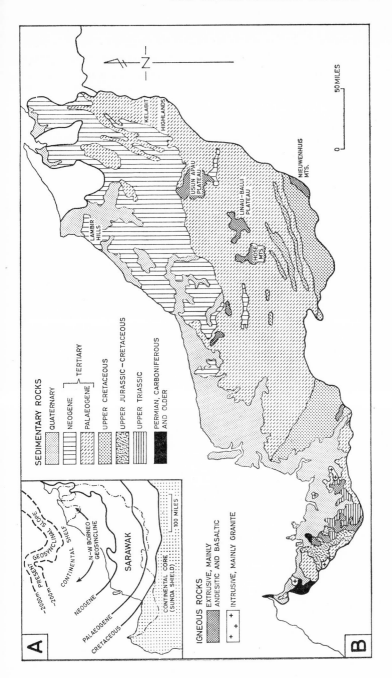

A

- – – –2000m PRESENT GEOSYNCLINAL SLOPE
- – – –200m CONTINENTAL SHELF
- N–W BORNEO GEOSYNCLINE
- NEOGENE
- PALAEOGENE
- CRETACEOUS
- SARAWAK
- CONTINENTAL CORE (SUNDA SHIELD)
- 100 MILES

SEDIMENTARY ROCKS

- QUATERNARY
- NEOGENE } TERTIARY
- PALAEOGENE
- UPPER CRETACEOUS
- UPPER JURASSIC–CRETACEOUS
- UPPER TRIASSIC
- PERMIAN, CARBONIFEROUS AND OLDER

IGNEOUS ROCKS

- EXTRUSIVE, MAINLY ANDESTIC AND BASALTIC
- INTRUSIVE, MAINLY GRANITE

KELABIT HIGHLANDS

USUN APAU PLATEAU

LAMBIR HILLS

LINAU–BALUI PLATEAU

HOSE MTS.

NIEUWENHUIS MTS.

N

0   50 MILES

B

The northern flank of the continental core was submerged during the Jurassic, and in late Cretaceous times a geosyncline or marine trough, known as the North-West Borneo Geosyncline, developed extending from the Lupar valley to Mount Kinabalu in a crescent concave northwards and including most of Sarawak (Fig. 2). The deepest part of the geosyncline lay adjacent to the continental foreland and, in late Cretaceous times, this area therefore experienced the high mobility characteristic of such a central belt. Towards the outer or northern part these conditions gave way to the more stable conditions typical of the marginal shelf-like character of the periphery of a geosyncline, and great thicknesses of sediments were laid down during most of the Palaeocene and Eocene. The first folding occurred in late Eocene times and affected mainly the Upper Cretaceous and Eocene deposits of central Sarawak. Folding was most intense close to the continental core and decreased towards the north and north-west. In these marginal areas extensive limestones began to develop chiefly at Melinau on the western side of the Mulu Massif in the Fifth Division.

The axis of the geosyncline migrated steadily north and north-west towards the present coastline during Tertiary times. There is, in fact, abundant evidence of almost continuous subsidence in north-west Borneo and enormous composite thicknesses of sediments of all descriptions were laid down as deposition gradually shifted in accordance with the movement of the geosynclinal axis.

Deposition apparently ceased by late Miocene times in almost the whole of central Sarawak, the exception being the Balingian Basin which received a thick sequence of late Miocene and younger sediments. Central Sarawak is therefore built largely of deposits of Palaeogene age comprising mainly hard sandstones, greywackes, siltstones, shales and slates; the major structural trend lines conform closely to the crescent shape of the geosynclinal axis running roughly west-east in the lower and middle Rejang. In northern Sarawak, on the other hand, deposition continued into the Pliocene and there is some evidence to suggest a Miocene structural phase that caused warping and led to the formation of isolated later Tertiary coastal basins, as for example the Lambir Hills to the south of Miri, each of which received huge thicknesses of late Miocene and Pliocene sediments. The greater part of northern Sarawak thus consists of a very wide range of sedimentaries of Neogene or late Tertiary age (Fig. 2).

During the periods of Pliocene and Quaternary sedimentation extensive volcanism occurred in the folded Palaeogene strata of interior central Sarawak. Volcanic eruptions and subsequent basaltic extrusions affected the Hose Mountains, the Usun Apau Plateau, the Linau-Balui Plateau and the Nieuwenhuis Mountains resulting in formations consisting of an andesite-dacite-basalt association. Further folding occurred in Pliocene and Pleistocene times; this brought virtually the whole of Sarawak above sea-level and initiated a period of severe erosion in post-Tertiary times.

Geomorphological evolution

Three major erosion cycles are recognized in the post-Tertiary evolution of Sarawak.[4] The first, the Peneplanation Cycle, probably occurred in late Pliocene or early Pleistocene times. Regional peneplanation occurred which was almost certainly polycyclic or composite, and this resulted in a general truncation of the Tertiary structure. Today remnants of the peneplain exist as truncated Tertiary hills often topped by a cover of sand and gravel; near the coast these hills are usually about 200-300 feet above sea-level but their height increases rapidly inland and they reach 3,000-4,500 feet in the interior of Kapit District. The strongest evidence of peneplanation is the altitudinal uniformity of the hills which form a 'summit plain' both in the coastal belt and the interior. This feature is marked in the Kelabit Highlands but is best preserved in the area bounded by the Hose Mountains, the Usun Apau Plateau and the Indonesian border, where the general summit height averages 4,000-5,000 feet; the remarkably constant height of the Klingkang and Bungo Ranges in western Sarawak appears to provide corroborative evidence. Clearly the highest peaks in Sarawak, including Gunong Murud (7,950 feet) and Gunong Mulu (7,798 feet), formed monadnocks throughout this cycle. Subsequently the peneplain was warped and the interior was uplifted considerably.

The resulting rejuvenation marks the beginning of a second cycle, the Jerudong Cycle, probably in Middle Pleistocene times. This lengthy cycle ran into full maturity, producing a generally smooth topography; a system of wide, mature valleys developed and these survive today as 'medium high' terraces formed mainly of sand usually 30 to 100 feet above present sea-level along the coast and which also occur, although less well preserved, at higher levels farther inland. Close to the Indonesian border in the Kelabit Highlands and in Kapit District the upper sections of the valleys remain largely unaltered by more recent erosion cycles.

[4] Liechti *et al.*, op. cit., pp. 303-321.

The present cycle, or Alluvial Cycle, may comprise three sub-cycles. It was probably initiated by a fall in sea-level of about 250 feet in the late Pleistocene as a result of which towards the coast the valleys were incised to a depth much greater than at present. Later, the sea-level rose by about 170-200 feet and the deposition of sand, sandy clay and gravel occurred in these new deep valleys. After a time, the sea-level fell again by about 15-20 feet; the former alluvial level was dissected and partly removed and is probably represented by the present 'low' terraces of the Rejang delta and the Balingian-Mukah area. This fall initiated the present sub-cycle of rapid coastal aggradation which is chiefly the result of deltaic deposition by the major rivers, the Baram and the Rejang. On these geologically recent alluvial and tidal flats, extensive peat swamps have formed in the last four or five thousand years.

Relief and Drainage

Essentially Sarawak comprises three topographic units (Fig. 3). A plain of swampy alluvium, generally rising but a few feet above sea-level, extends along most of the coast, narrowing considerably between the mouths of the Kemena and Suai Rivers and almost disappearing between Sibuti and Miri, but attaining a width of 50 miles or more in the lower Baram, Rejang, Saribas, Lupar and Sadong valleys. In south-west Sarawak the smooth expanse of alluvium is broken in places by isolated mountains and mountain groups close to the coast such as Gunong Sarapi (2,988 feet) and Gunong Gading (2.950 feet). Beaches consist largely of mud and only occasionally of sand; coastal waters are very shallow and the existence of bars at most river mouths hinders the development of ports. These low-lying, badly drained coastal plains occupy one-fifth of the total land area. Rapid aggradation continues and in places the coastal plains are extending seawards at an estimated rate of more than thirty feet per year.

The coastal plain gives way to a broad belt of rugged hill country. Most of this is less than 1,000 feet but its general height increases towards the interior. In much of central and northern Sarawak this zone is built of tightly-folded Tertiary sandstones and shales. Differ-

Figure 3 Relief.

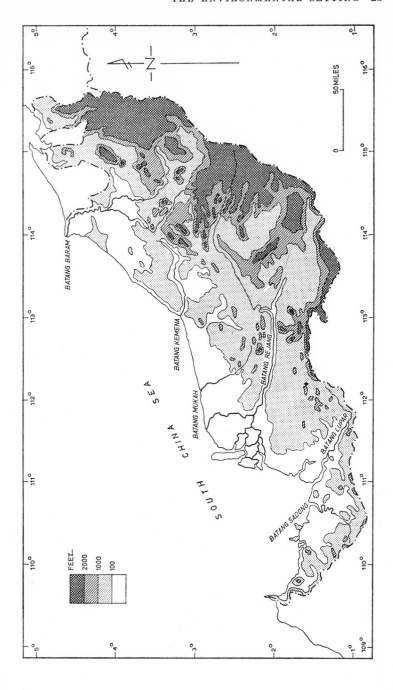

ential erosion has produced a dissected area of long, steep, high ridges alternating with narrow valleys whose alignment owes much to structural trend lines determined by the shape of the geosynclinal axis. Towards the north the very thick successions of massive younger Tertiary sandstones dominate the topography, forming a series of steep scarps and hogbacks whereas subdued, dissected lowlands occur where young Tertiary shales predominate from which rise sandstone ridges. Mountains bounded by cliffs characterize the main limestone formations as at Gunong Melinau and Bukit Subis. The large plateaux of Usun Apau and Linau-Balui are formed of young Tertiary and Quaternary lavas as are the more dissected Hose and Nieuwenhuis Mountains. In western Sarawak the oldest rocks form low, dissected country from which rise steep limestone hills and several sandstone ridges. The continuous sequence of ridges and valleys characteristic of much of this belt severely inhibits road construction, and communication lines necessarily focus on the rivers. Clearly the Iban system of shifting cultivation is well suited to local topography (see Chapter 3).

This belt of rugged hill country merges into the mountainous area of the interior of the Third, Fourth and Fifth Divisions. Here the boundary with Indonesia follows the watershed of a long and irregular mountain range forming part of the spine of Borneo Island. Much of this boundary is unsurveyed; the almost continuous cloud cover makes aerial photographic interpretation difficult, part of the area remains virtually unexplored and only preliminary reconnaissance mapping is available. Most of this interior mountain range lies above 4,000 feet, yet, except in the north-east, few peaks exceed 6,000 feet; basically it comprises irregular masses of dissected highland with occasional peaks. Interspersed among these are the broad alluvium-filled mature valley remnants of the Jerudong Cycle. Today these are settled and cultivated by hill peoples as is the upper Kelalan valley in the Fifth Division.

Sarawak is characterized by a multitude of rivers and streams. Apart from the scores of short minor streams, all the main rivers rise close to the Indonesian border and flow westwards or north-westwards to the South China Sea. The headwaters of most of these occupy broad, mature valleys formed during the Jerudong Cycle and as yet little affected by later erosional cycles. In contrast, in the central belt of rugged hill-country valleys are typically youthful and are experiencing the effects of the present erosion cycle. Here rivers flow swiftly, often through steep gorges and over numerous dangerous rapids as in the case of the Trusan, Limbang, Baram and Rejang. When they emerge on to the broad, flat coastal plain, however, they meander sluggishly and, particularly in the Rejang delta, they divide into numerous distributaries.

The Rejang is the longest Sarawak river with a total length of 350 miles. The course of its lower and middle reaches is clearly determined by the regional strike but its upper reaches show the effects of local volcanic activity. In the north, the Baram and the Limbang follow irregular courses and were affected by the Pleistocene uplift. In the west, the Saribas, Lupar and Sadong each have wide funnel-shaped estuaries which contrast markedly with the extensive deltas of the Rejang and Baram; the lower and middle reaches of both the Saribas and Lupar follow the regional strike. Rivers have always played a fundamental role in local life: they remain the chief lines of communication for much of the population, and all settlements, whether of sedentary or shifting peoples, are sited close to these, the arteries of Sarawak.

Climate

Located in the humid tropics between 0°50′ N and 5° N, Sarawak has a climate characterized by heavy rainfall, uniformly high temperatures and high relative humidity. There is little variation in the average length of day throughout the year but the high incidence of cloud reduces the mean number of sunshine hours received daily to between four and seven hours over most of the State. In consequence, temperatures rarely exceed 100°F (37·8°C); indeed, at mean sea-level they range between 72°F (22·2°C) and 88°F (31·1°C) with a mean annual temperature of 78°F (25·6°C). Temperatures vary little throughout the year and average monthly temperatures show a range of only about 4°F (2·2°C). The diurnal range, however, is much greater and in most coastal areas averages about 10°F (5·6°C) rising to as much as 20°F (11·1°C) in the interior. As is to be expected, temperatures are generally lower in the mountainous interior where at night they can fall below 60°F (15·6°C). At dawn mean relative humidity over the year is 98 per cent and at 2 p.m. 70 per cent.[5]

Practically the whole of Sarawak has a mean annual rainfall of over 100 inches and most of the State receives 120-160 inches per year

[5] J. Seal, 'Rainfall and Sunshine in Sarawak', *Sarawak Museum Journal*, Vol. VIII, No. 11, 1958, p. 500.

(Fig. 4). Figures in excess of this are recorded in the Kuching-Serian-Simanggang area, in the mountainous country bordering Indonesia and in the upper Baram valley. Rapid heavy downpours in these interior areas have marked effects on the rivers which rise suddenly as much as 50 feet above their normal level. The driest parts of the State are the Rejang delta, the extreme western tip of the First Division and an area in the Fifth Division between Bukit Pagan and Bukit Batu Lawi, each of which receives a mean annual rainfall of less than 120 inches.

There appear to be significant variations around these means, however, which merely emphasizes the fact that the climate is not as markedly uniform regionally, seasonally or over a period of years as is generally supposed. Thus the mean annual rainfall at Miri is 124 inches, but it varied from 167·5 inches in 1937 to 94 inches in 1940; similarly at Kuching, where the mean is 158 inches per year, only 109 inches were recorded in 1914 as against 226 inches in 1882. Wide variations of monthly rainfall have also been recorded over the years in all parts of Sarawak. The wettest month in Kuching is January with a mean of 26 inches, but this has varied from 69 inches in 1881 to 8 inches in 1950.

Usually the climatic year is divided on the basis of the distribution of monthly rainfall. Four seasons are recognized in Sarawak and their differing characteristics owe much to the location of the State on the north-west coast of Borneo Island. However, it must be emphasized that these seasons are most clearly apparent in coastal areas, particularly in the west, and that, towards the interior, seasonality is far less noticeable.

From the beginning of October until February is the period of the north-east monsoon, known locally as the *landas* season. This is characterized by generally persistent strong north-easterly winds, and it represents the main rainfall peak for the State as a whole (Fig. 5). The north-east monsoon blows fairly steadily across the South China Sea but once south of latitude 5°N its average speed decreases. Disturbances moving down the South China Sea bring heavy rain to the exposed coastal belt of Sarawak and many coastal stations record monthly totals in excess of 20 inches for December and January. The north-east monsoon has its greatest effects on Sarawak west of the Batang Mukah, and coastal stations in this area receive nearly three-fifths of their mean annual rainfall in the months of October to February inclusive (Fig. 5).

Figure 4   Mean annual rainfall.

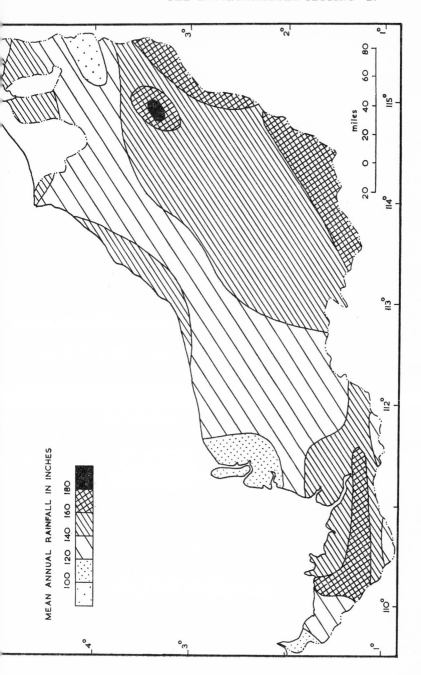

MEAN ANNUAL RAINFALL IN INCHES

100 120 140 160 180

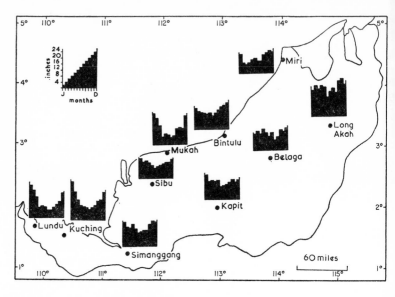

Figure 5   Mean monthly rainfall for selected stations.

From April to July or August is the period of the south-west monsoon. This is characterized by south-westerly winds which are feebler and less persistent than those experienced during the north-east monsoon. Rainfall is considerably lower over much of the State, the mean monthly total falling as low as 7·5 inches in July at Kuching, and most comes in the afternoons between 3 p.m. and 6 p.m. Rainless months are extremely unusual but occasional dry periods of three to four weeks occur and these can cause considerable harm to crops, a danger heightened by the fact that periods of bright sunshine are longer in this season than during the north-east monsoon; on the other hand they provide ideal burning conditions for the shifting cultivators. At Miri during this period the heaviest rain comes from thunderstorms of sharp intensity in the early hours after midnight. During this season the heaviest rain is experienced in the interior; in coastal areas it is a relatively dry season (Fig. 5).

Two shorter transitional seasons of about eight weeks each occur between the monsoons. During the first, extending through late February, March and early April, rainfall declines from the north-east monsoon peak whereas during the second, extending through most of

August and September it begins to rise again from the south-west monsoon minimum. With few exceptions it is the hilly interior of the Third and Fourth Divisions that receives most rain in these seasons; indeed, it is only at the height of the north-east monsoon that these interior areas are not the wettest in Sarawak.

Climatic conditions of the type experienced in Sarawak go far to explain its particular geographic characteristics. Constantly high temperatures coupled with high humidity foster the proliferation of fungal and bacterial diseases and continuous insect activity with direct effects on humans, livestock and crops. Traditional house designs and settlement sites clearly reflect local climatic conditions often in a way not recognizable in modern suburban development. Soils are generally poor, being deficient in nutrients, and, when exposed, they suffer rapid erosion and oxidization of organic material; in fact, rain normally falls as intense localized showers which can create immediate erosional, flooding, drainage and silting problems. To a very considerable extent the luxuriant natural vegetation is dependent upon climatic conditions and, moreover, the climate imposes certain restrictions on the possibilities of agricultural development and diversification.

Soils

Adequate knowledge of soils and their potentialities is essential for successful agricultural development. Yet, as with most aspects of the physical environment, soil survey remains in the exploratory stage in Sarawak, and the Soils Division of the Department of Agriculture only began work late in 1958. At that date about 1 per cent of the total land area had been covered by detailed or reconnaissance soil surveys. Since 1960, however, the Division has become increasingly active in providing a sound basis for the rising tempo of agricultural development and settlement schemes. By late 1962 information was available on the soils of almost one-fifth of the State, and the first approximation of a classification of Sarawak soils had appeared.

Soil survey in Sarawak now follows established methods suited to local conditions and requirements, and it takes one of three forms. Detailed surveys are undertaken in connection with drainage and irrigation projects, the *padi* and coconut planting schemes and the siting of agricultural research stations. Reconnaissance surveys, involving the combination of intensive air photo interpretation and ground checks along significantly located lines, are produced as a basis for Divisional Development Plans: these provide a broad assessment of general agricultural potential to aid in planning new road routes and to indicate large blocks of land suitable for Rubber Planting Scheme 'B'. Finally, rapid air photo reconnaissance surveys, unaided by field checks, are used to produce generalized land capability and suitability maps as the basis for planning in large undeveloped and inaccessible areas. In consequence, some information on soils is now available for much of Sarawak, although it is most reliable for the more accessible areas and for those with apparently the greatest immediate developmental potential.

It is generally recognized that the luxuriant forests of the humid tropics are not an indication of fertile soils and the majority of Sarawak soils are poor and often acid. They fall into five main groups, the differences depending on parent material, topography and the soil-forming processes involved.[6]

Much of the State has a cover of residual soils derived principally from the Tertiary sands and shales in the rugged hill country. These are characteristically thin with high acidity and low fertility, and they are all leached to a varying degree depending on the type of parent material and the local landforms. Most of these comprise yellow latosols a soil-type that occurs widely in South-East Asia. These develop on the gentler slopes of the hilly areas and are derived from mixed sandstone and shale formations. They are yellow clay-loams and clays low in plant nutrients, strongly acid, sometimes quite deep on gentler slopes and generally well drained. At present these soils are chiefly used for shifting cultivation but over large areas they are suited to rubber although the nature of the terrain and the dearth of roads would make planting expensive. On the steeper slopes of these same hillsides develop thinner, poorer soils known as lithosols; often planted with hill-*padi*, these have little agricultural value and are best left under forest, because clearance can promote severe erosion. Together these two soil-types occupy five-eighths or more of the total land area of Sarawak. Within this same broad group of residual sedimentary soils are the red and yellow podsols, also widespread in South-East Asia. These are derived from more sandy parent material in well-drained localities on gently undulating land and are highly susceptible to erosion. They are strongly acid loams or sandy-loams with the

---

[6] *Sarawak: Annual Report of the Department of Agriculture, 1959*, Kuching, Government Printer, 1960, pp. 23-24.

typical bleaching below the topsoil and are of even lower fertility than the related yellow latosols. They are relatively widespread in western Sarawak and may occupy one-eighth of the total land area. Used to some extent for hill-*padi* with a long fallow period, they have a low agricultural potential.

Small patches of residual soils derived from igneous rocks also occur, and despite their scattered nature they are of considerable agricultural significance. The most important are the fertile strong-brown deep, well-structured clay-loams derived from basalt and andesite which appear as patches along the Kuching-Serian road. Other soils derived from granite and basalt occur to a limited extent but they are generally more inaccessible.

Podsolic soils formed on the beach and terrace remnants of earlier erosion cycles are known locally as *kerangas* soils. These consist of a white sandy soil resting on stiff unconsolidated deposits of sand, gravel and clay with the typical leached horizon below a surface accumulation of undecayed matter. At a depth of one or two feet there is often a hard, very acid pan of sand cemented by organic matter which can impede drainage. *Kerangas* soils are sandy, extremely acid and generally infertile. They are commonly found in the drier areas between the coast and the peat swamps and on flat, undulating country inland; they also occur as islands in peat swamps and mangroves and at relatively high levels on ridges and hill-tops as in the upper Koyan valley on Mount Dulit and in the Gunong Selang Forest Reserve. They have very little agricultural potential, although where conveniently located they are not unsuited to intensive methods of Chinese market-gardening.[7]

Recently deposited coastal and riverine alluvial soils are widespread on the deltas and coastal flats and appear as narrow strips often half a mile or more wide along the valleys. These form low humic gleys characterized by a high water-table and periodic flooding and are predominantly grey to brownish clays. On the terrace margins they have increasingly coarser and sandier textures and merge into podsolic soils, whereas on the margins of basins they grade into semi-bog and muck soils with an increasing organic content. These alluvial soils vary but in general have better than average fertility by Sarawak standards. Throughout much of the State they are already devoted to wet-*padi*, and poor drainage inhibits the cultivation of most other crops.

[7] F. G. Browne, 'The Kerangas Lands of Sarawak', *Malayan Forester*, Vol. XV, 2, 1952, pp. 61-73.

Peat swamps cover twelve per cent of the total land area. These coastal and deltaic swamps are frequently deep and have a convex surface flattening out towards the centre. The greatest depths of peat occur in the inland rather than the coastal swamps and they overlay a stiff clay, probably of mangrove origin. It is believed that, as the coast extended seaward, the mangroves that had developed on the coastal silts and clays were progressively replaced by peat which increased in depth as the extending and aggrading rivers rose above the original mangrove level, a process that has been going on for the last 5,000 years. The water-table invariably lies close to the swamp surface and during the wet season may rise above it. The peats are characterized by complete stagnation of drainage indicated by the presence of undecomposed or semi-decomposed woody material at all levels. These organic soils are extremely acid, chemically poor and provide poor root foundations. Without drainage they are totally unsuitable for almost all crops except the sago palm. It is generally agreed that the highly developed peats are best left under their natural forest cover to be exploited for timber, because the work necessary to fit them for cultivation would be enormously expensive. The shallower peripheries of some of the domed swamps might be drained, as was proposed for the margins of the Tinjar-Baram swamp in 1956. But to be effective, peat drainage must be integrated on a large scale, and it appears unlikely that much will be done in the foreseeable future.[8]

Vegetation

Three-quarters of Sarawak is still covered by primary forest. High temperatures and an annual rainfall of 100-180 inches promote the continuous and luxuriant plant growth that has earned for Borneo the epithet 'the evergreen island'. Nevertheless, location, soil type and altitude produce marked vegetation zones varying from extensive stretches of swamp forest on the coastal plains to the montane forest on the Indonesian border (Fig. 6).

Mangrove and *nipah* palm forests develop on tidal swamps in sheltered

[8] J. A. R. Anderson, 'The Structure and Development of the Peat Swamps of Sarawak and Brunei', *Journal of Tropical Geography*, Vol. 18, 1964, pp. 7-16.

Figure 6   Land use and forest types. (Based on 'Land Use Map of Sarawak', (1:1,500,000), Sarawak Series NC 11, 1957, with the permission of the Director of Lands and Surveys, Sarawak.)

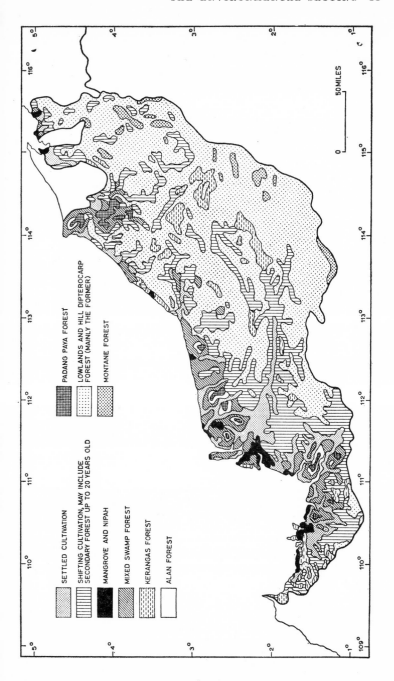

SETTLED CULTIVATION

SHIFTING CULTIVATION, MAY INCLUDE
SECONDARY FOREST UP TO 20 YEARS OLD

MANGROVE AND NIPAH

MIXED SWAMP FOREST

KERANGAS FOREST

ALAN FOREST

PADANG PAYA FOREST

LOWLANDS AND HILL DIPTEROCARP
FOREST (MAINLY THE FORMER)

MONTANE FOREST

50 MILES
0

places where aggradation is still active. In particular they occur at the mouths of the Sarawak, Rejang and Trusan Rivers and contain a succession of plant types ranging from those representing the pioneer stage on newly-formed mud banks at the seaward end to a vegetation closely resembling inland forest on the landward side. These forests comprise mainly species of *Rhizophera*, or *bako*, capable of growing in heavy saline clays and raised on stilt roots forming an impenetrable tangle; they also include *nipah* palm (*Nipa fruticans*), and *nibong* (*Oncosperma filamentosa*), in addition to very poor forest on the drier parts of the swamps. They occupy less than 2 per cent of the total forest area but are important as a source of firewood, charcoal and formerly cutch, the extract of mangrove bark used in tanning and dyeing. Thatch is manufactured from the *nipah* palm which is also used to produce a variety of other products including sugar and cigarette papers. In general, cultivation in these areas is impracticable because of periodic flooding by salt water.

Nearly one-sixth of the forest area is occupied by peat swamp forest. This is widespread between the Sadong and Saribas Rivers, covers a broad coastal strip from Kuala Paloh to Bintulu and occupies much of the lower Baram valley. The peat swamp forest includes several distinct sub-types apparently related to the age and state of development of the raised bogs. The most extensive and most important of these is known as mixed swamp forest which occurs on loose, relatively shallow peat on swamps of comparatively recent origin near the coast or as a peripheral zone on more ancient bogs farther inland. The peat swamp forest comprises trees of considerable commercial value and because of its accessibility is the chief source of Sarawak's timber exports; of these the most significant are *ramin* (*Gonystylus bancanus*), *meranti* (*Shorea* spp.), *medang jongkong* (*Dactylocladus stenostachys*), *semayur* (*Shorea inaequilateralis*) and *kapur paya* (*Dryobalanops rappa*). On very deep, badly-drained peat in the centre of the swamps, a dense forest of rather small trees occurs which is usually single species dominant. This is known as *padang paya* forest; it occupies a little more than 2 per cent of the total forest area and is most extensive in the lower Baram valley, appearing also between the Mukah, Oya, Igan and Lassa Rivers and at several places in the Sadong-Saribas area. Often associated with this, on the deep peats farther from the swamp centre, is a type known as *alan* forest dominated by *Shorea albida*. Some of the land under mixed swamp forest may prove suitable for cultivation, but that under *padang paya* and *alan* forests is totally unsuitable.

The leached sandy soils in the extreme west and on the higher parts of the belt of hill country in central Sarawak support an edaphic heath forest known as Kerangas which also appears at places along the coast. Kerangas forest occupies nearly 5 per cent of the total forested area. Much of it is of poor quality, trees are comparatively small and often there is a tendency for a single species to dominate in particular areas. Generally these forests are of little commercial value but in places they consist of almost pure stands of *ru ronang* (*Casuarina sumatrana*), one of the world's best fuel woods. Elsewhere the conifer, *bindang* (*Agathis alba*), has been extracted for export to Australia, although accessible supplies are very limited, and *kapur empedu* (*Dryobalanops fusca*) has been cut in Lundu District for use in Kuching. The soils on which Kerangas forest occurs are unsuitable for agriculture and most have been avoided by shifting cultivators who recognize this fact.

Virtually the remainder of Sarawak between the coastal plain and an altitude of about 1,500 feet has a cover of lowland dipterocarp forest. This occurs on all but the very poorest or most specialized soils and depends for its existence on a hot, moist climate which promotes the development of a lofty and luxuriant forest in which trees grow continuously. The forest is dense and trees reach a considerable height; they are almost unbranched below the canopy which is usually 140-160 feet or more above ground level. Little light penetrates to the ground so that there is scant undergrowth, although lianes and rattans are numerous.

These lowland dipterocarp forests have experienced a very long period of development uninterrupted by man or by marked climatic changes and this has produced their basic characteristic, the fact that they comprise a multitude of species and that these are closely intermixed.[9] Indeed, the number of indigenous tree species is estimated at well over 2,500, of which about one-tenth are of commercial importance as timber, and 250 different species were discovered on 15 acres of the Semengoh Forest Reserve.[10] As the name implies, this type of forest is dominated by dipterocarps but many other tree families occur, often in small numbers. These lowland forests yield a variety of hardwoods but they are difficult to work commercially partly because

[9] M. E. D. Poore, 'Vegetation and Flora' in *Malaysia: A Survey*, edited by Wang Gungwu, London and New York, Pall Mall Press and Frederick Praeger, 1964, p. 47.
[10] *Sarawak Annual Report, 1960*, Kuching, Government Printer, 1961, p. 73.

B

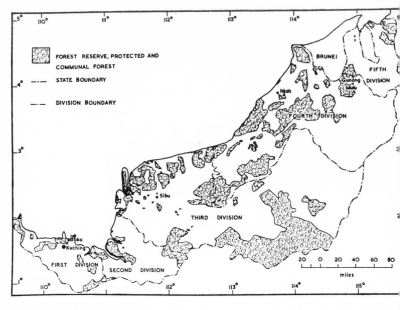

Figure 7   Forest reserves.

of the great diversity of trees which seriously reduces the yield of merchantable timber per acre and partly because of transport difficulties in the rugged hill country in which they occur, for only timbers that float can be extracted. Undoubtedly in many places these forests cover soils which are well suited to agricultural development. Where they have been cleared in the past by shifting cultivators they have been replaced by less well-developed secondary forest which may be of considerable age.

Above the level of this forest type is an ill-defined transition zone occupied by hill dipterocarp forest containing some species that do not occur at lower altitudes. With increasing height there is a rapid decline in the number of dipterocarp species until they finally disappear at about 4,000 feet. Here they are replaced by montane forests comprising chiefly oaks, chestnuts and conifers. Completely inaccessible, these montane forests are as yet of no economic importance. A type of moss forest appears in the areas of perpetual dampness on many of the highest peaks such as Gunong Mulu.[11]

[11] For a detailed discussion of vegetation see F. G. Browne, *Forest Trees of Sarawak and Brunei and their Products*, Kuching, Government Printer, 1955

Forest Reserves

The forests constitute an asset of immense potential commercial value. They also serve as a guard against soil erosion and deterioration and flooding, drainage and water supply problems. However, rapid population growth, agricultural development schemes and the growing timber industry are accelerating the pace of forest clearance in Sarawak.

In the post-war era, the Sarawak Forest Department has determined to ensure adequate conservation. It has aimed at setting aside a sufficient area of forest to form a 'National Forest Estate' which will be worked commercially under proper forest management. It is estimated that 25 per cent. of the country should be retained under forest to be worked in this way and by 1962, when the reservation programme was nearly complete, 24 per cent of the State lay within Forest Reserves and Protected Forests.[12] All suitable areas of mangrove and peat swamp forest have been so reserved as have large areas in the interior of the Third and Fourth Divisions (Fig. 7).

Other areas have been designated National Parks in which the existing natural vegetation will remain undisturbed; these include the Bako National Park north of Kuching, the Niah Caves area and Gunong Mulu. They are to be preserved for their botanical and faunal interest, not least to facilitate future research, and as scenic areas for recreational purposes; the archaeological significance of the Niah Caves is an additional compelling reason for preservation in that area.

[12] *Sarawak Annual Report, 1962*, Kuching, Government Printer, 1963, pp. 111-112.

2 Population and Settlement

By South-East Asian standards Sarawak is sparsely populated. Its population in 1960 totalled 744,529 with an average density of fifteen per square mile. This is comparable with the adjacent State of Sabah, but contrasts sharply with nearby Java and Singapore and is considerably lower than the average figure for Malaya of 124 per square mile in 1957.

Population Distribution and Growth

Sarawak's small population is far from evenly distributed. The heaviest concentrations occur on the coastal plains and in the valleys of the west in the area between the Kayan and Mukah Rivers, and almost three-quarters of Sarawak's population lives south of a line through Sibu and west of a line through Kanowit. Densities in all the Districts of the First and Second Divisions are above the State average; in fact, the First Division accounts for only seven per cent of the land area of the State but contains a third of its population and very nearly a quarter of the people of Sarawak live in the Kuching-Serian area. If the three largest urban centres, Kuching, Sibu and Miri, are excluded, the Districts of Kuching Rural and Bau, with 105 and 72 per square mile respectively, stand out as the most densely settled in the State. Elsewhere, apart from occasional concentrations at and around the smaller towns of Bintulu, Marudi, Limbang and Lawas, population is sporadically distributed in the major valleys and becomes progressively sparser in their isolated upper sections. Indeed, very few people live in the hilly interior of the Third, Fourth and Fifth Divisions, and both the huge Districts of Kapit and Baram (which together comprise almost half the total area of Sarawak), have average densities of only three per square mile (Fig. 8).

No attempt at a complete enumeration of the total Sarawak popula-

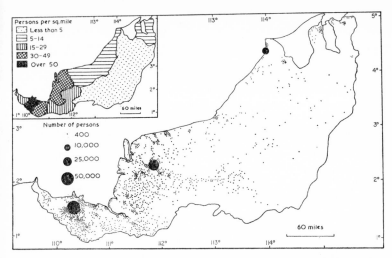

Figure 8 Population distribution, 1960. Inset: Density of population, 1960.
(N.B.—Excluding Kuching, Sibu and Miri Municipalities.)

tion was attempted before 1939, although several estimates for different areas were produced at various dates. The frontiers of Sarawak were extended several times during the nineteenth century so that by 1905 the State was over twenty times its original size when Brooke rule began in 1841; coupled with the suspect nature of many of the earlier figures this makes it impossible to gauge the rate of population change during the nineteenth century.

In 1841, when the State extended only from Tanjong Datu to the Samarahan, it was estimated to contain about 10,500 people. Thirty years later, when the State had grown to include all the lands west of Tanjong Kidurong, a confessedly inaccurate census placed the total population at 141,546. By 1908, when Sarawak had attained its present extent, the total population was estimated at 416,000. Clearly, however, three factors caused major population changes in the nineteenth and early twentieth centuries. First, immigration, principally of Chinese, caused changes both in total numbers and composition; immigration tended to be very uneven, varying from a mere trickle at some periods to a flood at others. Secondly, the internal migration of native peoples, particularly the Ibans, caused marked distributional changes. Finally the ravages of disease, especially cholera and smallpox, which at times reached epidemic proportions among native groups in many parts of the country, resulted in serious population declines in many localities.

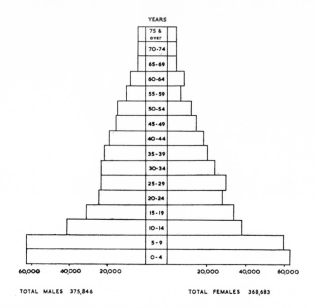

Figure 9   Age pyramid, total population, 1960. (Source—*Sarawak: Census of Population, 1960*, p. 44.)

Table 1   Population Growth, 1939-1965

	Number	Increase %
1939	490,585	
1947	546,385	11·4
1960	744,529	36·3
1965	838,000 (estimate)	12·7

Despite the inadequacies of the earlier figures, there is little doubt that the rate of population growth in pre-war Sarawak was extremely low and, indeed, between 1939 and 1947 population rose at an annual rate of only 1·4 per cent. The post-war era has witnessed a remarkable change in this trend; both immigration and emigration are now insignificant, yet between 1947 and 1960 Sarawak recorded an annual rate of increase of 2·5 per cent and evidence indicates that this has increased since 1960.[1] To a large extent this is the result of improved health conditions; disease control and the spread of medical and child welfare services have induced rising fertility rates, considerably reduced infant mortality and extended life expectancy among much of the

[1] *Sarawak Development Plan, 1964-68*, Kuching, Government Printer, 1963, p. 2.

population. Although the Chinese community shows the most rapid rate of increase, a similar trend is apparent in each of the other major groups. A result significant for future planning is that in 1960 more than half the total Sarawak population was less then twenty years of age (Fig. 9); thus the rate of population increase is likely to reach an even higher figure in the near future and economic development plans must cater for a rapidly expanding labour force.

It is difficult to assess spatial changes in the Sarawak population between 1947 and 1960 because changes occurred in the boundaries of eight Census Districts. Marked numerical and percentage increases occurred, however, in the administrative Districts of Kuching, Sibu and Miri, which include their respective towns and, in general, population increased most markedly in the Kuching-Serian and middle Rejang areas. Undoubtedly these areas have experienced in-migration in the post-war period. Elsewhere, only Lundu, Baram and Lawas Districts had percentage increases greater than the State average, and increases of between twenty and thirty per cent were recorded over very wide areas. Population did not decline in any District but Lubok Antu emerges as a region of limited growth and probable out-migration; only modest increases occurred in the coastal District of Saribas, Kalaka and Mukah and this may reflect the departure of people from these depressed sago-producing areas (Fig. 10).

Population Composition

Thus far the Sarawak population has been treated as a whole but it is, in fact, ethnically very mixed. Indeed, for its size, Sarawak is one of the most multi-racial countries in the world and the welding of its diverse ethnic groups into a loyal and united people is the major problem facing Sarawak no less than Malaysia as a whole.

Demographically Sarawak presents a picture of bewildering complexity and the division of the population into its constituent communities or ethnic groups presents almost insuperable difficulties because no standard criteria can be applied. The basic accepted division is that between indigenous and immigrant peoples, but even here the line is hard to draw, for at some time in the past a considerable part of the total population has moved into the present territory of Sarawak from elsewhere.

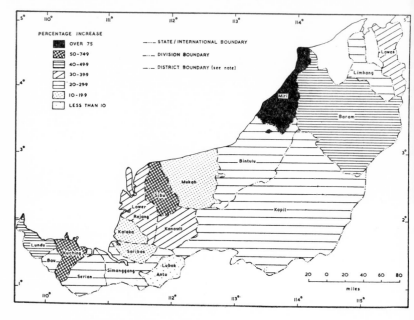

Figure 10   Population increase, 1947-1960.

Note—The 1947 boundaries of Kanowit and Lower Rejang Districts have been retained. In 1957 an area around Pakan, containing some 6,000 people, was transferred from Sarikei to Kanowit and allowance has been made for this in calculating the increases in the Districts of Lower Rejang (now divided into Binatang and Sarikei Districts), and Kanowit. The former Serian District (now divided into Serian and Sadong Districts), has been treated as a single unit for the purposes of this map.

Indigenous peoples

The 1947 Population Census defined indigenous peoples as

> ' those persons who recognise no allegiance to any foreign territory, who regard Sarawak as their homeland, who believe themselves to be a part of the territory and who are now regarded as natives by their fellow men.'[2]

This definition was used again in 1960 when half a million people, or 68 per cent of the total population, were classed as indigenous. This

[2] L. W. Jones, *Sarawak: Report on the Census of Population, 1960*, Kuching, Government Printer, 1962, p. 47.

general term covers a diversity of groups of varying cultural and
economic levels with different forms of social organization and showing
noticeable regional concentrations. It is usual to classify these broadly
into Iban (Sea Dyak), Malay, Land Dyak, Melanau and Other
Indigenous.

Table 2   Major Indigenous Groups, 1939, 1947 and 1960

	1939		1947		1960	
Group	*Number*	*%*	*Number*	*%*	*Number*	*%*
Iban	167,700	46	190,326	48	237,741	47
Malay	92,709	26	97,469	25	129,300	26
Land Dyak	36,963	10	42,195	11	57,619	11
Melanau	36,772	10	35,560	9	44,661	9
Others	27,532	8	29,867	7	37,931	7
Total Indigenous	361,676	100	395,417	100	507,252	100

(Source: *Sarawak: Report on the Census of Population, 1960*, p. 50.)

N.B.   The apparent decline of the Melanau population between 1939 and 1947
probably represents some confusion between Malays and Muslim Melanaus
on the part of the Census enumerators.

Iban.   The Iban, or Sea Dyaks, form the largest single indigenous
group in Sarawak. Formerly notorious headhunters, they are largely
pagan rice cultivators, some growing wet-*padi* in the riverain and deltaic
swamps of the lower Lupar, Saribas and Rejang Rivers, although the
majority still practise shifting cultivation of dry-*padi* in hilly areas
some fifty to a hundred miles from the coast. Many have also taken to
rubber planting and some are employed on the oil-field.

The Iban form a comparatively homogenous group speaking a
common language and with a distinguishable culture and social
organization. Their characteristic form of settlement remains the
longhouse (Plate I). These contain several 'doors' or *bileks*, each of
which represents an economically self-sufficient, essentially autonomous
family unit. Basically the Iban longhouse community is a federation of
families, because their society is classless and egalitarian.

Today the Iban are spread widely throughout rural Sarawak, but
there are heavy concentrations in the Second and Third Divisions;
as yet, very few have moved into the towns. The main Iban strongholds
are the Lupar and Rejang River systems and they constitute more

B*

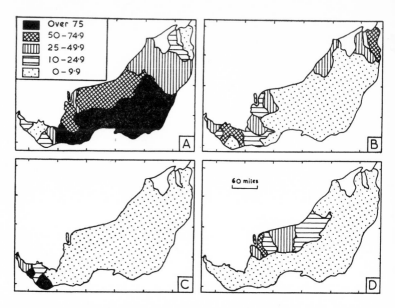

Figure 11 (A) Iban, (B) Malays, (C) Land Dyaks and (D) Melanaus as a percentage of the total indigenous population, by district, 1960. (Source of data: L. W. Jones, *Sarawak: Report on the Census of Population, 1960,* Table 1.)

than three-quarters of the total indigenous population in the Districts of Simanggang, Lubok Antu, Kanowit and Kapit (Fig. 11A).

The Iban population has increased steadily in the recent past. It is perhaps significant, however, that between 1947 and 1960 they recorded the lowest rate of increase of any major group in Sarawak, and today they may be numerically less important than the Chinese.

The last century and a half has witnessed a very marked territorial expansion of the Iban population. Having migrated north-westwards from the Kapuas headwaters in Kalimantan across the watershed into Sarawak territory some considerable time earlier, at the opening of the nineteenth century they were probably restricted to the upper reaches of the Batang Lupar and Batang Saribas and their tributaries in the area that now forms the Second Division. By 1960 over three-fifths of the total Iban population was located to the north of the boundary between the Second and Third Divisions, a line which follows the watershed between the Lupar and Saribas on the one hand and the Rejang on the other. Thus, particularly during the nineteenth century, the Iban pushed constantly northwards into the Rejang basin, and thence even farther north, into an almost uninhabited forested area. In the manner of pioneers looking for new land, they spread the shifting cultivation of hill *padi* through the valleys of the fast-flowing rivers of central Sarawak.

These great nineteenth-century Iban migrations have yet to be studied in detail, but Freeman recognizes a two-pronged movement northwards into the Rejang.[3] Beginning in the early decades of the century, groups of Iban moved from the headwaters of the Batang Lupar and the Kanyau (a tributary of the Kapuas in Kalimantan) into the Katibas valley. This movement was well under way by 1850 and within a short while they had reached the main Rejang River, settling first in the vicinity of Song, but subsequently fanning out into all the Rejang tributaries upstream of the Sungei Ngemah.

In the 1830's and 1840's other groups began a second movement from the valleys of the Lemanak, Skrang and Layar into the Entabai and Julau valleys and the headwaters of the Kanowit River. Thus, early in 1859 Charles Brooke wrote of the Kanowit River,

'This stream is inhabited by Sea Dayaks, who have for the last fifteen or twenty years been migrating from the Saribas and Skrang districts for the purpose of obtaining new farming grounds. These exoduses took place overland between one river and another. Such parties would do their four or five days' march, then build their houses, and proceed to farm for one or two years, after which they would recommence their march, and so on . . .'[4]

During the 1850's and early 1860's there was considerable enmity between the newly-arrived Ibans and the people of the upper Rejang— the Kajangs and Kayans. After October 1863, however, when formal peace was declared between the Ibans and the interior tribes, Iban occupation of the main Rejang valley and its tributaries continued apace. Although occasionally subjected to punitive Government expeditions for their headhunting activities or for contravening Government orders, as for example in 1881 when the valley of the Batang Baleh was closed to Iban settlement, by the end of the century

---

[3] J. D. Freeman, *Iban Agriculture: A Report on the Shifting Cultivation of Hill Rice by the Iban of Sarawak*, London, H.M.S.O. (Colonial Research Studies, No. 18), 1955, pp. 11-20. See also A. J. N. Richards, 'The Migration of the Ibans and their Poetry', *Sarawak Museum Journal*, Vol. V, No. 1, 1949, pp. 77-87.
[4] C. Brooke, *Ten Years in Sarawak*, London, Tinsley Brothers, 1866, Vol. I, p. 327.

they had occupied the greater part of the middle Rejang basin. Despite further punitive measures, by the early 1920's the Ibans had occupied the Batang Baleh and its numerous tributaries.

By the 1870's groups of Iban had begun to push farther north in their search for new land, driven only partly by population increase, for their methods of land use were adapted to a system of constant expansion into virgin areas. By the 1880's Ibans from the Rejang and Kanowit valleys had settled at the headwaters of the Mukah and Oya Rivers. At the end of the century the Rajah gave the Ibans permission to settle on the rivers on the coast between Igan and Tanjong Kidurong, and by 1900 a considerable number had availed themselves of this permission, and Iban settlers were moving into the valleys of the Balingian, Tatau and Kemena systems (Fig. 12).

This Iban movement into the areas north of the Rejang continued well into the present century. It is undoubtedly a relatively recent phenomenon and, as Freeman observes, it raises a significant point. The territory between the mouth of the Rejang and Tanjong Kidurong was ceded to the first Rajah in 1861; it therefore passed into Government hands at least a decade before the Ibans began to move north

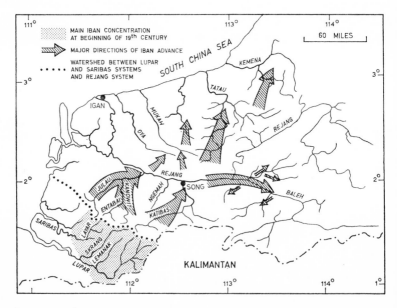

Figure 12 Iban migrations.

of the main Rejang River. Today many of these people claim traditional rights over their land, maintaining that it was handed down to them from remote ancestors, a claim that is clearly specious. As Freeman remarks, 'if Government policy in the area is to be properly implemented, it is of cardinal importance that the historical facts be fully established, and clearly understood by all'.[5]

Malays. Islam first reached north-west Borneo in the mid-fifteenth century. Slowly but steadily the faith took hold among many of the peoples of the coastal plains, the interior population remaining animist pagans. To a very considerable extent therefore the present-day 'Malay' population of this area comprises indigenes converted to Islam and the Malay way of life at some time during the last half millenium; only a minute proportion is of immigrant Malayan origin. But religion alone is not the distinguishing mark of the Malay in Sarawak for there are, in fact, other Muslim groups, such as the Melanaus and Kedayans, who consider themselves to be different from the Malays. Nor, for that matter, is it possible to take physical characteristics as a criterion. Essentially, in the Borneo territories a Malay is one who regards himself as such and is so regarded by his fellow-men.

Brunei is the traditional focus of Malay settlement in north-west Borneo. A powerful and extensive sultanate in the fifteenth and sixteenth centuries, it remained a centre for the diffusion of Islam and Malay culture in this part of the island despite its subsequent loss of prestige and territory under a succession of weak sultans.

By the early decades of the nineteenth century subsidiary points of Malay settlement had emerged in the Lupar estuary and in the vicinity of Kuching in an area that had recently acquired a new significance as a centre of antimony production. In the mid-1830's the miners revolted against the Brunei Sultan's local representative. Rajah Muda Hassim, heir-presumptive to the Sultanate, was sent from Brunei to quell the rebellion but proved ineffective. James Brooke, who first arrived in Sarawak in August 1839, came back a year later and in return for suppressing the rebels was offered and accepted a block of territory that now comprises most of the First Division. Thus, from the start there existed a special relationship between the Brookes and the Malays, and Malay influence has always been strong in Sarawak.

The Malays form slightly more than a quarter of the indigenous population of the State. They are essentially a coastal and riverine

[5] Freeman, op. cit., p. 20.

people rarely found above the limit of tidal influence.[6] Their settlements consist of individual wood and *atap* houses which are invariably raised on stilts several feet above ground level and as a general rule Malay villages are larger and characterized by a greater degree of permanence than those of the other indigenous groups (Plate II). They have also shown a greater predilection for urban life and every coastal town or bazaar has its distinctive Malay section, often physically separate from the remainder of the settlement, as in Kuching, and invariably close to the water's edge.

Malays engage in a variety of occupations including fishing, boat-building, wet-*padi* farming, mixed gardening, fruit growing and rubber and coconut planting; some collect and prepare *nipah* palm thatch and other swamp and jungle produce; others work as hired agricultural labourers, usually as rubber tappers. There are also considerable numbers employed at various levels in government service, but the proportion has declined noticeably in the post-Brooke era.

Malay settlements occur at intervals along the length of the Sarawak coast. They are frequent in the coastal areas of the First and Second Divisions and significantly the major Malay stronghold is Kuching District, to which some migration from other parts of Sarawak has occurred in the recent past. Malays also constitute an important component of the population of the Sarawak Districts that border Brunei, still an important centre of Malay influence in the area; however, there has been some movement of Malays from Lawas and Limbang into Brunei partly to take up work on the oil-field (Fig. 11B).

The Malays have a social organization based on an aristocratic tradition with a relatively rigid heredity ranking in which traceable ancestry plays an important role; considerable social prestige is also gained by making the pilgrimage to Mecca. Preoccupation with rank has led to widespread connections among the upper class Malay families.

'These wider horizons and the experience of government under the sultans and the rajahs have brought a segment of the Malays closer to a consciousness of ethnic unity and regional political entity than other indigenous Borneans whose lives are confined to the village community.'[7]

[6] See T. Harrisson, 'The Malays of South-west Sarawak before Malaysia', *Sarawak Museum Journal*, Vol. XI, Nos. 23-24, 1964, pp. 341-511.
[7] Country Survey Series, Human Relations Area Files, *North Borneo, Brunei, Sarawak*, New Haven, 1956, p. 42.

When this comment was made a decade ago it was a fair view of the situation; in the interim profound changes have overtaken Sarawak. Although on the new national Malaysian scene, the Malays are in the political ascendancy, they must now share the local Sarawak political stage with these other indigenous peoples as well as with the immigrant population. As Harrisson observes,

'Borneo is *not* a Malay country in the Malayan sense, and for the successful achievement and survival of Malaysia, it is very necessary to face this fact clearly and at all times.'[8]

Land Dyaks. Having originally moved northwards from the south-west corner of Borneo, the Land Dyaks already concentrated very heavily in the area which formed the initial core of the Sarawak Raj when James Brooke first arrived in 1839. A mild and very conservative people, they have shown no tendency to move out from this traditional area despite continuous population growth and increasing impoverishment of their land. Today they are almost entirely restricted to the Districts of Lundu, Bau, Kuching and Serian (Fig. 11c).

In general they occupy the higher reaches of the various branches of the Kayan, Sarawak, Sadong and Samarahan Rivers. Longhouse dwellers, they are, like the Iban, primarily shifting cultivators of hill-*padi*. The Land Dyaks, however, are characterized by an elaborate system of labour exchange in working their land and by their complex system of land inheritance. Their attitudes to life in general, conditioned to some extent by the long periods of suppression they suffered in the past, have tended to make them less aggressive, adventuresome, ambitious and adaptable than the Iban, and they have been much slower to adjust to new external influences, economic or otherwise. Government effort is now directed towards facilitating the necessary changes.

Although they form a broadly recognizable ethnic group and have a restricted geographic distribution, the Land Dyaks fall into several distinct sub-groups between which there are marked dialect differences and some variations in custom. These groups represent small localities or collections of villages, each a complex of several small longhouses which, in the past, were characterized by their relative isolation, because few Land Dyaks ever left the confines of their own village areas. Only with the political awakening attendant upon developments in the last

[8] T. Harrisson, 'The Peoples of North and West Borneo' in *Malaysia: A Survey*, edited by Wang Gungwu, London and New York, Pall Mall Press and Frederick Praeger, 1964, p. 164.

half decade have attempts been made to develop any feeling of unity among the Land Dyak peoples.

Melanaus. The Melanaus numbered a little less than 45,000 in 1960. Although some small groups are found up-river, they are primarily a people of the low-lying coastal plains of the Third and Fourth Divisions, and the main concentrations occur on the lower reaches of the Igan, Oya, Mukah and Balingian, Tatau and Kemena Rivers. The Melanaus have long been famous as sago producers and these coastal and riverine swamps are their traditional strongholds and were important sago-exporting areas as early as the 1840's. Today over nine-tenths of the Melanau population lives in the Districts of Sarikei, Sibu, Bintulu, Binatang and Mukah, by far the largest number being in the latter two Districts (Fig. 11D).

As will be shown later, the sago industry has been severely depressed in the last decade and this is causing changes in the traditional social and economic patterns of the Melanau. Advantage has been taken of the limited opportunities offered by these coastal swamps for the planting of rubber, fruit trees and rice; fishing, the collection of jungle produce and the weaving of baskets and mats provide minor sources of income. But the major economic development has been the growth of the local timber industry which now employs many Melanaus.

In some respects the Melanau are considered to be intermediate between the Malays and the peoples of the interior. Their traditions, customs and habits bear a resemblance to those of the latter; although there are differences of local dialect, language similarities also point to a connection with the up-river groups. Moreover, the Melanau were originally longhouse dwellers but this settlement form began to break down a century ago. Now the characteristic Melanau village consists of a ribbon of individual wood and *atap* houses lining a river bank, similar in general appearance to the typical Malay village.

A considerable number of Melanaus have been converted to Islam and this has accelerated the 'Malayanization' of this group of people, many also adopting Malay-style dress and inter-marriage with Malays has occurred; others, however, have become Christians and the re-mainder are pagans, often termed *Likaus*. The Melanau remain, nevertheless, a distinct group with their own peculiar problems, a fact clearly reflected in the establishment, in September 1965, of a new Sarawak political party (The Tugau United People's Party), aimed specifically at serving Melanau interests.

Other Indigenous Peoples. Numerically and economically the category 'other indigenous peoples' is less important than any single group so far discussed. A convenience adopted merely for census purposes, this category includes many small groups, living for the most part in the deep interior of the country, most of whom have little in common. Their importance lies chiefly in the problems they pose for a Government intent upon improving the lot of the indigenous peoples.

Table 3   Other Indigenous Communities, 1947 and 1960

	1947	1960
Kenyah	5,507	8,093
Kayan	6,183	7,899
Kedayan	5,334	7,207
Murut	3,290	5,214
Kelabit	1,612	2,040
Bisaya	2,058	2,803
Punan and others	5,883	4,675
Total	29,867	37,931

(Source: *Sarawak: Report on the Census of Population, 1960*, p. 55.)

The Kenyah and Kayan are frequently grouped together for, though their languages differ, they are closely related peoples. Originally migrants from the Batang Kayan area of Kalimantan, they now concentrate in the valleys of the upper Rejang and Balui, the Baram and Ulu Kemana. Until the mid-nineteenth century they dominated the whole area between the Rejang and the Limbang. They retreated before the incoming Iban, a process hastened by the great Kayan expedition of 1863 when the Tuan Muda, Charles Brooke, attacked the upper Rejang with a force of some 15,000 Iban. Their numbers were further reduced by malaria, endemic in the inland valleys, and by introduced diseases, especially smallpox and cholera. Malaria control has done much to reverse this trend and between 1947 and 1960 the Kenyah-Kayan population apparently increased by over a third. Although they live in longhouses and have an economy similar to that of the Iban and Land Dyaks, the Kenyah-Kayan have a markedly different social structure, being very class conscious and with an inherited aristocracy.

The Kedayans are a Muslim group with strong ties with Brunei in which State they form an important element of the population. They are found at intervals along the coast of the Fourth and Fifth Divisions where they cultivate *padi* and have the reputation of being very efficient and industrious farmers. Two related groups, the Muruts and Kelabits, are important in the interior valleys of northern Sarawak. The former now concentrate in the Trusan valley and although at one time they were more widespread and certainly more numerous, during the last century they too have suffered severely from the depredations of disease; the latter inhabit the headwaters of the Baram River. Skilled agriculturists, these two groups are among the most productive *padi* planters in Sarawak. The Bisayas are a small group located in the middle Limbang valley. They are noted for their peculiar style of longhouse and they plant sago, *padi* and rubber and keep buffaloes. Finally, scattered throughout the deep forests of the upper Rejang and Baram are small, nomadic, non-cultivating communities of people known as Punans. In general they subsist on wild sago, vegetable collecting and hunting; they collect jungle products and weave mats and *rotan* bags which they barter with their neighbours at government-supervised trade meetings.

Immigrant peoples
In 1960 immigrant peoples comprised 32 per cent of the total population. During the last three-quarters of a century this group has continuously enlarged its numerical share of the Sarawak population. For long this was the result of the arrival of increasing numbers of new immigrants, but more recently, with the virtual cessation of immigration, it has resulted from the higher rate of natural increase recorded by the immigrants. The immigrant peoples include Chinese, Europeans, Indians and Indonesians; the latter three communities numbered 1,600, 2,400 and 3,200 respectively in 1960 and the Chinese alone comprise 96·5 per cent of this miscellaneous group.

Chinese. The Chinese population of Sarawak more than doubled between 1939 and the mid-1960's and today they may form the largest single community in the State, outnumbering even the Iban. Immigration has played a negligible part in this increase, for it is now rigorously controlled, and there was a net gain by immigration of only 7,800 Chinese between 1948 and 1960. The Chinese community reveals, in fact, a greater rate of natural increase than any other group and in the period 1947-1960, its number rose at an annual rate of 3·5 per cent.[9]

[9] L. W. Jones, op. cit., p. 57.

Table 4   Chinese Population, 1939-1965

	Number	Increase %	Total Population %
1939	123,626	—	25·2
1947	145,158	17·4	26·6
1960	229,154	57·9	30·8
1965 (estimate)	272,000	18·7	32·4

As elsewhere in South-East Asia, the Chinese tend to concentrate in and around the towns; indeed, over three-fifths of the Sarawak Chinese live in the three largest towns or in their surrounding rural areas. 'Every district has its Chinese settlement of over 1,000 people but in the remoter districts in particular few live far from the centre where shops, the company of compatriots and a school for the children are present'.[10] The rate of growth of the Chinese population in the vicinity of the three largest urban centres suggests some movement towards them in the post-war era and this is supported by birthplace statistics in the Census. The resettlement of approximately 8,000 Chinese in three 'new villages' on the Kuching-Serian road in July 1965 had the effect of increasing the degree of 'urbanization' among the Chinese, as did similar earlier resettlement in Malaya.[11] In the recent past there has also been an internal movement of Chinese in connection with government-sponsored agricultural settlement schemes such as those at Sibieu near Bintulu and at Karap on the Sungei Bakong in Baram.

Dialect Groupings. The *Hua Chiao*, or Overseas Chinese throughout South-East Asia originated almost entirely from the maritime provinces of south-east China—principally Fukien, Kiangsi, Kwangtung, Hunan, Kwangsi and Hainan. This is an area of considerable linguistic diversity marked by local differences in dialect, many of which are mutually unintelligible, the distribution of dialect groups showing little conformity with provincial boundaries.

Drawn from these south-eastern provinces, the Sarawak Chinese shared a common body of customs, values and beliefs but preserved their local dialects, as did their countrymen elsewhere in South-East

[10] L. W. Jones, op. cit., p. 58.
[11] See Hamzah Sendut, 'Resettlement Villages in Malaya', *Geography*, vol. XLVII, 1962, pp. 41-46.

Asia. Despite the use of Mandarin, or *Kuo Yü* (the Chinese national spoken language) in Chinese schools and the growing division between the 'old guard' Chinese and a more youthful, communist-oriented element, these dialect differences continue to serve as important dividing lines within the Sarawak Chinese community. They frequently reflect occupational differences and regional concentrations, both owing much to the dates at which particular groups entered the country and the continued strength of clan and other association ties.[12]

Table 5   Chinese Dialect Groups, 1947 and 1960

	1947		1960	
	Number	%	*Number*	%
Hakka	45,409	31·3	70,221	30·6
Foochow	41,946	28·9	70,125	30·6
Hokkien	20,289	14·0	28,304	12·4
Cantonese	14,622	10·1	17,432	7·6
Tiechiu	12,892	8·9	21,952	9·6
Henghua	4,356	3·0	8,278	3·6
Hainanese	3,871	2·6	5,717	2·5
Others	1,773	1·2	7,125	3·1
Total	145,158	100·0	229,154	100·0

(Source: J. L. Noakes, *Sarawak and Brunei: A Report on the 1947 Population Census*, London, 1950, p. 93, and *Sarawak: Report on the Census of Population, 1960*, Table 4, p. 128.)

The Sarawak Chinese community falls into seven major dialect groupings (Table 5). The Hakkas and Foochows have retained their overall dominance in the post-war era and today comprise almost two-thirds of the Chinese population. Hokkiens form the third most important group, but in terms of numbers they have declined in relative importance since 1947, as also have the Cantonese, whose fourth-ranking position in 1947 is now held by the Tiechius, a group which increased by over 70 per cent in the intercensal period. These are followed by the two smallest groups, the Henghuas and Hainanese, the former recording the most marked rate of increase of any group with the exception of the miscellaneous collection of 'other Chinese'.

[12] See T'ien Ju-K'ang, *The Chinese of Sarawak*, London, 1953, London School of Economics and Political Science, Monographs on Social Anthropology, No. 12.

The 1960 census report does not contain information on the distribution of these dialect groups so that the following comments are based on the 1947 enumeration; it is unlikely, however, that the basic patterns have shown any marked change in the interim.

Hakkas dominate the rural areas of the First and Second Divisions and in 1947 the Districts of Bau, Serian and Kuching Rural contained two-thirds of their total number; they also form a majority of the Chinese population of Miri District. In sharp contrast, Foochows are almost completely absent from the First and Second Divisions but provide the principal component of the Chinese population of the Third Division, concentrating heavily within a triangle bounded by Igan, Kanowit and Sarikei; they also comprise two-fifths of the Chinese population of Bintulu and Baram Districts. Cantonese are also virtually absent from the First and Second Divisions; like the Foochows most live in the lower Rejang basin where they form the largest dialect group in Kanowit District. Principally traders and merchants, Hokkiens are the largest Chinese group in Kuching town; they appear in small numbers in most parts of Sarawak, particularly in the towns and bazaars, but form a majority group only in the Oya-Mukah sago-producing areas and in the Fifth Division. Well over half the Sarawak Tiechius live either in Kuching town, where many are grocers, or in its surrounding rural areas. They are an important group in the Second Division but, apart from a small number in Bintulu, there are very few elsewhere in Sarawak (Figs. 13, A to F). The Hainanese community is as closely associated with the coffee-shop business in Sarawak as it is in most other parts of South-East Asia and it is, therefore, a largely urban community. As noted later, most of the Henghuas are fishermen.

History of Chinese settlement. Chinese traders began to visit Sarawak early in the Christian era. Archaeological evidence of several trading settlements has been discovered at coastal sites which suggests that intercourse between China and Sarawak continued until the early fourteenth century, or possibly the mid-fifteenth century, but that it then ceased.

The modern period of Chinese migration to Sarawak began in the early nineteenth century and the first migrants did not come direct from China but from the Sambas-Pontianak region to the south-west of the present Sarawak boundary. Chinese gold-mining *kongsis*, composed mainly of Hakkas, were at work in this region by the 1760's; the settle-

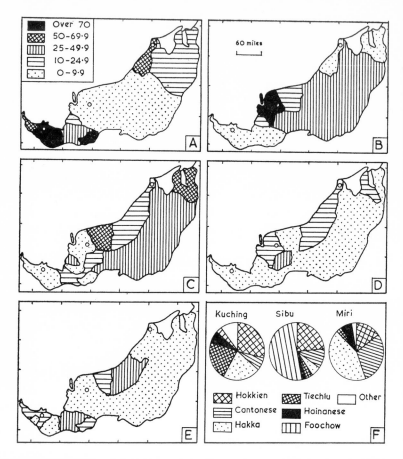

Figure 13   Chinese dialect groups, 1947. (Source of data: J. L. Noakes, *Sarawak: A Report on the 1947 Population Census*.)

(A) Hakka, (B) Foochow, (C) Hokkien, (D) Cantonese and (E) Tiechiu as a percentage of the total Chinese population, by District, 1947. Kuching, Sibu and Miri Municipal Areas are excluded from the above maps; the composition of their Chinese populations is shown by comparable divided circles in (F). (The total Chinese population of these towns in 1947 was Kuching, 21,699; Sibu, 6,201; Miri, 6,879.)

ments flourished and by the late 1830's there may have been more than 30,000 Chinese in the area. The chief mining settlements were Sambas, Monterado and Mandor. Large Chinese agricultural and trading communities also existed at Pamangkat, Mampawa and Pontianak. The Dutch took possession of west-coast Borneo in 1823 and the extension of Dutch control was accompanied by increasingly arduous restrictions upon the Chinese; moreover, by the 1830's the gold deposits in the chief mining areas started to show signs of exhaustion and Chinese settlement began to spread into new areas.

Chinese gold-mining probably began in the Bau area of the First Division of Sarawak in the 1820's; the Sambas *kongsi* gained entrance to the Bau goldfields in 1841 and thereafter the Chinese population of western Sarawak increased rapidly as migrants moved in from Dutch territory. These were mostly Hakkas and although some turned to agriculture, chiefly vegetable gardening, the majority engaged in mining. By the 1840's some Hokkien traders had settled in Kuching and a small group of Cantonese were market-gardening near the town.

In August 1850 a considerable body of Chinese refugees from Pamangkat arrived in Sarawak to escape the tyranny of their rivals at Monterado. Some of these settled in Kuching and its vicinity and some in nearby small agricultural colonies such as Batu Kawa. Most moved into the goldfields of upper Sarawak where the Chinese mining camps of Bau, Bidi, Paku and Tundong now lay under the control of a *kongsi*, itself dominated by a secret society, with its headquarters in Bau. By 1857 there were about 4,000 Chinese in western Sarawak, located primarily on the mining fields.

The secret society grew in strength and became increasingly turbulent and rebellious. Roused by various rumours and by the conviction of its members for opium smuggling, the *kongsi* attacked and captured Kuching in February 1857 with the intention of replacing the Rajah's Government. The insurrection was quickly suppressed and Kuching re-occupied; the Chinese rebels retreated to the interior, under constant pressure from the Rajah's supporters, and, after crossing into Sambas territory, the small group of survivors were captured by Dutch officials. It has been estimated that not far short of a thousand rebels were killed during the retreat, and the insurrection was a severe setback to Chinese settlement and the gold-mining industry in western Sarawak.

Within a short time Chinese refugees began to return to western Sarawak and new immigrants started to arrive from over the border, from the Straits Settlements and direct from China. Many mines were reopened, but the industry never fully recovered; however, the Chinese agricultural and trading communities grew, stimulated in particular by the introduction of gambier and pepper planting in the 1870's. Immediately after the insurrection the Chinese population had fallen sharply. By the early 1870's there were probably between 3,500 and

4,000 Chinese in the present First Division; subsequently, increased immigration brought the number in the whole of Sarawak to about 7,000 in 1877 when the State comprised the present First, Second and Third Divisions. By 1908, when Sarawak had extended to its present boundaries, the total Chinese population was estimated at 45,000, representing perhaps a tenth of the total population.[13]

Throughout the nineteenth century the First Division remained the dominant centre of Chinese settlement. A merchant, trading and artisan community, consisting mainly of Hokkiens, developed in Kuching town; mining in the Bau area remained a Hakka-dominated enterprise and Tiechiu and other agriculturalists, many planting gambier and pepper, opened plantations locally.

The spread of the Rajah's influence brought more peaceful conditions to the lands east of the Batang Lupar and the Chinese started to penetrate new areas. Small groups began mining gold at Marup in the upper Lupar valley in the 1850's. Hokkien and Tiechiu traders opened small posts, many in close proximity to the newly-erected government forts, at which they bartered cloth, jars, salt and other necessities of life in exchange for jungle produce. Penetrating the Lupar and Saribas valleys in the early 1850's, Chinese traders had ventured as far as Kanowit before 1860 and a few years later Hokkien merchants from Singapore were establishing trading posts on the Rejang River. By the early 1880's Cantonese had moved into the timber trade and were exporting logs and sawn *belian* from the Rejang to Hong Kong, and Chinese traders had already penetrated the Baram and Tinjar valleys of the Fourth Division (Fig. 14).

This extension of Chinese influence continued hand in hand with the territorial growth of the Sarawak Raj in the last four decades of the nineteenth century. However, Chinese interest in these newly-acquired lands was restricted to small-scale trade and commerce. Tiny Chinese communities appeared in the many small bazaars and administrative centres but, apart from a government-sponsored plan to settle Chinese in the lower Rejang in the 1880's, little attempt was made to develop other fields of enterprise. The pioneer Chinese east of the Lupar came to trade; here the nineteenth century was the era of the traders' frontier; the extension of Chinese agricultural settlement into these vast, forested and swampy tracts had to await the twentieth century.

In 1900 a native of Fukien, Wong Nai Siong, visited Sibu in the

---

[13] S. Baring-Gould and C. A. Bampfylde, *A History of Sarawak under its Two White Rajahs, 1839-1908*, London, Henry Sotheran and Co., 1909, p. 33.

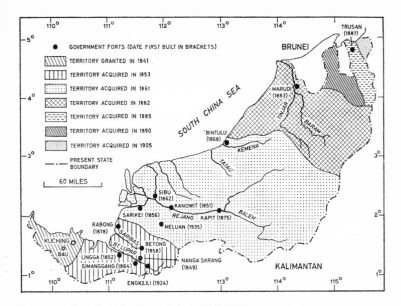

Figure 14 Growth of the Sarawak Raj, 1841-1905.

Third Division and made an agreement with the Second Rajah, then actively encouraging immigration, to import Foochow agriculturalists to develop the area. Granted a loan by the Rajah to cover their passage money, he introduced about 1,000 Foochow settlers during 1901 and 1902. The government undertook to provide at least three acres of land for each adult, rent-free for twenty years, and also to support the families for the first six months, after which the total loan was to be repaid in instalments. The initial settlement was at Sungei Merah, close by Sibu town (known to the settlers as 'New Foochow'). At first they planted vegetables and *padi* but soon pepper was introduced and within a short while Foochow settlement spread up-river towards Durin and down-river to Bukit Lan (Fig. 15).

When Wong Nai Siong returned to China, the Rev. James Hoover, a missionary of the American Episcopal Church, was appointed by the Sarawak Government to supervise the Foochows at Sibu. Rubber was introduced in 1906 and planting proceeded rapidly. The profits achieved during the boom induced the settlers to write home to persuade their relatives to join them and large numbers of Foochows arrived in Sibu during the 1910's. Settlements spread down the Rejang River and large areas were cleared and planted with rubber. Rising rubber prices follow-

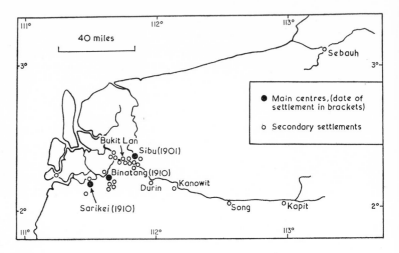

Figure 15   Foochow settlement in central Sarawak, 1900-1930.

ing the world depression of 1920 produced a new rush for land among the local Foochows; in the early 1920's Sibu had a boom and part of the community left agriculture for commerce, trade and industry.

Foochow settlement began at nearby Binatang and Sarikei about 1910 and an increasing number of immigrants entered these areas in the second and third decades of the century. These were also primarily agriculturalists, planting both rubber and pepper, and Foochow settlement spread outwards from both towns as official permission was granted for the creation of new villages (Fig. 15). Concurrently, Foochows moved into other parts of the Rejang Basin; small agricultural and trading communities appeared in Rejang, Kanowit and Song, and in the 1920's a group moved from Sibu to Kapit where they opened land for rubber. At the same time other groups moved from Sibu to Sebauh, near Bintulu, and to Puyoh on the upper Baram where the majority also planted rubber. By the 1920's, the Rejang valley had already become the stronghold of Foochow agriculturalists and the pattern has persisted (Fig. 13B).[14]

The Second Rajah's policy of encouraging immigration resulted in the contemporaneous introduction of batches of immigrants of other

[14] See Chiang Liu, 'Chinese Pioneers, A.D. 1900: the New Foochow Settlement of Sarawak', *Sarawak Museum Journal*, Vol. VI, No. 6, 1955, pp. 536-548, and S. Runciman, *The White Rajahs*, Cambridge, Cambridge University Press, 1960, pp. 208-209.

dialect groups. In 1900, 300 Hakka families were brought to the suburbs of Kuching where they opened agricultural holdings. The following year another agreement was made to provide government backing for the introduction of Cantonese to the Sibu district; a large block of land was granted for pepper planting and about 500 Cantonese arrived before the end of 1901. Subsequently some of these began trading ventures in local bazaars and some turned to other forms of agriculture. Ten years later a further element was added to Sibu's Chinese population when a Methodist missionary introduced a large party of Henghuas.

Many of these settlers remained in the areas to which they were first brought and in addition there was considerable privately-organized immigration. Successful settlers sent for their relatives and these tended to move into the same occupations and districts as their kinsmen. Thus in the 1920's and early 1930's there was a marked immigration of Hakkas, most of whom moved into the First Division while some eventually settled in Miri District. Although restricted by individual permit to the relatives or dependents of those already resident in Sarawak, Chinese immigration continued until the beginning of the Second World War; indeed the immigration records (which unfortunately were destroyed during the Japanese Occupation) showed a net gain of 19,165 Chinese immigrants in the period 1935-1939. By the latter date there were 123,626 Chinese in Sarawak, comprising a quarter of the total population and the economy of the territory was very largely in their hands.[15]

Political significance of the Chinese community. In few parts of the world have the Overseas Chinese been assimilated to any extent into indigenous society; intensely proud of their Chinese origin, they remain a distinct, if not aloof, community. Lacking the religious barriers of Malaya, intermarriage with indigenes has been more frequent in Sarawak, but nevertheless the Chinese population still forms a discrete entity. Retaining their customs, values and languages, the Chinese are marked off from the indigenous population by their greater wealth, their higher levels of literacy and their more rapid rate of natural increase. Significantly, more than half the Chinese population was less than 15 years old in 1960.

Chinese control most of the business, trade and industry of Sarawak,

[15] J. L. Noakes, 'The Growth of the Population of Sarawak', L. W. Jones, op. cit., p. 321.

and the main development of the two major cash crops—rubber and pepper—has been in their hands. Yet until recently, they were content to remain apart from public affairs, desiring only to be left in peace to pursue their goal of monetary gain, wealth remaining the major determinant of class in the Chinese community. The initial immigrants came with the hope of acquiring sufficient wealth to return to spend their final years in the homeland. Few did so, and the Chinese have become an increasingly settled community; in fact, four-fifths of the Sarawak Chinese were born in the country and well over half those born elsewhere (principally China), were over 45 years old in 1960 so that the proportion of foreign-born Chinese will now decline rapidly.

For long, developments in China and their economic stake in Sarawak have caused the Chinese to regard Sarawak as home. Rising indigenous nationalism and the urge to protect their cultural and economic attributes in the face of official policies designed to favour the indigenous peoples, have drawn some of them deeper into local politics in the last decade than ever before.

Political developments in Sarawak in the 1960's in some respects resemble those in Malaya a decade or more earlier. A communist organization (the Clandestine Communist Organization, or CCO) growing out of a small wartime communist-inspired body, gained strength in the later 1950's, seeking recruits particularly among Chinese-medium schoolchildren and penetrating the Trade Union movement. The Sarawak United People's Party (SUPP) was registered in June 1959; avowedly socialist and multi-racial, from the beginning it was Chinese-dominated and was viewed by the Government as a front for the CCO.[16]

Initially desirous of extending their influence by peaceful means, the communists began to change tactics in 1961 and members undertook training in jungle guerrilla activities locally or over the Indonesian border. The inclusion of Sarawak in the Federation of Malaysia, first suggested in May 1961, and effected in September 1963, aroused fears as to their future position among many Sarawak Chinese. The SUPP opposed the formation of Malaysia on the proposed terms; the communists were actively against the plan and this, together with Indonesian 'confrontation', has dominated the situation in Sarawak in the mid-1960's, culminating in a wave of terrorism in the Chinese-dominated Kuching-Serian area in June 1965, the subsequent resettle-

[16] Sarawak Information Service, *The Danger Within: A History of the Clandestine Communist Organization in Sarawak*, Kuching, Government Printer, 1963.

ment of the local Chinese population in 'new villages' and an intensification of the Government campaign against the communists.

However, the communist movement does not reflect the views of the overwhelming majority of local Chinese any more than the similar movement in Malaya did in the 1950's. Indeed, Leigh has suggested a three-fold grouping of the Sarawak Chinese community for purposes of political analysis.[17] First, there are the 'Sarawak-oriented' Chinese who have renounced all ties with China and regard Sarawak as their home. Most of them are town-dwellers, relatively well-off and English-speaking. Secondly there is a very large 'floating' group or Chinese prolateriat which includes the majority of the illiterate and the less-highly educated in Chinese medium, most of whom are concerned simply with earning a basic living and have little interest in politics. Finally, the 'China-oriented' group consists mainly of the young chauvinistic urban Chinese wholly educated in their own medium to a relatively high level but most frequently faced with employment difficulties. It is among this group that communist influences find their greatest support. As Leigh says,

'Most are fundamentally loyal to Sarawak but are proud of the restoration of China, her heritage and culture. They cling tenaciously to all that is Chinese and resist any pressure toward assimilation . . . [they] . . . are arrogant in their disregard for other races and would be a problem even if China was not Communist.'[18]

Urbanization

It is impossible to establish a standard criterion by which 'urban' may be distinguished from 'rural'. A combination of particular functions, amenities and physical characteristics marks a town off from its surrounding rural areas and, as with all geographic 'regions', there is rarely a clear dividing line but rather a transitional zone. Nevertheless, urban and rural areas have distinctively different personalities and these are recognized by their inhabitants.

[17] M. B. Leigh, *The Chinese Community of Sarawak: A Study of Communal Relations*, Singapore, University of Singapore, Singapore Studies on Malaysia No. 6, 1964, pp. 31-32. See also R. O. Tilman, 'The Sarawak Political Scene', *Pacific Affairs*, Vol. XXXVII, No. 4, 1964-5, pp. 412-425.
[18] Ibid., p. 32. See also C. P. FitzGerald, *The Third China: The Chinese Communities in South-East Asia*, Singapore, Donald Moore for the Australian Institute of International Affairs, 1965.

Usually the distinction is made in terms of the number of people resident in a settlement. A specific 'threshold' figure is chosen (which varies according to local conditions in different parts of the world), and all settlements with a population greater than this figure are classed as urban centres. This itself raises problems, particularly obvious in the case of Sarawak. Generally population statistics come from census returns and these refer to town boundaries established either by law or by census officials; often these boundaries have little geographic meaning and the figures may exclude part of the 'urban' population resident in suburban or dormitory areas. Moreover, it is questionable whether the threshold figure applicable today has a similar relevance in the past.

Degree of urbanization

No definition of the term 'urban' appears in the 1960 Sarawak population census; by implication, however, it seems that 3,000 was taken as the threshold figure.[19] On this basis there are seven towns in the State, of which the largest is the capital, Kuching Municipality, with a population of a little over 50,000. Only three towns have a population of over 10,000 so that by world standards the towns of Sarawak are very small and there is nothing remotely comparable with the 'million' cities of South-East Asia: Bangkok, Djakarta, Manila, Saigon and Singapore (Table 6).

Table 6   Urban Centres, 1960

	Population
Kuching Municipality	50,579
Sibu Urban Area	29,630
Miri Urban Area	13,350
Simanggang Town	5,648
Bintulu Town	5,307
Sarikei Town	4,204
Lutong Town	3,039
Total	111,757

Apart from these seven centres, Sarawak contains many 'urban' or 'overgrown' villages, often locally known as bazaars (Plate XIII). Most

[19] L. W. Jones, op. cit., p. 6.

contain between one and two thousand people and, like the larger centres, they usually act as the local administrative headquarters and perform various services for the surrounding rural areas. A considerable proportion of their inhabitants is engaged in non-agricultural activities, but they all have residents involved directly in farming. In fact, town and country are still very closely related in Sarawak irrespective of the size of urban centre.

Taking the total population of the seven largest towns, 15 per cent of the population of Sarawak may be classed as urban; to include the multitude of smaller centres would give a grossly inflated impression of the degree of urbanization, as over four-fifths of the total labour force is engaged directly in agriculture. Moreover, this figure is comparable with those recorded for neighbouring Sabah and, indeed, for most of South-East Asia. Within the region only Malaya, Singapore and the Philippines reveal a markedly greater degree of urbanization.

Characteristics of the urban population
Chinese comprise two-thirds and Malays one-fifth of the total urban population. Bintulu and Lutong are the only towns in which the Chinese do not predominate; in the former, a small river-mouth trading and administrative centre, Melanaus form the largest community and in the latter, a small town which grew up around the oil refinery constructed there in 1917, Malays, the largest component of the oil company's work force, are slightly more numerous than Chinese (Fig. 16).

Nevertheless, only one-third of the Sarawak Chinese live in urban centres. Europeans are the most highly urbanized community: most of them live in Kuching, for they still form an important section of the higher echelons of the administration and its technical branches, and many are employed by the larger commercial organizations, but there are also significant numbers in the Miri-Lutong area in connection with the oil company's operations. Many of the other non-indigenous peoples also live in towns so that the urban population is characterized by its very small indigenous component; indeed seven-tenths of all town-dwellers are non-indigenous and in the case of the two largest towns, Kuching and Sibu, the proportion rises to over three-quarters. Of the indigenous communities only the Malays show any real tendency towards urbanization and, with the peculiar exception of the Melanaus in Bintulu, very few indigenes have yet taken to urban life (Table 7).

Sarawak as a whole is characterized by the youthfulness of its population and well over half the people living in the three major

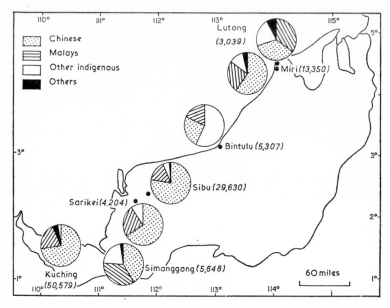

Figure 16   Ethnic composition of main urban centres, 1960. (Source of data: *Sarawak: Census of Population, 1960*.)

towns are less than twenty years old. Moreover, more than two-fifths of the population of Kuching Municipality and the Sibu Urban Area are Chinese in this age-group. This creates many planning problems.

Table 7   Degree of Urbanization by Community, 1960

	Total Population	*Urban Population*	*Urban* %
Chinese	229,154	74,915	32·7
Malay	129,300	23,502	18·2
Melanau	44,661	4,833	10·8
Iban	237,741	4,081	1·7
Land Dyak	57,619	924	1·6
Other indigenous	37,931	400	1·1
Europeans	1,631	1,147	70·3
Other non-indigenous	6,492	1,955	30·1
Total	744,529	111,757	15·0

Currently the demand is for expanded educational, child welfare and recreational facilities but in the very near future the urban population is likely to rise at an even more rapid rate than at present and the demand for housing and employment will increase in consequence.

Major urban centres
Over four-fifths of the total urban population lives in the three largest towns. Although in many respects these differ from each other and from the smaller towns, at the same time they epitomize the character and the problems of Sarawak's urban centres.

Kuching. Sited on the banks of the Sarawak River where small hills rise above the surrounding swamps and some eighteen miles from the sea, the State capital is the largest town in Malaysian Borneo and has the longest history. When James Brooke arrived, Kuching was a collection of wood and *atap* buildings with a population of perhaps a thousand; since then it has always dominated the Sarawak urban scene. It became Brooke's headquarters and as piracy declined and the Raj was extended, trade developed. Despite the setback of the 1857 insurrection, a Chinese quarter appeared on the south bank and by the late 1860's, when the town's population was estimated at nearly 8,000, this contained the principal shops, warehouses and commercial establishments, there being Malay *kampongs* on the north bank in the vicinity of the Rajah's Astana, and Chinese market gardens on the expanding fringes of the town. Although the town was mainly a trading centre, small-scale processing industries had already appeared, including sago factories and an antimony-smelting works.

Steady economic development in the late nineteenth and early twentieth centuries channelled an increasing amount of business through Kuching and the town expanded and was improved; already by the late 1880's 'a well built and planned town [had] sprung up, with good roads, handsome public buildings, and efficient police—all the essentials of civilization in fact'.[20] By 1939 the town had a population of 34,500 of whom 55 per cent were Chinese. Although retarded by the effects of the Japanese Occupation in the ensuing intercensal period, Kuching escaped war damage. In 1947 its population totalled 38,000, there being a slight increase in the proportion of Chinese.

Kuching 'agglomeration' has grown rapidly in the post-war era. A marked intensification of buildings in the town itself has been more than matched by the rapid growth of settlement on its periphery. Notable Malay concentrations have emerged at Kampong Tabuan, a

[20] Baring-Gould and Bampfylde, op. cit., p. 400.

C

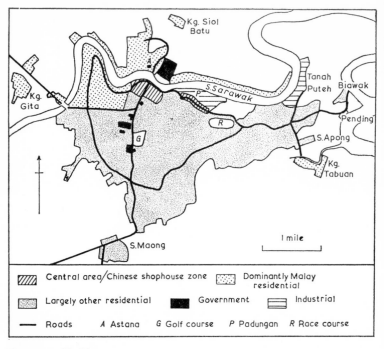

Figure 17   Kuching.

village to the east of the town on the southern bank of the Sungei Tabuan; at Kampong Gita, another predominantly Malay settlement across the Sarawak River to the west, and at Kampong Siol Batu, also across river, to the north. Suburban areas, some with Chinese majorities, have also developed on the southern fringes and to the west near the new port at Tanah Puteh, opened in mid-1961 (Fig. 17). House building has boomed in Kuching in the 1960's. The June 1960 housing census indicated about 4,000 permanent and semi-permanent housing units in the town. It is estimated that a further 1,400 units were completed in the period June 1960 to October 1962, the majority representing private development of low-cost housing.[21]

This post-war growth is completely hidden by the census statistics for Kuching Municipality which indicate that the town's population increased by only one-third between 1947 and 1960. In the intercensal period the municipal boundaries were altered very considerably: they were extended on the west to include Pending, but shrank on the north

[21] *Sarawak Development Plan, 1964-1968*, p. 4.

to exclude the *kampongs* across the river. As noted, settlement here had extended greatly in the interim, and it is estimated that the villages concerned housed about 10,000 people, the bulk of whom were Malays. Indeed it is probable that the population of Greater Kuching, including these cross-river *kampongs* and the various new suburbs, was about 77,500 in 1960 and that its rate of growth was at least twice that suggested by the census figures.[22]

This change in census boundaries had another important effect, for it gives the impression that the Malay population of Kuching declined between 1947 and 1960, whereas all available evidence suggests that there was, in fact, a very substantial increase in the number of Malays residing in the Kuching urbanized area. In part this was the result of natural increase, but to an important extent it represents the immigration of Malays from rural areas. Rural-urban migration has been a significant process in post-war Sarawak, as elsewhere in South-East Asia; for a variety of reasons, some economic, some social, towns and the life in them have drawn an increasing number of people away from their agricultural background in the rural areas and have proved particularly attractive to the young and the educated. Some Chinese have also moved into the town, but the growth of its Chinese population owes more to natural increase. It seems likely that, in 1960, Chinese comprised three-fifths and Malays one-third of the total population of the Kuching 'agglomeration'.

Kuching contains the main government and commercial offices in Sarawak together with an increasing number of small manufacturing concerns. The central area on the south bank remains a predominantly Chinese shop-house area, containing also the market and most of the offices. It is bounded on the west by a predominantly Malay area similar to that on the north bank; immediately on the east, on the way to the port area, lies the new Padungan industrial estate, opened in 1959 and designed to encourage the establishment of small factories, together with the blocks of flats constructed by the Government as a low-cost housing project. To the south of the central area is a more spaciously laid-out zone of larger buildings, including the Museum, the General Hospital and several schools, beyond which lies suburban development. A considerable section of the town's population forms part of the extending bureaucracy, but the port, the oil depot at Biawak, the government-owned shipyard and engineering works (the Brooke Dockyard and Engineering Works), the building and construction industries and an expanding

[22] *Sarawak Annual Report, 1962*, Kuching, Government Printer, 1963, p. 69.

range of processing industries provide other sources of employment. Trade, commerce and retailing also absorb many, particularly Chinese.

Sibu

Many of Sarawak's smaller towns and bazaars owe their existence to the construction of forts as Brooke rule extended in the nineteenth century. Often built where no permanent settlement had existed previously, these soon drew to them small groups of Chinese traders; many became centres of the expanding local administration and eventually emerged as small towns with this dual function. In some respects Sibu, the second town of Sarawak and headquarters of the large Third Division, is an example of this type of development.

Fort Brooke was built at Sibu in 1862 and this became the headquarters of the newly-acquired Rejang area. Development was slow and by the early 1880's the settlement consisted of about thirty *atap* huts housing a band of Chinese traders. In 1900 a Methodist Mission was established and immediately afterwards there was an influx of Foochow agricultural settlers. The subsequent growth of the local Chinese population, aided by Sibu's natural river anchorage, stimulated the growth of trade and a small town developed. Sibu was destroyed by fire in 1928 and the town, then developing fast, was completely rebuilt and provided with a modern drainage system. By 1939 Sibu had a population of 8,500. The town suffered little damage as a result of the war and its total population had risen by 1947 to nearly 10,000, over 60 per cent of whom were Chinese.

Sibu has grown at a phenomenal rate since 1947 and its total population in 1960 was almost 30,000; here again, however, census boundaries changed, the Sibu urban area having been considerably enlarged, chiefly in this case because the town had outgrown its old boundaries. The town is sited some eighty miles from the sea at a point where the southward flowing Igan enters a large bend of the Rejang proper. The main Chinese shophouse area, government and commercial offices, wharves and warehouses lie on what was once a small, flat, swampy island on the eastern bank of the Igan mouth. Residential areas extend outwards from here along the major roads.

The population remains heavily Chinese-dominated and this post-war growth is connected with the rapid development of the timber industry and commerce in general in the Rejang area. A $2.2 million town development scheme was begun in Sibu in 1954 and is now completed. The greater part of the town centre has been rebuilt and now consists of modern three- or four-storey shophouse and office blocks. The port has been greatly improved and Sibu has emerged as a very important centre for the rubber and timber trades. Some small-scale industries have been established and there is a modern cigarette factory and a large timber-processing plant (Plates VI and IX). Sibu is still a rapidly-expanding port because in late 1961 a new deep-water channel to the town was discovered: this, the Kuala Paloh Channel, enables much larger ships to reach the port, now in many respects the main centre of commercial progress in Sarawak. As in the case of Kuching, it is attracting increasing numbers of indigenous migrants from rural areas.

Miri

Headquarters of the Fourth Division, Sarawak's third town is located on a narrow strip of flat land on the coast some fifteen miles south of the mouth of the Baram. It is entirely a twentieth-century creation and the history of the town is closely linked with that of the oil-field.

At the beginning of the century, a small Malay *kampong* existed on the site. The first oil well was sunk in December 1910 and production rose steadily during the 1910's and 1920's to reach a peak in 1929. By this time the jungle had been cleared, the swamps drained, roads built and 'an area which was almost uninhabited [was] now a centre of bustling life'.[23] In consequence, the Resident moved his head-quarters from Marudi on the Sungei Baram to Miri which became the administrative centre for the Fourth Division. By 1939 the town had a population of 11,000, almost two-thirds of whom were Chinese.

At the end of 1941 Miri was invaded by Japanese forces; it suffered severe damage as a result of the war and the town proper was almost entirely destroyed. Reconstruction began in the late 1940's, but the town's population was still slightly smaller in 1947 than it had been before the war. Production from the local oil-field declined steadily and most of the oil refined and shipped from nearby Lutong now originates from the Seria field in Brunei discovered in 1929. As a result, Miri has not experienced the marked post-war growth of Sarawak's other major towns and its population rose by only 22 per cent between 1947 and 1960 to stand at 13,350 at the latter date.

Nevertheless, much development has occurred in Miri since the end of the war, and the whole town has been rebuilt. Miri lies on low-lying land at the mouth of a small river of the same name which flows

[23] C. Hose, *Fifty Years of Romance and Research or a Jungle-Wallah at Large,* London, Hutchinson, 1927, p. 237.

parallel and very close to the coast before finally entering the sea over a dangerously shallow bar. The town centre, including the bazaar, hospital and government and commercial offices, lies on the landward side of the river mouth and is hemmed in by steeply-rising land immediately to the east where a small amount of oil is still obtained. Some two miles to the south at Tanjong Lobang lies the government residential area and about the same distance to the north, halfway to Lutong town, lies the oil company's large residential area at Piasau. There are plans to build a new airport at Miri and, if the oil company's attempts to discover off-shore deposits meet any success, further urban expansion could occur; if not, Miri's future prosperity will depend on the nearby agricultural development schemes and local forestry development possibilities.

Town development programme

It was not until late 1960 that a Town and Country Planning Section was established within the Sarawak Land and Survey Department; in the last half decade this Section has done a great deal to produce adequate development plans for the State's towns.

Nevertheless, since the end of the war the Sarawak Government has had an extensive programme of town and bazaar development. Road improvement and drainage works have been undertaken widely in town areas and the centres of many small towns have been completely rebuilt in brick. During the 1950's, slum clearance and squatter re-settlement were undertaken extensively in the three major towns. In Kuching, government-sponsored, low-cost housing projects comprising both terrace houses and blocks of flats were developed at, for example, Padungan and Kampong Pinang and a new settlement was created at Kampong Gita to which some of the squatters were moved. New suburban shopping centres were also developed, such as those at Batu Lintang and Maong. At Sibu the former slum area at Pulau Babi was reclaimed and, at Miri, slum clearance was undertaken at Kampong China and Kampong Dagang and low-cost housing built with government aid. More recently, however, housing development in these centres has been undertaken by private enterprise. Although $7.5 million as been allocated for the low-cost housing programme in the period 1966-1970, it is now the explicit aim of the Government to make the rural areas more attractive places in which to live and work and the 1960's are witnessing a very heavy concentration of government effort and expenditure on rural-development projects.

3 Agriculture and Fishing

About four-fifths of the economically active population derive their living from agriculture and fishing, and, in 1965, agricultural products earned 51 per cent of total export income, excluding petroleum. However, although the Sarawak economy is basically agricultural, less than 6 per cent of the total area is devoted to settled cultivation; almost one-fifth comprises land used for hill-*padi* farming on a bush-fallow system and the remainder is under primary forest (Fig. 6). Agriculture in Sarawak is characterized by its smallholding nature; holdings are largely owner-operated and few engage hired labour on either a temporary or permanent basis. Of the holdings enumerated in the 1960 Agricultural Census, 45 per cent were operated by Iban and almost 20 per cent by Chinese; the Malay and Land Dyak communities each owned about one-tenth of all farm holdings and one-twentieth were held by Melanaus.

Agricultural operations fall into three basic types: export crop production (chiefly rubber, pepper and sago); sedentary peasant farming based on wet-*padi* and other food crops for local consumption; and hill-*padi* farming on a bush-fallow system. The divisions between these are blurred, however, for there is widespread integration of different crops and farm activities; thus wet-*padi* farmers frequently also have rubber or coconuts and a rising proportion of hill-*padi* farmers own rubber lots, whilst some plant pepper. Moreover, the current agricultural development programme is serving to increase the degree of this integration by encouraging the extended planting of cash crops.

The extension and improvement of farming is the cornerstone of development planning in Sarawak for, despite the recent growth of the timber industry, agriculture will remain the basis of the economy and ultimately social and economic progress depends on the upgrading of rural incomes. However, in terms of agricultural development, Sarawak faces severe difficulties. Over vast areas soils are poor, and often acid; the steep slopes characteristic of much of the interior and the extensive peat swamps of the coastal plains inhibit development and enhance costs, as does the lack of roads. The widespread existence of the bush-fallow method of hill-*padi* farming presents a complex and urgent problem which must be solved before agricultural development can proceed much further in interior areas. Training schemes are required to overcome the general ignorance of good farming practices and there is a shortage of suitable staff. Finally, development is hampered by land-tenure problems.

Land Classification and Tenure

The first land laws were introduced in 1863 and these and all subsequent legislation formed the basis of the Land Ordinance of 1932. The Land Settlement Ordinance of 1933 provided for the establishment of a new Land Register based broadly on the Torrens system whereby ownership recorded in the Register constitutes a guarantee of title. The classification of land into major categories according to tenure was placed on a legal footing by the Land (Classification) Ordinance of 1949. Work on a new Land Code to consolidate and enlarge the scope of all previous legislation began in 1954 and culminated in the Land Code of 1958; despite its inadequacies, this remains the basis of land administration.

Land is divided into the following five categories, only the first two of which may be held under title. Almost one-tenth of Sarawak is classed as 'mixed zone land', most of which lies in the First and Second Divisions, in the Sibu-Sarikei area, along the banks of the middle Rejang and in the coastal zone of Mukah District. Anyone can hold title to this category of land, which may also be occupied by indigenous peoples under customary tenure. It is the sole category of land that Chinese may own or occupy, and currently non-indigenous peoples hold less than one-quarter of all mixed zone land. There is considerable pressure on land in the main Chinese areas, particularly in the First and Third Divisions where little accessible unencumbered land is available, and, in places, customary land is occupied illegally by Chinese farmers. Wherever possible the Government is reclassifying land as mixed zone land to make more available for alienation to new settlers, chiefly to provide for the extension of rubber planting both on individual holdings and on block developments.

A little over 5 per cent of the State comprises 'native area land', of which there are sizeable amounts in the Second Division, the Rejang delta, Bintulu District, the Miri-Marudi-Bekenu area and the lower Limbang valley. Only indigenous peoples may occupy or hold title to this land, much of which remains under customary tenure. More than one-fifth of Sarawak is classed as 'native customary land' which is extensive in the interior and includes some areas designated 'native communal reserves'. All land held under customary rights falls into this classification. These rights were created in the past by the felling of virgin jungle and the land concerned is still used mainly for bush fallow; these are, however, rights of user only and cannot exceed the area that can be used by the holder, nor can they be retained if the person or community moves elsewhere and transference outside the community is prohibited. Under the Land Code, new customary rights can be created only by the felling of jungle under permits issued by the government, but the vast and inaccessible areas involved make enforcement difficult. When title is issued to land in this category it ceases to be native customary land and becomes either mixed zone land or native area land.

The fourth category, 'reserved land', includes forest reserves, protected forests, national parks and other State land used by or reserved for the government. All remaining land, much of which lies in the deep interior, is classed as 'interior area land'. Most of this is under primary forest; it cannot be held under title, but customary rights may be created with permission.

Shortly after its introduction it became clear that the 1958 Land Code suffered serious defects. In the absence of a general land policy it merely perpetuated the existing outdated and confusing system of land tenure. Land problems were already delaying rural, social and economic development, chiefly by restricting the amount of land available for extended settled cultivation. The existence of customary rights over all land used for bush fallow, and over much of that under settled cultivation, inhibited development, particularly in areas served by new roads, because, before any land could be alienated, the existing complicated customary rights must be investigated and this was a slow process. Essentially these rights applied to a pattern of subsistence agriculture and it was felt that 'the present system of Native land tenure is therefore unsuited to sound economic development'.[1]

Clearly there was an urgent need for a complete review of existing

[1] *Sarawak Annual Report, 1962*, Kuching, Government Printer, 1963, p. 52.

c*

legislation and a Land Committee was appointed to study the problem in 1962. Its report, published in 1963, recommended major changes of which the most important was the abolition of land classification in its present form, coupled with a provision to protect the interests of indigenes by stipulating that they may not dispose of their land without official consent. It further recommended that in areas of settled agriculture, customary rights should be recognized as ownership by issue of title, but that land used for bush fallow should remain under customary tenure and it was proposed to establish special reserves for this purpose. Changes were also proposed in the system of land alienation and administration. These changes would have expedited official land development schemes and opened up more land to non-indigenous farmers. The recommendations were accepted in principle by the Government; however, they aroused bitter antagonism among some indigenous groups and bills for the proposed new legislation to give them effect tabled in May 1965 were swiftly withdrawn. Land classification and tenure remains a basic problem, the solution to which must precede any large-scale agricultural development; moreover, as a problem with racial overtones, involving an apparent contradiction between the desires of the land-hungry Chinese and the idea of respecting and safeguarding 'native' traditions and rights, it could again emerge as an explosive political issue.[2]

Development Area Concept

The rapid social and economic up-grading of the large rural population is the fundamental aim of development planning in Sarawak. For this purpose development committees co-ordinate the work of government departments in each Division under the overall supervision of a State development planning committee. In recent years the basic feature of rural development planning has been the 'development area' concept whereby effort is concentrated on schemes within selected areas to achieve maximum effect with the limited resources available.[3] Un-

[2] See Y. L. Lee, 'Agriculture in Sarawak', *Journal of Tropical Geography*, Vol. 21, 1965, pp. 27-29.
[3] See *Sarawak Development Plan, 1964-1968*, Kuching, Government Printer, 1963, pp. 27-32, and M. R. Read, 'Problems of Agricultural and Rural Development in Sarawak', *Development Seminar*, Commonwealth Development Corporation, Kuching, April 1964 (mimeographed.)

fortunately the continued existence of the old land tenure arrangements hinders the full application of these plans.

The concept is based on three considerations. First, the most satisfactory means of developing State land for agricultural purposes is by planned, block settlement. However, many blocks of unencumbered land suitable for the purpose lie in inaccessible areas to which new roads must be built. To encourage farmers to settle on these blocks, 'facilities will have to be provided for them in advance, and the necessity of establishing a new community positively demands integrated planning and a concentration of Government's resources'.[4] Secondly, intensive effort is required to improve indigenous agriculture on the lines envisaged. By persuading hill-*padi* farmers to turn to wet-*padi* and to introduce cash crops into their economy, their annual income can be raised substantially, in the case of those joining rubber-planting schemes, to over four times their present levels. To achieve these changes considerable agricultural extension work is necessary to supplement existing crop-subsidy schemes. This is best done by concentrating on selected, suitable areas and so economizing in the use of the limited trained staff available. Finally, it is impossible to provide social and other amenities, such as schools and medical facilities, to the small, isolated and scattered communities that characterize hill-*padi* farming areas. The development of more intensive agriculture based on tree crops or wet-*padi* will induce these farmers to adopt a more stable form of settlement. This will foster greater population concentration and facilitate the provision of amenities. In many areas this entails the redistribution of holdings to achieve a more rational layout and this remains a complicated procedure under existing land regulations.

Apart from the rubber-planting scheme discussed on pp. 94-6, schemes have been proposed for hill-*padi* farming areas. These will involve the selection of blocks suitable for intensive cultivation, within which village sites will be chosen. Holdings will be redistributed to give each family a ten-acre plot within the block, the land will be brought into intensive cultivation, the families moved into the village and amenities provided. Subsequently the additional land formerly used by these communities for bush-fallow cultivation might be allowed to revert to forest or be used for planting purposes by other people. Under the land development programme it is hoped to settle 11,750 families on about 80,000 acres of land by 1970. Substantial crop subsidies are available

[4] *Sarawak Development Plan, 1964-1968*, p. 29.

to finance this programme, and \$13.1 million has been allocated for land purchase, settlers' houses and village development.[5]

Rice Production

Rice is the staple food of the people of Sarawak and *padi* cultivation has long been a basic feature of the local economy. Rubber now occupies a larger acreage but in 1960 almost 58 per cent of the economically-active population was engaged in rice production and over 46 per cent of the total population depended either entirely or mainly on this single industry for a livelihood. Rice farming is predominantly the activity of the interior indigenous peoples and almost two-thirds of all rice farmers are Iban; less than half the Sarawak Malays engaged in *padi* planting and only a very small proportion of the Chinese are so employed (Table 8).

Table 8   Peoples engaged in Rice Farming, 1960

	No. engaged entirely or mainly in rice farming	Percentage of all rice farmers	Total economically active population	Percentage total economically active population engaged in rice farming
Malay	20,220	11·9	42,975	47·1
Melanau	4,599	2·7	17,712	26·0
Iban	108,889	64·2	122,701	88·7
Land Dyak	19,878	11·7	23,498	84·6
Other indigenous	13,959	8·2	17,042	81·9
Chinese	1,734	1·0	67,171	2·6
Europeans	—	—	769	—
Others	387	0·2	2,417	16·0
Total—Sarawak	169,666	99·9	294,285	57·6

(Source: L. W. Jones, *Sarawak: Report on the Census of Population, 1960*, Table 21, pp. 260-261.)

[5] *First Malaysia Plan, 1966-1970*, Kuala Lumpur, Government Printer, 1965, pp. 117 and 119.

Despite this heavy dependence on rice farming, for long Sarawak has imported a considerable proportion of domestic rice requirements. Throughout much of the Brooke era, concern was expressed over growing rice imports. As population increased, largely through immigration, imports rose even higher, not least because the Chinese immigrants, themselves engaged in other activities, preferred imported rice. This dependence on food imports raised serious problems during the Japanese Occupation. For almost a decade after the war, therefore, developmental policy aimed at increased rice production to reduce the need for imports. Rice exports were prohibited and a government *padi* purchase scheme was introduced in 1946, both measures remaining in force. Little success attended this policy, however; rice imports are now treble those of 1950 and currently almost half the rice requirements are imported, largely from Thailand and mainland China. It is no longer considered possible, or desirable, to attempt to achieve self-sufficiency in rice production; it is hoped, however, to improve the lot of the rice producer and thereby increase output.

In a few favourable areas, farmers depend on the sale of *padi* as their chief source of cash income These sales are most significant in the Districts of Miri, Baram and Lawas in northern Sarawak; elsewhere, only a very small proportion of rice farmers achieve a cash income from their crop and, indeed, a mere 9·6 per cent of all rice farms sell surplus *padi* (Fig 18). The results of the 1960 Census of Agriculture reveal the bare subsistence level of Sarawak's rice farmers, for only 35·9 per cent of all the *padi*-growing farms enumerated, produced sufficient rice for family requirements. In only five Districts (Sibu, Miri, Baram, Limbang and Lawas) did more than half the enumerated farms satisfy domestic needs; over large areas less than one-third of the farms were in this position, and certain areas of serious shortage emerge (Fig. 19). Rice farming, therefore, 'is more a way of life than an economic source of livelihood'.[6] Even where surpluses are sold, rice gives a poor cash return for the labour expended; indeed on average it gives a lower cash return per acre than any other crop. Many rice farmers grow other crops and it is a significant fact that less wet-*padi* tends to be planted when prices for export crops are high.

Rice is grown in both the wet (or swamp) and dry (or hill) forms, and of the 290,000 acres planted in the 1964-65 season almost two-thirds comprised the latter. In both cases the crop is traditionally planted on

[6] Sarawak Information Service, *Information on Sarawak*, Kuching, Borneo Literature Bureau, 1960, p. 33.

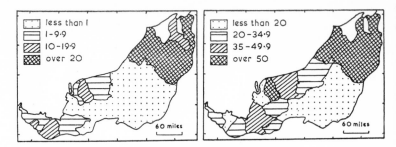

Figure 18   Percentage of rice-growing farms selling surplus *padi*.
Figure 19   Percentage of rice-growing farms producing sufficient *padi* for family requirements. (Source of data: *Sarawak Census of Agriculture, 1960*, Table 24.)

a shifting basis, techniques of cultivation are primitive depending on rudimentary hand methods, holdings are small, the use of fertilizers is uncommon and yields are extremely low. Yields of dry-*padi* average 600-720 lb. per acre; yields of wet-*padi* average 1,150-1,375 lb. per acre. Although the latter remain below averages recorded in other parts of Asia, efforts are now directed towards reducing the acreage of dry-*padi* and expanding and improving the area devoted to wet-*padi*.

Shifting hill-*padi* cultivation can cause serious land deterioration; but it provides other major impediments to the improvement of the social and economic position of the indigenous peoples for whom it is the chief form of sustenance. Productivity per acre is low and, although an inexpensive seed dressing has been introduced, yields cannot be increased by any significant margin. Output in many interior areas is already at or below subsistence level. Moreover, returns are unreliable, depending entirely on the vagaries of the climate, and bad years bring serious shortages; as Freeman remarks, 'the Iban are no strangers to failure and scarcity'.[7] Productivity per worker is also low. Hill farms produce a very small return for much arduous work and it has been shown that the hill-*padi* farmer might expect an annual return on his labour equivalent to only about $150 to $200.[8] Finally, it is estimated that about 70 acres are necessary to support each family of hill-*padi* farmers, only a small part of which is planted annually. The interior population is therefore widely scattered in small isolated groups, thus inhibiting the provision of social and welfare services. Without doubt

[7] J. D. Freeman, *Iban Agriculture: a Report on the Shifting Cultivation of Hill Rice by the Iban of Sarawak*, London, H.M.S.O. (Colonial Research Studies, No. 18), 1955, p. 71.
[8] *Sarawak Development Plan, 1964-1968*, p. 20.

the widespread existence of this type of farming presents the government with one of its most complex and pressing problems.

Hill-padi

The cultivation of hill-*padi* forms the basis of the economy of about two-fifths of Sarawak's total population; it is the dominant activity of perhaps four-fifths of the Iban, Land Dyak and other indigenous peoples. However, although their economy is based heavily on *padi*, all these farmers grow supplementary food crops, including sugar-cane, maize, pumpkins and cucumbers, either intermixed with their *padi* or around the edges of their farm clearings. Many now also have small plantings of cash crops, such as rubber and pepper, the income from which is often used to buy the extra rice needed to supplement domestic production.

It is difficult to assess the total acreage of hill-*padi* with any degree of accuracy but it is estimated that 171,400 acres were planted in the 1964-65 season, of which 55 per cent lay in the Third Division, 16 per cent in the Second Division, 14 per cent in the Fourth Division and 9 per cent in the First Division. The crop is grown on a shifting system, or more correctly a 'bush-fallow' system, chiefly on the poor, thin and often acid soils of the steep interior hillsides frequently on slopes of over 40°. Vast areas of virgin forest have been felled by shifting cultivators in the past and it is estimated that 18 per cent of the total land area has been used for this purpose.[9]

The annual cycle of activity among these farmers is geared to the growing of hill-*padi*, itself closely surrounded by ritual and superstition which inhibit change. The land selected for the new *padi* fields is felled and allowed to dry in June and July. Burning takes place in the period early August to late September depending on the weather; a good burn is of supreme importance for it simplifies sowing and provides large quantities of ash which have beneficial effects on yields. Sowing follows almost immediately and may continue well into October, the seed being sown in holes made with a dibbling stick. Grass and other weeds soon begin to grow among the newly-planted seed and weeding is necessary until the *padi* approaches maturity in January, when it must be guarded against marauding animals. Reaping takes place in March and April and ritual demands that the individual heads should be cut by hand. The *padi* is then carried to the main longhouse where

[9] See B. J. C. Spurway, 'Shifting Cultivation in Sarawak', *Malayan Forester*, Vol. VI, April, 1937, pp. 124-128.

it is threshed by treading, for there are also spiritual taboos on the use of flails. Winnowing is followed by ceremonial storing in bins.

Among the Iban and the Land Dyaks, family ownership of land within the longhouse territory is established by the felling of primary jungle and the rights so acquired are passed on by inheritance. The Iban have pioneered vast areas of virgin forest in interior central Sarawak in the last hundred years and Freeman provides a detailed account of their traditional methods.[10] When pioneering new territory a group of families starts farming in the lower reaches of a tributary stream, each family working a spur by moving up from its foot to the ridge crest and rarely using land above 1,000 feet (Plate IV). The Iban *umai*, or farm clearing, averages three to five acres, and there is a tendency to farm virgin land for two successive years under a system known as *krukoh* farming whereby half to two-thirds of the initial clearing is planted in the second year and the difference is made up by felling further virgin jungle. This system, deeply rooted in the traditional Iban economy, is a means of getting maximum returns from virgin land in the shortest possible time. When all the virgin forest in the lower reaches of the valley is exhausted, the entire group of families moves upstream, each family beginning work on a new spur. In this way a stream basin is gradually worked over and the land falls under family ownership. They then move to a new stream basin and follow the same procedure. Ultimately, when several valleys have been used, they return to the original farms, now covered with secondary forest; these are cleared and farmed for a single year and the grand cycle of shifting cultivation round the territory begins again. The length of this grand cycle varies according to local conditions, but, in 'pioneer' areas, it may be fifteen to thirty years. Because of this system of gradual advance in groups, the total holding of a single family lies in small blocks scattered in different valleys throughout the whole longhouse territory, although each family manages its own farm as an independent unit.[11] Traditionally, after a while the Iban often moved to an entirely new area and abandoned the whole of their former territory. By means of this true or 'pioneer' system of shifting cultivation they have migrated into and through the valleys of central Sarawak in the last century and a half.

[10] Freeman, op. cit., pp. 22-24.
[11] Freeman (op. cit., p. 22) quotes the example of a family at Rumah Nyala on the Sungei Sut which in 1949 owned about 150 acres of secondary jungle divided into 24 different lots and scattered over an area of 4 to 5 square miles in 6 different valleys.

Often Iban longhouse territories are too large for the farmers to live permanently in the main longhouse. When the cultivated clearings lie too far away to make daily travel feasible, the population splits into groups of families which move to smaller, temporary longhouses known as *dampa* sited close by the farms. These are rarely occupied for more than five to six years in succession, and when the land nearby

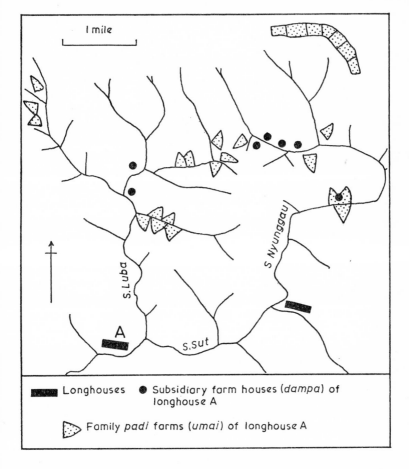

Figure 20   Subsidiary farm houses and family *padi* farms of an Iban longhouse on the Sungei Sut, 1949-1950. The Sungei Sut is a left-bank tributary of the Batang Baleh a little above its confluence with the Batang Rejang. (Redrawn from J. D. Freeman, *Iban Agriculture*, Sketch Map 3, p. 36, by permission.)

has been used they are dismantled and the most valuable parts carried to a new site where cultivation begins again. Eventually, when the grand cycle is complete, the group of families returns to the main longhouse to farm their secondary jungle in its vicinity. With a grand cycle of twenty years, less than one-quarter of the period is spent farming from the main longhouse and the rest of the time is spent operating from three or four different *dampa* within the territory (Fig. 20). This system has been used widely by the Iban, and Freeman regarded it as 'inevitable as soon as a community increases beyond about eight *bilek* families, and farms become removed by more than a mile or two from the original centre of cultivation'.[12] Many Iban now have small rubber holdings; these are generally near the main longhouse and one or more members of each family remain there much of the time to tap the trees.

The system of 'pioneer' shifting cultivation described by Freeman is adapted to areas where virgin forest is available in unlimited quantities. In many parts of Sarawak this is no longer the case: population growth, the extension of settled cultivation and the creation of 'forest reserves' all tend to restrict the amount of virgin forest available. This traditional Iban system of almost continuous migration, so prodigal in its use of land, is therefore giving way to the permanent occupation of existing longhouse territories. Of necessity this entails changes in land-use practices as the farming system is rationalized to permit stabilization. It is recognized that hill-*padi* farming will remain a basic feature of the economy of the indigenous peoples of much of interior Sarawak for some considerable time. Stabilization implies, therefore, a change from this 'pioneer' system of shifting cultivation to a system of 'bush fallow' where the population-land ratio within specific territories permits land to be cultivated for a single year and then left to recuperate for twelve to fifteen years before being re-cultivated; this, in turn, implies the abandonment of *krukoh* farming which can damage the land permanently by stimulating erosion and weed-growth.

Many hill-*padi* farmers already utilize a bush-fallow system and some, particularly Land Dyaks in the First Division and Iban in parts of the Second Division, have done so for some considerable time. However, if it is not to cause serious land degradation, this system requires that population density in a given territory be less than the carrying capacity of the land, because, if it rises above this level, the

[12] Freeman, op. cit., p. 35.

fallow period becomes too short for adequate forest regeneration and *lalang* and scrub gain control.

A minimum fallow period of twelve years is considered essential and fifteen years is regarded as more favourable. Using cycles of this length the average carrying capacity of a longhouse territory varies between thirty-four and forty-six persons per square mile. Clearly, when the population-land ratio exceeds about fifty per square mile, danger of land degradation through too frequent clearance is imminent, and, if it exceeds seventy persons per square mile, it definitely occurs.[13] In much of central Sarawak, population-land ratios remain well below these levels so that here problems of land degradation resulting from the Iban use of a bush-fallow system are as yet minimal, and traditional shifting methods can give way to greater stability without necessitating the abandonment of hill-*padi* farming. The general policy has been to evolve an improved bush-fallow system into which selected cash crops can be integrated to broaden the general economy and the process of stabilization has been greatly fostered by the extension of rubber planting under government subsidy.

In parts of the First and Second Divisions, on the other hand, the population-land ratio already exceeds the danger level. Settled cultivation is most extensive here, the available virgin forest has been exhausted and fallow periods are too short to permit adequate regeneration so that many areas have suffered soil erosion. Much Land Dyak land, for example, is now seriously impoverished and over-worked, as are old-established Iban areas in the Second Division. A complete change in farming patterns appears unavoidable and some groups have voluntarily abandoned their traditional economy for the cultivation of cash crops such as rubber and pepper, while others have turned to wet-*padi* planting. However, to initiate this change on a major scale is one of the urgent problems facing the Government. Almost a decade ago, as a short-term measure, a propaganda drive was started to persuade hill-*padi* farmers to develop swamp *padi* land farther down-river to supplement their existing inadequate production. Some success was achieved and there was, for example, a regular seasonal movement of hill farmers down-river to swamp *padi* areas at Lubok Nibong in the Second Division, but hill-*padi* farming is a way of life and change therefore comes very slowly. Land settlement schemes provide one of the best answers and in this respect Rubber Planting Scheme 'B' could play a major role (see pages 94-6).

[13] Freeman, op. cit., pp. 133-135.

Wet-padi

In the 1964-65 season nearly 120,000 acres were planted with wet-*padi*. This is double the acreage planted in the 1956-57 season and represents almost a 50 per cent increase over the 1959-60 season. A marked expansion of acreage has occurred in all Divisions in the last decade, reflecting the growing success of the policy of expanding and improving wet-*padi* cultivation (Table 9).

Table 9   Acreage of Wet-*Padi*, 1956-57, 1959-60 and
1964-65 Seasons

Division	1956-57	1959-60	1964-65
First	16,874	21,949	28,818
Second	17,488	28,336	31,680
Third	14,040	17,610	27,677
Fourth	8,547	8,754	23,172
Fifth	1,200	4,832	7,130
Total	58,149	81,481	118,477

(Source: *Sarawak: A Digest of Agricultural Statistics, 1966*, Agricultural Economics Section, Department of Agriculture, Kuching, March, 1966, Table 24, p. 40.)

Large expanses of wet-*padi* are rare. The crop is mainly confined to small scattered patches in delta areas and on coastal flats and the strips of alluvium flanking the lower reaches of the rivers although, where suitable, inland swamps are also used. Muruts and Kelabits have small irrigated *padi* fields on the patches of level land (known locally as *bah*), in the upper Trusan and were famed for their double-cropping here even in the nineteenth century; elsewhere in Sarawak double-cropping is virtually unknown. Although considerable development has occurred recently in the Fourth Division, the major wet-*padi* areas lie on the coastal and riverine flats between Kuching and the Rejang mouth. The coastal Malay villages of the First and Second Divisions have an economy in which wet-*padi* planting, fishing and coconut and rubber planting are inter-related. Some Iban communities particularly in the lower reaches of the Lupar, Saribas and Rejang Rivers, are engaged in wet-*padi* planting; Land Dyaks cultivate the swamps of the First Division as an adjunct to their hill-*padi* fields, and among them mixed fields, in which low-lying parts are under wet-*padi* and rising ground is planted with hill-*padi*, are very common. About a quarter of the Melanau community plants wet-*padi* on the coastal plains of central Sarawak, and in places small groups of Chinese do likewise.

There is little tradition of intensive wet-*padi* cultivation and this form of agriculture is probably a relatively recent innovation in most parts of Sarawak; certainly much of the current acreage represents twentieth-century development. The principles of controlled drainage and irrigation are largely unknown and only 2 per cent of the total wet-*padi* acreage recorded in the 1960 Census of Agriculture was irrigated; output therefore depends on the vagaries of the weather. Many wet-*padi* areas have poor natural drainage. The lack of bunds and drainage systems, coupled with the high, and relatively evenly-distributed, rainfall, means that fields are almost continuously inundated which encourages acid soil conditions and makes off-season cropping difficult; moreover, in some coastal areas farmers face problems of salt-water ingression. Transplanting from nurseries is general, but animal-drawn implements are rarely used and in most areas cultivation is by simple hand methods (Plate II). This restricts the area that can be planted by a farmer and holdings average 2½ acres in size; it also makes the suppression of off-season weed growth difficult and it means that the simple manuring that would result from animal grazing is absent. In consequence, yields are low and, because farmers are generally convinced that the returns will be uneconomic if the same land is planted in successive years, wet-*padi* is usually grown on a short-term fallow basis which leaves large areas of potential wet-*padi* land unplanted each year. This belief that even wet-*padi* land requires a fallow period is deep-rooted and has, on occasion, militated against the success of official efforts to improve cultivation methods. Nevertheless, much is being done to increase the productivity of existing wet-*padi* land, to encourage the development of new areas and, where necessary, to stimulate the diversification of the local economy to reduce the dependence on rice.

In 1959 an 'Assistance to Wet-Padi Planters' scheme was introduced to encourage and assist the development of wet-*padi* areas by the farmers themselves with technical advice, tools and materials provided by the Department of Agriculture; small cash subsidies were also available. This scheme was designed to stimulate the construction of drainage and irrigation works for areas of less than 300 acres and a sum of $50,000 was provided annually for this purpose under the 1959-63 Development Plan. The scheme proved moderately successful and by the end of 1962, 90 separate areas, aggregating 5,120 acres, had been improved; subsequently public investment in the scheme was greatly increased.[14] There remains considerable scope for increasing rice production by introducing and extending improved methods of water control both into existing areas and into potential wet-*padi* land. A total of $6.5 million has therefore been allotted for the drainage and irrigation programme in the period 1966 to 1970. It is planned to open up 7,800 acres of new land for wet-*padi* and to improve 19,500 acres for the production of *padi*, coconuts and other crops.[15]

It has been shown that the use of buffalo-drawn cultivation implements can augment wet-*padi* yields. Yet, of the farm holdings enumerated in the 1960 Census of Agriculture only 1,520 had buffaloes and over four-fifths of these were in the Fifth Division; throughout much of Sarawak, however, the use of animals in wet-*padi* cultivation is not traditional and even in the Fifth Division many are kept for other purposes. At the end of 1960, approval was granted to a scheme to encourage the use of buffaloes in wet-*padi* cultivation. Farmers are taught how to use these animals and because the number of buffaloes available locally is insufficient, animals are imported for training for use in wet-*padi* fields and these are provided to farmers at a subsidized price.

A major *padi* research programme was initiated in the 1959-60 season and experiments are in progress on the types of fertilizer, *padi* varieties and cultivation methods that can be best introduced into Sarawak to increase productivity among wet-*padi* farmers. A main *padi* research station in the First Division is supported in this work by *padi* test stations in other Divisions. Ultimately this will promote a significant increase in average yield per acre for wet-*padi* farmers. Nevertheless despite a growing total population, it is doubtful if most farmers will ever achieve a satisfactory living from *padi* alone. Greater diversification of their economic base is therefore essential. In many cases this will mean the integration of suitable cash crops into their farming patterns; in others it can be achieved by the more widespread use of off-season crops, such as soya-beans, groundnuts and sweet potatoes.

[14] *Sarawak Development Plan, 1964-1968*, p. 35. [15] *First Malaysia Plan*, p. 116.

Cash Crop Production

The four major cash crops—rubber, pepper, sago and coconuts—occupy over 420,000 acres; they account for the bulk of export earnings and provide the main source of cash income for much of the population.

Rubber

Rubber was Sarawak's chief export product for almost thirty years until it was displaced by timber in 1964. It remains the most valuable agricultural export and in 1965 accounted for almost 28 per cent of total export earnings, excluding petroleum. Essentially a smallholder industry, rubber planting has permeated much of the rural economy and many longhouse communities now have rubber which serves as a good safeguard against possible shortages of rice. There are only four large privately-owned estates (over 1,000 acres each), and comparatively few medium-sized holdings, Chinese-owned and averaging 100-300 acres each. Over nine-tenths of the rubber lies on smallholdings, most of which are less than five acres in size. Although it is the most widely-grown permanent crop, the main concentrations lie in the middle and lower Rejang in the Districts of Kanowit, Sibu, Binatang and Sarikei, in the First Division in the Districts of Kuching Rural and Bau, and in the Kalaka and Saribas Districts of the Second Division. Accurate statistics of acreage are not available, but the total area under rubber in 1965 is probably between 310,000 and 330,000 acres which is largely in the hands of Chinese and Iban smallholders.

Hevea brasiliensis was first introduced into Sarawak in 1881 when two or three seedlings were planted in Kuching. As elsewhere, the new exotic failed to attract the attention of planters until after the turn of the century and commercial planting only began in earnest in 1905. It was Brooke policy to discourage any large-scale capitalist development that might dislocate the lives of the indigenous peoples so that to a very considerable extent the growth of the new industry lay in the hands of smallholders, both immigrant and indigene.

Nevertheless, early development did not totally exclude the establishment of estates. Planting began on part of the Borneo Company's Poak concession in 1902; Javanese labour was imported for the work and the 2,500-acre property became known as the Dahan Estate. Five years late planting was under way on the Sungei Tengah Estate which also belonged to the Borneo Company. In the meantime, H. H. Everett, proprietor of a local cutch factory, had opened two small estates at

Bongkissam to the south of Santubong. The first rubber was exported from Sarawak in 1910 when boom prices were at their zenith. Only a very small acreage had as yet been planted, but continuing high prices aroused great interest and smallholders began to rush to plant the new crop.

Marked expansion of rubber as a smallholder crop occurred during the 1910's and again in the decade following 1923. Members of all ethnic groups had planted some rubber before 1910 and good returns from these initial plantings stimulated a planting boom in the years of the First World War. Planting extended among the Malays of the south-west; coastal Melanaus began to abandon or neglect their sago; the Foochow settlers at Sibu, augmented by the arrival of new immigrants, opened holdings on the low-lying peat soils flanking the Rejang river and in the Sarikei area; and rubber planting spread to the Iban communities of the near interior. This spate of activity was halted temporarily by the general depression of the immediate post-war years. By the mid-1920's about 100,000 acres had been planted with rubber in Sarawak; much of this was immature, and exports in 1924 totalled only 6,700 tons. Rising prices in the early 1920's brought renewed activity. Planting was widespread in western Sarawak and the Chinese invested considerable amounts in rubber around Sibu, Binatang and Sarikei whilst other Foochows opened holdings at this time near Kapit and Sebauh and in the Baram valley. Many Iban communities also planted the crop during the 1920's, and when the Great Depression ushered in the era of restriction the total area devoted to rubber exceeded 220,000 acres.

In 1931 rubber exports totalled 10,450 tons and, as the large acreage planted in the previous half-decade reached maturity, the crop was rapidly becoming Sarawak's most important export product. The crashing prices of the depression therefore had severe and widespread effects; although tapping continued, often at increased intensity, many holdings were neglected, others abandoned. The first attempt to restrict rubber exports in Sarawak was the introduction of the 'tapping holiday' system in June 1934, under which tapping was prohibited between fixed dates. This achieved limited success and under the *Rubber Regulation Ordinance* of February 1938 the Sarawak Government instituted a 'coupon system' resembling that in use in Malaya whereby individual planters were allotted a production quota based on an assessment of their holdings. This scheme was still in force when the Japanese invaded Sarawak in 1941. By that time the total area under rubber amounted to 239,557 acres. There were six large estates aggregating 10,580 acres and thirty-eight medium estates occupying 7,428 acres. The remaining planted acreage lay on nearly 97,000 smallholdings; 51 per cent of this acreage was owned by indigenes whose holdings averaged less than 1½ acres, and the balance belonged to Chinese in holdings averaging nearly 6 acres each.

Some rubber was destroyed during the Occupation, although there is no accurate estimate of the amount involved; conversely, there was probably some haphazard planting of seedling rubber during the war years, and of this there is also no statistical measure. As a smallholder enterprise, the Sarawak rubber industry recovered quickly from the effects of the Occupation and exports in 1947 slightly exceeded those of 1940. Moreover, like their counterparts elsewhere, the rubber small-holders of Sarawak responded immediately to the marked fluctuations of natural rubber prices in the post-war era and exports soared to an all-time peak of over 55,000 tons in 1950 in tune with the temporarily high prices induced by the Korean War. When prices fell equally spectacularly, so did output, and, in 1954, Sarawak exported less rubber than in any peace-time year since 1938. The high prices of 1951-52 aroused much interest in new planting and replanting with high-yielding rubber. It is estimated that almost 19,000 acres were newly planted between 1946 and 1951 and measures were taken to prevent planting on land required or suitable for wet-*padi*. As prices fell this interest declined: in some areas tapping ceased and one European-owned estate was closed.

In this immediate post-war period, rubber was regarded as a declining asset in Sarawak; official effort was not directed towards the rehabilitation of this industry but towards the discovery of an alternative cash crop to relieve the heavy dependence on rubber. By the early 1950's at least four-fifths of the total rubber acreage comprised the old, unselected seedlings initially planted by individual smallholders and nearing, or past, an age when tapping was to become or had become uneconomic even for smallholders except at times of very high prices. Much of this rubber was poorly planted, often on unsuitable low-lying peat soils. Techniques of maintenance, tapping and processing were of a low standard, yields were poor and most of the product was exported as low-grade sheet. Eventually, however, it was accepted that rubber had long become the main cash stand-by for many Sarawak farmers and that, despite earlier hopes, there was no easy alternative to rubber as the main smallholder cash crop in Sarawak. Of all the important tropical cash crops, rubber is the only one tolerant of a very wide range of soil and topographic conditions: it is sufficiently hardy to withstand considerable neglect and is relatively free from pests and diseases; it provides an assured and regular source of income for the smallholder; and it is comparatively simple and cheap to extract the latex and to process it sufficiently for sale to dealers.

Moves to rehabilitate the industry were first made in 1954 but did not materialize until two years later. The task was immense and urgent, for rubber remained Sarawak's major export product, the existing holdings lay in the hands of a multitude of small-scale, conservative and scattered producers, and the recently-developed high-yielding varieties were already being planted in other producing countries. The dearth of estates, a legacy of the Brooke era, meant that the substantial external private capital investment in the planting of high-yielding rubber that has occurred in post-war Malaya could not be expected in Sarawak nor, for that matter, could smallholders be expected to draw inspiration from developments on neighbouring estates. It was essential for the Government to stimulate, by financial and other means, the rapid expansion and improvement of a small-holder industry forming the basis of much of the rural economy; new land must be planted with high-yielding material, old rubber must be replanted where suitable, and standards of maintenance, tapping and processing must be greatly improved.

A Rubber Planting Scheme to subsidize replanting and new-planting with high-yielding material was introduced in 1956 and for various reasons was back-dated to 1955. Although subsidies were also available to estates, the prime object of the scheme was to 'expand and diversify a smallholding agricultural economy based on rubber as the cash crop and not to replace traditional systems of agriculture with one wholly dependent on rubber'.[16] The extension of rubber planting was regarded as a good means of inducing greater stability in areas of shifting cultivation and the scheme was designed, among other things, to reduce the dependence of the population on subsistence farming and to draw them into the money economy as a means of improving rural living standards. Smallholders received grants in the form of cash, planting material and fertilizers totalling $200 per acre for those new-planting and $450 per acre for those replanting. Subsidies to estates were of the same order but were made only in cash.

---

[16] *Sarawak: Annual Report of the Department of Agriculture, 1957*, Kuching, Government Printer, 1958, p. 27.

From the start the scheme proved to be extremely successful, initially particularly among Chinese smallholders, and the original target of 10,000 acres to be planted with high-yielding material in five years 'was well encompassed in less than half that time'.[17] In 1957 the planting target was increased to 40,000 acres, and in 1958 to 60,000 acres. Response continued to be excellent, and a rapidly increasing number of indigenous farmers took advantage of the scheme; the target was therefore increased again in 1959 to stand at 90,000 acres of high-yielding rubber to be planted before 1964. Since 1st January 1959 a cess has been levied on all rubber exports to help finance the scheme and this permitted the grant for new planting to be raised to $250 per acre. A total of $37.41 million was set aside in the 1959-63 Development Plan for the purposes of the scheme.

The target was not fully achieved, but over 80,000 acres had been planted under the scheme by the end of 1963. This was an immense achievement in the face of severe difficulties. Topographic conditions in much of Sarawak made terracing essential; *lalang* grass proved a serious pest on new holdings, particularly those on or adjacent to areas of former shifting cultivation; eradication was laborious and expensive; lack of communications made the distribution of planting material and the supervision of the holdings difficult; limited staff were available; and most of the holdings concerned were less than 5 acres in size, their owners requiring guidance in planting and maintenance techniques. Over one-third of this planted acreage lay on Iban holdings, chiefly in the Second and Third Divisions, and another third lay on Chinese holdings, mainly in the First and Third Divisions and the coastal section of the Fourth Division. Most of the remainder was planted by Land Dyaks in the First Division and only a very small proportion of the total represented planting on estates. Replanting of existing rubber proved very much less popular than new planting and over nine-tenths of the acreage planted under the scheme by the end of 1963 represented newly-created holdings. In part this reflects the general unwillingness of smallholders to forego income from existing rubber necessitated by replanting, but many indigenous people feel that there is plenty of land available and that it is therefore better to plant new land rather than replant existing holdings. Moreover, much of the existing rubber in the Rejang valley, planted as it is on low-lying peat soils, is not considered suitable for replanting. Under the existing land

[17] Ibid., p. 8.

regulations it is more difficult for Chinese to acquire new land, particularly adjacent to the areas in which they are already settled in numbers, and four-fifths of the replanted smallholding acreage was Chinese-owned, largely in the First Division. Replanting has also been undertaken on several estates. Since 1964 this scheme has been known as Rubber Planting Scheme 'A' and the grants now stand at $600 per acre for replanting and $400 per acre for new planting. By the end of 1965 over 100,000 acres had been planted with high-yielding material under its auspices; in addition some rubber has been planted outside the scope of the scheme, but it is generally of poor standard.

Apart from planting by individuals, the scheme gave top priority to 'communal, mixed racial and block plantings' and several such projects were undertaken. At a Foochow settlement near Bintulu, almost 4,000 acres had been planted by 168 families by 1959 and is now in tapping. A small Malay project was started at Engkilili in the Second Division and another small mixed racial settlement developed at Senga in the Fourth Division. Iban in the Third Division and Land Dyaks in the First Division followed a system of block planting.

Chiefly because of transport difficulties and the shortage of trained staff, the Rubber Planting Scheme was restricted to the more accessible areas. To meet the needs of farmers in the remote interior, a special Assisted Rubber Planting Scheme was introduced in 1960 and planting began the following year. Planters from isolated areas attend selected centres where they receive basic training in land selection, preparation, planting and maintenance; on their return home they prepare the land and then collect free planting material and fertilizer sufficient to plant one acre. Planting and maintenance are their responsibility but after a year the new holdings are inspected and if satisfactory, the planters receive planting material and fertilizer sufficient for a further two acres. By the end of 1965 about 8,000 acres had been planted with high-yielding material in interior areas under this scheme.

A new scheme, the Rubber Planting Scheme 'B', was introduced in 1964. Under this it is hoped to establish a total of 50,000 acres of high-yielding rubber by 1968 in a number of large blocks for alienation by title to settlers in individual holdings comprising 8 acres of rubber, 2 acres of *dusun* (mixed fruit and vegetables) and a ¼-acre house-lot. These are essentially land-development schemes based on rubber and thus far eight are in progress (Table 10, Fig. 21 and Plate III). The blocks vary in size according to local terrain and other factors and, before work begins, existing rights in the land are extinguished by

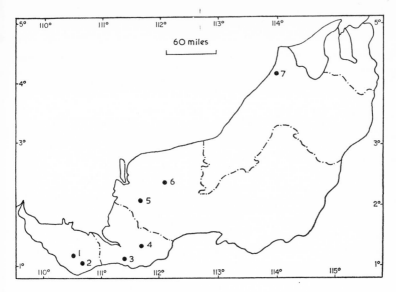

Figure 21   Rubber Planting Scheme 'B'.

Schemes

1	Simuja	5	Meradong
2	Gunong Sadong	6	Sibintek
3	Melugu	7	Lambir.
4	Skrang and Bukit Batu		

surrender or by adjudication and compensation. Development of each is phased and is the responsibility of the Department of Agriculture until the rubber is two years old when it will be subdivided into holdings and allotted to selected settlers with each scheme catering for about 200 families. Most prospective settlers are drawn from the surrounding area and in some instances include indigenous peoples formerly holding customary rights over the land. The schemes are generally multi-racial and in some cases, notably the Melugu Scheme, settlers from areas close to the Indonesian border have participated. Supervision is largely in the hands of experienced European officers who were formerly rubber planters in Malaya. Central villages with various amenities are provided as the schemes progress; subsequently, processing centres will be established and marketing will be organized by co-operatives. The Sarawak Development Finance Corporation has agreed to a scale of loans, method of advances and terms of repayment for all participants to provide for the cost of housing, fertilizers and personal subsistence until the rubber matures. By the end of 1965 a total of 8,000 acres had been planted on the schemes already in progress (Table 10). Topographic conditions, the lack of roads and the shortage of trained staff make these land development schemes extremely expensive; but they could prove very important in terms of rural development in Sarawak.

Table 10   Rubber Planting Scheme 'B', 1965

Scheme Name	Planned Acreage		Acreage planted by 31st December 1965	
	Phase 1 (1964)	Phase 2 (1965)	Phase 1	Phase 2
Simuja	559	224	559	224
Gunong Sadong (i.e. Kg. Taii)*	Nil	Nil	Nil	Nil
Melugu	600	977	600	350
Skrang	770	1,000	770	1,000
Bukit Batu	500	Nil	500	Nil
Meradong	642	1,910	642	1,830
Sibintek	600	1,066	600	100
Lambir	635	1,000	290	630
Total	4,306	6,177	3,961	4,134

* Work on this scheme began in January, 1966.

(Source: *Sarawak: A Digest of Agricultural Statistics, 1966*, Table 5, p. 11.)

As a result of these planting schemes, over one-third of the total workable rubber acreage in 1965 comprised high-yielding material, only a small part of which is as yet in tapping. Exports of rubber from Sarawak have fallen slightly in recent years as declining prices made tapping uneconomical on many very old holdings (Fig. 22). As the new plantings mature later in the decade, output will rise sharply and average yields, now between 400 and 450 lb. per acre, will show marked improvement. Moreover, a sum of $61 million has been allocated under the First Malaysia Plan to finance the planting of a further 105,000 acres of rubber in the period 1966 to 1970.[18]

However attempts to improve the industry are not restricted to planting: smallholders are also being taught improved management

[18] *First Malaysia Plan*, p. 111.

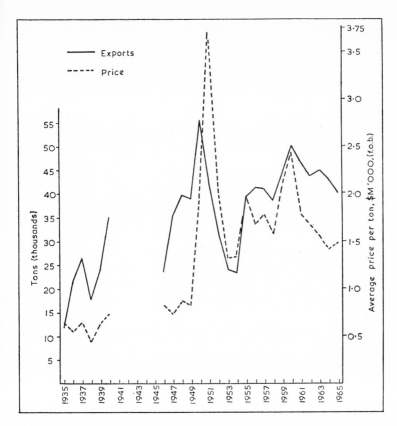

Figure 22   Exports of rubber, 1935-1965. (Sources of data: Colonial Office, *An Economic Survey of the Colonial Territories*, Vol. V, p. 140; *Sarawak: A Digest of Agricultural Statistics, 1966*, Table 2, p. 4.)

and processing techniques. The typical rubber sheet exported from Sarawak receives poor grades for it suffers from serious defects. Many smallholders are ignorant of correct processing techniques and use crude methods and equipment, and 'too small quantities of latex are handled to warrant exceptional attention, price margins may be negligible and as often as not a state of indebtedness requires as rapid a turnover as possible'.[19] Most smallholders sell unsmoked sheet to the numerous sundry goods merchants licensed to handle rubber and these frequently do the smoking themselves or do it on behalf of the smallholder for a fee. In 1959 the Department of Agriculture began

[19] *Sarawak: Annual Report of the Department of Agriculture, 1957*, p. 5.

a scheme to encourage the establishment of communal or group processing centres at strategic points at which smallholders can learn
improved processing methods. A simple processing shed and smoke-
house is built, the farmers co-operating to supply much of the building
material while the Department subsidizes them with other material
and equipment. The scheme has had marked effects on the quality
of sheet produced by participants. Use has also been made of in-
structional films. Nevertheless, much remains to be done, for only 8
per cent of the ribbed smoked sheet exported in 1965 received R.S.S.
Grades 1 and 2.

Pepper

Pepper is the second most valuable agricultural export and for much
of the post-war era Sarawak has ranked with India and Indonesia as
one of the three leading world producers. Brunei was noted as an ex-
porter of pepper 150 years ago and there is evidence of early pepper
gardens far up the Limbang River in the present Fifth Division. The
modern Sarawak pepper industry, however, developed in the late
nineteenth and early twentieth centuries and began in the west.

Although Chinese planted both pepper and gambier in west Sarawak
at an earlier date, the foundations of the industry were laid in 1876
when the Rajah offered free passages to planters from Singapore and
allocated land for pepper gardens to some local Chinese merchants.
Attracted by 'liberal concessions of land and monetary assistance'
from the Government, immigrant planters arrived from Singapore,
and the Hakka Chinese in the vicinity of the depressed Bau gold mines
quickly adopted the crops. By 1885 exports totalled 392 tons of pepper
and 1,370 tons of gambier and ten years later 'pepper gardens had
sprung up everywhere' in the former mining district of upper Sarawak.[20]

Money was advanced to many of these small-scale planters by the
Borneo Company, and high prices for gambier in the 1890's persuaded
the Company to acquire the 20,000-acre Poak Concession near Bau
on which Chinese smallholders planted the crops on the ratio of one
acre of pepper to ten acres of gambier; the refuse gambier-leaves were
used as manure for the pepper vines.[21] Continuing into the second

[20] W. H. Treacher, 'British Borneo: Sketches of Brunai, Sarawak, Labuan and
North Borneo', *Journal of the Straits Branch, Royal Asiatic Society*, No. 21, June,
1890, pp. 25-28, and S. Baring-Gould and C. A. Bampfylde, *A History of Sarawak
under its Two White Rajahs, 1839-1908*, London, Henry Sotheran, 1909, pp. 431-436.
[21] H. Longhurst, *The Borneo Story*, London, Newman Neame, 1956, p. 65.

decade of the twentieth century, this joint cultivation declined rapidly thereafter and gambier soon became unimportant as a Sarawak export.

Pepper production almost doubled between 1890 and 1900 and it exceeded 5,000 tons in 1906 when the industry concentrated in the Kuching and Bau Districts.[22] The new Foochow immigrants began to plant pepper near Sibu in the early 1900's but, although some gardens remain, rubber quickly became the basis of cash-crop agriculture in this area. The extension of Foochow settlement to Binatang and Sarikei saw the opening of a multitude of new gardens on the southern bank of the lower Rejang between the 1910's and the early 1930's. Nevertheless, a serious outbreak of disease and falling prices caused a continuous decline in production after the peak of 1906; by 1920 exports had dropped to about 1,000 tons. Many gardens were abandoned at this time and the industry was revived only by high prices in the late 1920's. Sarawak produced an average of 2,700 tons per annum between 1935 and 1939 and ranked as the second world producer of pepper after Indonesia. The industry was firmly established in the hands of Hakkas in the Kuching-Serian area of the First Division, and of Foochows and Cantonese in the Sarikei-Binatang area of the Third Division. This pattern has persisted.

Table 11   Number of Holdings and Area under Pepper, 1960

District	Number of holdings	Acreage	Average size of holding (acres)
Lundu	556	465	0·83
Bau	953	441	0·46
Kuching Rural	1,762	1,908	1·08
Serian	1,109	857	0·77
Simanggang	877	387	0·44
Sarikei	1,759	1,183	0·67
Binatang	585	362	0·61
Miri Rural	813	659	0·81
Others	1,118	914	0·82
Total	9,532	7,176	0·75

(Source: *Sarawak Census of Agriculture, 1960*, Table 10.)

[22] G. Dalton, 'Pepper Growing in Upper Sarawak', *Sarawak Museum Journal*, Vol. I, No. 2, 1912, p. 55.

D

Recently pepper has been planted by Land Dyaks in the First Division and by Iban in the Second and Third Divisions, but the industry remains largely a Chinese preserve. Holdings are small, averaging three-quarters of an acre. Most are tended by full-time gardeners with family assistance, although temporary labour may be hired at harvest time. Only about 26 per cent of the households sampled in a survey of the industry in 1959 depended entirely on pepper for their cash income.[23] The majority earn additional income from rubber, fruit orchards, vegetable plots or fish ponds and this supplies part of the investment capital (estimated at $7,000 per acre) needed to bring the pepper gardens into production; the remainder is usually borrowed from money-lenders at high interest rates, although a loan scheme is now operated by the Sarawak Development Finance Corporation.[24]

Vines will grow on a wide variety of soils, but success depends on the soil having good drainage, adequate water-holding capacity, a friable structure, low acidity and sufficient nutrient reserves. Planting is usually on well-drained hill slopes, for the vines are intolerant of excessive soil moisture (Plate IV). Forest on newly-opened land is felled and burnt and all stumps are removed before the cuttings are planted on specially prepared mounds of earth or terraces. Constant attention is required during the growing period; the vines are trained up hardwood posts, clean-weeding is practised, careful and regular pruning is undertaken to maximize the fruiting area and fertilizers are applied frequently. Indeed, the system of cultivation practised in Sarawak has been described as 'probably the most intensive of any pepper-producing country in the world'.[25]

Harvesting begins in the third year and yields reach a peak when the vines are five or six years old. The main harvest months are June to August and the work is laborious for the berries are picked by hand from ladders. For the production of black pepper, the berries are collected just before they are ripe, placed in boiling water and then dried. For white pepper they are left until fully ripe when the outer hull has become partly separated from the white centre, they are soaked in water, the hull is removed by rubbing and the white seed is dried. Black pepper is easier and cheaper to produce and yields a larger

---

[23] *Sarawak Census of Agriculture, 1960*, Kuching, n.d. (mimeographed), p. 23.
[24] See P. W. F. de Waard, 'Pepper Cultivation in Sarawak', *World Crops*, September 1964.
[25] *Sarawak: Annual Report of the Department of Agriculture, 1962*, Kuching, Government Printer, 1963, p. 15.

amount from a given quantity of berries; thus the price margin betweeen the two grades must be sufficiently large to induce planters to produce white pepper.

The economically productive life of vines in Sarawak averages ten to fifteen years. For long the crop was planted on a shifting basis: old gardens were abandoned and new land was cleared and planted when the productivity of the original vines declined. In part this system was related to the liberal use of burnt earth as a fertilizer, because about four acres of jungle land were required to supply the burnt earth necessary to support one acre of pepper for ten to fifteen years. In the post-war era burnt earth has been largely replaced by manufactured organic and inorganic fertilizers and this traditional system of shifting pepper cultivation has virtually ceased, although there is still a tendency to replace old vines with rubber, mixed crops or, in some instances, poultry farming, and to plant young vines on new land nearby. There is, however, a general shortage of land in the main pepper areas and recently Chinese planters have pioneered land on several newly-opened roads, including those to Simanggang and Ulu Oya; many of these newer gardens are very small and the average size is therefore declining.

The present method of cultivation is costly, requiring considerable capital outlay on, for example, fertilizers and posts, and most planters are in debt to pepper dealers. Despite the high capital investment and the large recurrent labour demand, pepper gives good returns when prices are high; there is, however, a rapid deterioration in standards of cultivation and a reduction in acreage when prices are low.

Pepper planting has always been essentially speculative; the world pepper market is characterized by cyclic price fluctuations to which planters are extremely sensitive. Prices vary in tune with changes in world production which is affected by several unpredictable factors relating to output in the major producing countries. Inclement weather, such as the heavy rains in Sarawak in early 1963, attacks of pests and diseases which, for example, seriously threatened the Sarawak industry in the 1910's and, more recently, Indonesian 'confrontation' and the embargo on imports of Indonesian pepper into Singapore—all have immediate effects on world prices. Occasionally these effects are amplified by the speculative influences which the special structure of the pepper market allows. For long, most Sarawak and Indonesian pepper exports have passed through Singapore and in 1959 a syndicate of Singapore dealers pushed prices up by accumulating very large stocks.

The fluctuating fortunes of the Sarawak pepper industry are directly attributable to price movements. High prices produce a spate of new planting; the new vines give a maximum yield some five to six years later so that there is always a time-lag between the movements of prices and production. Liquidation of stocks and increased production usually cause a subsequent fall in prices which acts as a brake on new planting and is accompanied by a decline in standards of maintenance.

Pepper prices rose steadily in the immediate post-war years to reach a peak in 1951. Most gardens had been abandoned during the Occupation and replanting and new planting were actively undertaken in the years up to 1952, by which time the number of tended vines was at least equal to the pre-war total. As these vines matured, output soared and in 1956 Sarawak was the leading producer of pepper in the world. Prices fell annually in the mid-1950's; a serious disease affected many vines, new planting was insignificant, some older gardens were abandoned and others neglected, and there was a tendency either to replant partly with rubber or to diversify with vegetable growing and pig-rearing. Production therefore declined in the late 1950's. The sharp rise in prices in 1959 and early 1960 stimulated considerable new planting, estimated to total about 1,000 acres in 1960.[26] Although partly offset by the abandonment of old gardens, this caused a marked increase in production in the present decade and exports in 1965 were the highest since 1956. Prices fell again between 1962 and 1964 with the usual effects on new planting which may be reflected in declining output in the later years of the decade. At present, however, there is an upswing of prices and planting is active in many places (Fig. 23 and Plate IV).

Total world consumption of pepper is lower than in pre-war days largely because its use as a food preservative has diminished. Pepper is now used chiefly for seasoning freshly cooked and prepared food and much of the world output of black pepper is absorbed by the meat-processing industry. There appear to be only modest prospects for an expansion of world pepper consumption and development plans for Sarawak do not envisage any marked extension of the planted area which stood at 5,228 acres in 1965. Instead, efforts are directed towards reducing production costs, increasing output from the existing acreage, improving the quality of the product, controlling disease and limiting the effects of price fluctuations.

In 1959 machinery was installed at Sarikei to enable exporters to

[26] *Sarawak: Annual Report of the Department of Agriculture, 1960*, Kuching, Government Printer, 1961, p. 14.

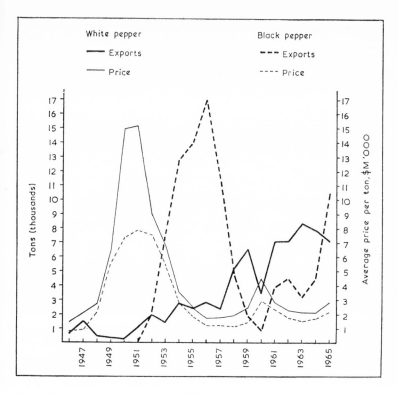

Figure 23   Exports of pepper, 1946-1965. (Sources of data: *Sarawak: A Digest of Agricultural Statistics, 1965*, Table 11, p. 15; *Sarawak: A Digest of Agricultural Statistics, 1966*, Table 13, p. 21.)

dry, clean and grade their pepper by modern methods, and the Sarawak Development Finance Corporation began to provide storage and short-term credit facilities to encourage crop release on the most advantageous terms to exporters. It is now proposed to operate similar processing and storage schemes at Kuching and Miri in the near future. In 1960 the rate of export duty on pepper was revised with the object of helping growers when prices are low and discouraging excessive speculative planting when prices are high. The problem of stabilizing prices has also been reviewed both by representatives of producing countries and by the FAO Committee on Commodity Problems. Moreover, long-term research aimed at improving cultivation practices and counteracting the effects of disease is now in progress; it has been shown, for instance, that hedge-planting can double output per unit area and planters in the Sarikei area are already abandoning their traditional system of planting vines to grow up separate poles in favour of the new method.

Sago

Sago flour was Sarawak's major agricultural export throughout the nineteenth century, a position it ultimately lost first to pepper and then to rubber in the present century. The flour is produced from the pith of a cultivated palm (*Metroxylon sagus*) which grows well on the swampy soils of the coastal plains of the Second and Third Divisions. Although much is planted on the deep peat which is extensive here, the best gardens lie on the strips of loam left by the meandering rivers. The industry here is traditionally a Melanau specialization and for long the local economy has depended heavily on this single export crop.

The palm takes 10 to 20 years to mature, depending on soil conditions and cultivation methods, and requires considerable attention during the growing period; constant protection against marauding animals is necessary, as is regular cleaning. Making new gardens, tending them, felling the palms and transporting them to the village are men's work; traditionally processing was almost exclusively the job of women. The usual working unit was the family, and it was suggested that in 1950 the average family working their palms throughout the year required income from about 20 acres. There is scant information on yields, but it was estimated in 1950 that one acre yielded on average a little over four palms per year and that an average of 2·8 *pikuls* of flour was obtained from each palm.[27] Accurate information on acreages is also unavailable. During the 1950's the Department of Agriculture estimated that 150,000 acres were under sago, but the Census of Agriculture in 1960 gave an estimate of 90,000 acres; a sample survey, based partly on up-to-date air photographs, produced an estimate of 34,000 acres in 1965.[28] The main producing areas remain Matu, Oya, Dalat, Mukah and Balingian in the Third Division and Saratok, Beladin and Pusa in the Second Division (Plate IX).

Sago production was important here before the area became part of the Sarawak Raj and Low reported in 1846 that large quantities of

[27] H. S. Morris, *Report on a Melanau Sago Producing Community in Sarawak*, London, H.M.S.O. (Colonial Research Studies No. 9), 1953, pp. 16, 39 and 162. 1 *pikul* = 133⅓ lb.
[28] *Sarawak: A Digest of Agricultural Statistics, 1966*, Kuching, Department of Agriculture, Sarawak, March 1966 (mimeographed), p. 37.

'rough sago' were exported to Singapore.[29] By about 1850 Chinese had established refineries in Kuching, but the increasing sago trade was severely affected by troubles in the producing districts in the later 1850's. The whole area was ceded to Brooke in 1861. With the restoration of peace the industry revived and the sago trade began to expand, organized largely by immigrant Malay traders. The Borneo Company also took an interest, opening a mill at Mukah, and, by 1874, was 'advancing money to numerous independent families to grow trees of their own'.[30]

Sago became a very profitable cash crop in the 1870's and 1880's and, with official encouragement, the last quarter of the nineteenth century witnessed the opening of many new gardens. Production increased accordingly. By the late 1880's Sarawak was said to produce more than half world output and exports rose from 8,700 tons in 1887 to 14,330 tons in 1897. Ten years later exports had risen to 20,400 tons and it was claimed that

'. . . the markets of the world are mainly supplied by Sarawak with this commodity. . . . On the low, marshy banks of the rivers, lying between Kalaka and Kedurong Point, are miles upon miles of what might be termed Jungles of the cultivated palm, where fifty years ago there were but patchy plantations'.[31]

During this period of rapid growth, marked changes occurred in the social and economic life of the Melanaus. By 1900 they had virtually abandoned their former subsistence or semi-subsistence economy for one based on a single export crop; concurrently, the old longhouse organization broke down to be replaced by the ribbon settlements of individual houses that line river banks in the area today. Moreover, a Chinese trading community had appeared on these rivers soon after the establishment of Brooke administration; by the end of the century the sago trade was passing increasingly into their hands and today it is dominated by them. Subsequently, rubber emerged as the main cash crop in coastal areas but sago has remained the staple product of most of this community. Exports averaged 21,000 tons per year during the 1930's, varying annually according to price conditions (Fig. 24).

[29] H. Low, *Sarawak: Its Inhabitants and Productions*, London, Richard Bentley, 1848, pp. 38-9.   [30] Longhurst, op. cit., p. 60.
[31] Baring-Gould and Bampfylde, op. cit., p. 430. See also S. St. John, *Rajah Brooke: The Englishman as Ruler of an Eastern State*, London, T. Fisher Unwin, 1899, pp. 211-212.

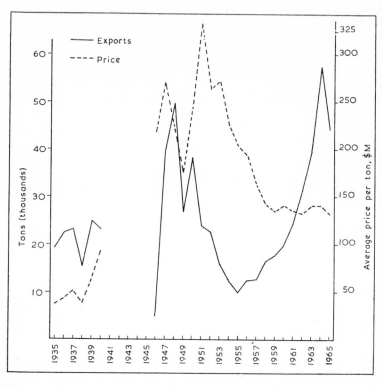

Figure 24   Exports of sago, 1935-1965. (Sources of data: *Sarawak: A Digest of Agricultural Statistics, 1965*, Table 27, p. 33; *Sarawak: A Digest of Agricultural Statistics, 1966*, Table 2, p. 4.)

Holdings were neglected during the Occupation, but when peace came a considerable income had accumulated in the gardens, for palms can be felled for the production of flour at several stages between their tenth and twentieth years. Prices were very high in the late 1940's and exports rose to a peak in 1948 as speculative traders poured large quantities of very poor quality flour on to the market. Legislation was passed that year in an attempt to ensure minimum standards for exports, but it never proved successful and was eventually repealed in 1959. Considerable over-felling had occurred during the boom so that, although prices rose markedly in 1950 and 1951, production declined. Prices fell drastically after 1953. Most of the flour was destined for the United Kingdom where a large proportion was absorbed by a single food-processing firm. When this was taken over by an American company closely allied to maize-growing interests, it substituted maize flour for sago flour and the Sarawak sago industry was almost ruined.[32] Exports dropped continuously to less than 10,000 tons in 1955; thereafter, paradoxically, although prices continued to fall, production increased, partly because new buyers emerged and partly because the sago producers have few alternative sources of income. The growers had been in a depressed condition for several years and, to provide some relief for the industry, the export duty on sago was waived in 1957 and has not been reimposed. The very rapid growth of output in the last half decade is not, therefore, a response to rising prices, for these remain at very low levels. Rather it reflects the increased concentration of processing in mechanized factories now supplying low-grade flour to the Monosodium Glutamate industry; it is also at least partly attributable to the interruption of Indonesian shipments to Singapore. The United Kingdom remained the major customer until 1962; since then it has been supplanted by Japan, which took 46 per cent of total exports in 1965.

Traditionally the production of wet sago flour, or *lemantak*, was a cottage industry. The men felled the palms and transported them to the village where the bark was stripped and the logs split. The pith was then reduced to a coarse sawdust by rasping with a nail-studded plank. The women processed this by placing it on a platform over the river, mixing it with water and trampling on it to express the starch which passed into a wooden trough below. Here the starch settled, leaving, after the water was drained off, crude wet sago flour. This was then collected on behalf of a local Chinese refining factory and paid for at a price based on Singapore market quotations. Usually a Chinese dealer tied several producing households to his factory by supplying goods on credit in order to ensure regular supplies of wet sago; the amount of credit allowed, however, always remained small, for unsettled debts could not be converted into land. The refining of wet sago has long been a Chinese monopoly, although it is neither capital- nor labour-demanding. The *lemantak* was merely washed and strained, placed in the sun to dry, hand sieved and then bagged; factories were invariably primitive, inefficient and dirty and 'profits came from keeping costs low and not troubling to produce flour of good quality'.[33]

[32] H. S. Morris, *A Report on the Sago Industry on the Oya and Mukah Rivers*, Department of Social Anthropology, London School of Economics and Political Science, University of London, 1964 (mimeographed), p. 8.
[33] Morris, op. cit., p. 3.

D*

The severely depressed condition of the Melanau sago producers, resulting from declining prices in the last decade, has been exacerbated by the breakdown of this traditional cottage industry. In response to the high prices of the post-war years production was accelerated by the introduction of power-driven rasping at refining mills close to the villages. This replaced the earlier domestic hand rasping, but the pith was still processed into wet flour in the households by the women. By the mid-1950's, when prices were falling, the refiners started to introduce mechanical means of processing wet flour in their factories. The whole sequence of sago processing has therefore become concentrated in a few refineries, each requiring a relatively small labour force. Almost the entire cottage industry which formerly supported the Melanau population has disappeared and a major source of their income has been removed; moreover, almost all household credit has been withdrawn by the factory owners.

Mechanization and factory processing has not resulted in an improved product, but it is quicker, slightly cheaper and simplifies factory management. The gardens are still owned by the Melanaus whose share of the industry has been reduced to tending the palms and felling and transporting them to the factories. This provides limited employment opportunities, and under-employment is widespread. Already there is a tendency to sell the whole crop of palms to a factory owner before they are mature and recently Morris predicted that 'it can only be a question of time, unless the process is checked, before sago gardens are sold in quantity to the owners of refineries, and the industry comes to be based on plantations in the hands of a few factory owners'.[34] The changed structure of the industry has had its greatest effect on the women who have lost their old economic role. Many men, however, have found employment in the local timber industry and this helps to counterbalance the greatly reduced income from sago. There is an urgent need for economic diversification in these depressed sago-producing areas but much of the land is unsuitable for other crops, because the soils are peaty and drainage presents serious problems. A wet-*padi* planting scheme is in progress, large-scale coconut planting might be attempted and marine fishing could be developed.

Coconuts

An estimated 73,300 acres were devoted to coconuts in 1965. Over large parts of Sarawak coconut trees are planted in small stands around

[34] Morris, op. cit., p. 4.

houses to supply domestic requirements of fresh nuts for cooking purposes; indeed one-third of the holdings with bearing coconuts recorded in the 1960 Agricultural Census did not sell any of their produce. However, the coconut is also grown as a cash crop either to supply copra to local oil mills or to furnish fresh nuts for sale on the internal market.

Essentially a smallholder activity, with holdings averaging 5 to 10 acres, the commercial cultivation of coconuts concentrates on the coastal and riverine flats of the First and Second Divisions which together contain over eight-tenths of the total planted acreage. The two Districts of Kuching Rural and Sadong have long been the dominant centres of the industry, which is largely a Malay enterprise, although recently the acreage under coconuts in the Second Division has increased markedly. Evidence suggests that the extension of coconut planting in south-west Sarawak is a development of the last hundred years. In the 1840's the crop was not widely planted in this area and Sarawak was supplied by imports from the Natuna Islands. Planting probably began here in the 1830's and was intensified and extended with the establishment of Brooke rule and the growth of Malay settlements during the nineteenth century.[35] Commercial cultivation is chiefly a product of the present century.

Standards of husbandry are poor and methods of copra production are crude so that the product is of low grade. Small quantities of copra are sun-dried but under local climatic conditions this results in a product of very variable quality. Most is prepared in simple open-hearth kilns, often fed with coconut husks and in which the drying time allowed is inadequate. The sale of copra is concentrated in the First and Second Divisions and oil production centres on Kuching.

Exports of copra rose to a post-war peak in 1950. Thereafter they declined rapidly and for much of the last decade Sarawak has not exported copra; moreover, since 1959 imports have been substantial. This does not indicate, however, that the industry declined and, indeed, local production of copra rose from 3,884 tons in 1959 to 9,000 tons in 1965. Rather it indicates the growth of coconut oil production both for export and for use locally in cooking and the soap industry. Thus output of coconut oil rose noticeably in the early 1960's and the removal of the export duty on this product in December 1960 stimulated an increase in exports of refined oil from 18,350 *pikuls* in 1959 to

[35] Low, op. cit., p. 38; T. Harrisson, 'The Malays of South-west Sarawak before Malaysia', *Sarawak Museum Journal*, Vol. XI, Nos. 23-24, 1964, pp. 379 and 426.

45,000 *pikuls* in 1961. Subsequently exports of refined oil fell and crude oil now comprises the bulk of overseas shipments, most of which go to Singapore.

There are now seven copra mills in Sarawak, all in the First Division. In 1965 these produced 76,600 *pikuls* of crude oil of which one-third was exported and over half was sold to the two local refineries which produced a total of 38,400 *pikuls* of refined oil; four-fifths of this was consumed locally, and exports of refined oil totalled 6,900 *pikuls* [36] The output of copra cake (the residue of milled copra) has also risen and most is used locally as animal feed. The total capacity of the existing copra mills is almost double present 'through-put' so they should have little difficulty in absorbing the expanded copra production expected in the next few years. In 1965 coconut products were 0·9 per cent of the total value of Sarawak's exports, excluding petroleum.

About a decade ago the coconut was recognized as a potentially valuable cash crop that could be easily integrated into existing farm patterns and thereby diversify the local economy, particularly of wet-*padi* farmers. The planted acreage at that time was inadequate to meet local needs and in some areas prices of coconut products were highly inflated and nuts were imported from neighbouring territories. Moreover, although exports of copra almost ceased, there were good prospects for increased local consumption of oil and for the export of coconut products. Many of the existing palms were old: frequently of poor genetic type, they were badly planted on inadequately drained land, the use of fertilizers was almost unknown and yields were low. There was an urgent need to rehabilitate and extend the industry and plans were completed in 1958 to launch a subsidized Coconut Planting Scheme the following year. The aim was to stimulate the new planting of coconuts to make Sarawak self-sufficient in coconut oil production, to make copra and oil available as export products and to increase the supplies of fresh nuts for home consumption.

The Coconut Planting Scheme takes two forms. To encourage the planting of coconuts in small stands near houses to provide for domestic requirements, seedlings are issued free to persons wishing to plant fifteen palms or less; no further subsidy is provided and this planting is referred to as 'unsubsidized'. To increase the diversification of local agriculture, the scheme is also designed to stimulate interest in the coconut as a smallholder cash crop. Seedlings are issued free to small holders at the rate of fifty palms per acre, subject to the holding having

[36] *Sarawak: A Digest of Agricultural Statistics*, 1966, p. 35.

suitable soils and adequate drainage, and a total cash subsidy of $2 per palm is paid over three years if planting and maintenance are satisfactory. In the first instance smallholders receive aid for a maximum of five acres, but if this proves successful they are eligible for assistance to plant a further five acres. Seed nuts to provide planting material for distribution come almost entirely from the First Division and are transported to other Divisions by sea and river. Seed nuts have also been obtained from Labuan to supply planters in the Fourth and Fifth Divisions.

The initial aim of the scheme was to plant a minimum of 10,000 acres during the 1959-63 Development Plan period and a sum of $1.2 million was set aside for the purpose. Response was very good and in 1960 the target was raised to 20,000 acres and the capital sum to $2 million. This enlarged target was exceeded and almost 22,000 acres had been planted by the end of 1963. This success encouraged the further enlargement of the scheme under the 1964-68 Development Plan and $9.5 million were allocated to subsidize the planting of 50,000 acres.[37]. Most coconuts are planted on coastal muck soils on which adequate drainage is essential. To achieve the increased rate of planting now planned, it is necessary to build bunds and provide water gates in many areas. The allocation for drainage and irrigation works under the current Development Plan is intended to cover these requirements, for in many instances wet-*padi* and coconuts already form part of an integrated economy which it is hoped will become more widespread. Coconuts demand relatively little labour and their cultivation does not interfere with the cycle of wet-*padi* planting. Although the cash returns they provide are lower than those obtainable from rubber, they are a profitable supplement to the economy of wet-*padi* farmers lacking a permanent cash crop. Moreover, inter-cropping permits further diversification and crops such as vegetables, maize and bananas are being planted increasingly among new coconuts.

By the end of 1965 almost 44,000 acres had been planted since the inception of the scheme. Almost half this new acreage lies in the Second Division. Much new planting has also occurred in the First Division, particularly during 1964 and 1965 (Table 12). The greatest response to the scheme has come from Malays in the coastal areas and over three-fifths of the total newly-planted acreage lie on Malay holdings. The local demand for coconuts and coconut products still exceeds supply. There seems every likelihood, therefore, that the greatly increased

[37] *Sarawak Development Plan, 1964-1968*, p. 35.

acreage which this planting scheme will provide by the end of the decade will prove a valuable addition to Sarawak's economy.

Table 12   Acreage planted under the Coconut Planting Scheme, 1959-1965 (to the nearest 10 acres)

Division	Subsidized	Un-subsidized	Total
First	12,360	860	13,220
Second	18,910	1,710	20,620
Third	2,940	1,570	4,510
Fourth	1,720	1,320	3,040
Fifth	1,570	800	2,370
Total	37,500	6,260	43,760

(Source: *Sarawak: A Digest of Agricultural Statistics, 1966*, Tables 17 and 18, pp. 28 and 29.)

Oil-palm

In recent years the acreage under oil-palm in mainland Malaysia has expanded rapidly and planting is extending in neighbouring Sabah. Despite some fears that recent additions to total world acreage may affect future prices, oil-palm remains a remunerative export crop whose introduction to Sarawak could play an important role in diversifying the economy. An abortive attempt was made to establish an oil-palm estate near Kanowit before the Occupation; since then the crop has not been planted on a commercial basis.

In 1960 plans were finalized between the Government and the Colonial (now Commonwealth) Development Corporation for a pilot oil-palm planting project at Danau in the Fifth Division. A twenty-acre block was planted and if results proved satisfactory it was intended to develop about 5,000 acres as an estate to be followed by smallholding development. Subsequently, a large area between Miri and Bintulu was shown to possess soils well suited to oil-palm planting. The Commonwealth Development Corporation now proposes to develop an estate of about 5,500 acres to the south of Bukit Subis in the vicinity of the Rivers Luak and Kabuloh which will be served by the new road from Miri. Under the 1964-1968 Development Plan, $2 million were allocated for Government expenditure on oil-palm development. It is hoped that at least two estates will be established in the plan period and a tentative planting target of 10,000 acres has been fixed.[38] Proposals have also been made for the development of oil-palm on smallholdings.

Minor Crops

Many minor crops are grown both for sale and for domestic consumption and although these occupy only small areas they are often of considerable importance in the local economy. Several crops, including maize, tapioca and sweet potatoes, are widely planted as rice supplements by hill farmers, and local fruits such as durian and rambutan are grown in mixed cultivation in most villages. Many other crops (e.g. groundnuts, chillies and soya-beans), are cultivated on a small scale and often occur as cash crops.

Most of these are grown for home consumption, but part of the output is sold locally and provides a welcome source of cash for many farmers. Maize, for example, which occupied a total of over 1,000 acres in 1960, is grown to a limited extent as a cash crop in many areas. Bananas are widely cultivated and have gained in popularity as a cash crop on newly-opened rubber and coconut holdings; considerable quantities are sold locally and some are exported. There is, in fact, a constant demand for fruit of all types, but quality is sometimes poor and fruiting is irregular; thus nurseries of certain local fruits have been established in all Divisions to provide improved seedlings for distribution to farmers. Pineapples grow well on the widespread peaty soils; entirely a smallholder activity, pineapple-growing concentrates in the First Division and around Sarikei in the Third Division. The canning of pineapples for export is a thriving industry in Malaya, and similar development could occur in Sarawak; however, although representatives of the Malayan industry have investigated local possibilities, nothing has materialized.

Market-gardening near the main towns is almost exclusively a Chinese preserve as it has been since the beginning of the Brooke era. Vegetables occupied an estimated 2,000 acres in 1960, of which more than a quarter lay in the Districts of Kuching Rural and Serian; they are also important in the Miri area, which exports fresh vegetables to Brunei. In recent years some success has attended attempts to persuade farmers in the interior to plant more vegetables for home use.

Citrus fruits are one of the most important minor cash crops, and

[38] *Sarawak Development Plan, 1964-1968*, p. 22.

occupied a total of 1,240 acres in 1960. Comprising mainly mandarin oranges, the groves are concentrated in the Binatang and Sarikei Districts of the Third Division and in the Districts of Bau, Serian and Kuching Rural in the First Division, although small areas have been planted in all Divisions. Standards of maintenance are high, the groves are manured regularly and, on the low-lying muck soils of the Binatang area, trees are often planted on broad flat-topped mounds two or three feet high. Citrus production is a Chinese enterprise and a sizeable capital investment in the Binatang area. In 1962 a factory was opened in Binatang town to produce fruit juice and other drinks from oranges and these find a ready sale locally. Part of the output of fruit is exported.

Tobacco is a relatively important minor cash crop in certain areas and occupied about 1,000 acres in 1960. Low-grade, sun-dried tobacco is produced in the First, Third and Fourth Divisions for sale in local bazaars. The opening of a cigarette factory at Sibu in 1959 aroused local interest in the crop and trials have been made with imported seed to improve the quality of leaf produced. This factory absorbs much of the output which it mixes with imported tobaccos to produce cigarettes sold locally under various brand names (Plate IX).

About 1,300 acres were planted with coffee (chiefly *Robusta*) in 1960. Coffee is grown to a limited extent in all Divisions and can serve as a useful cash crop for many indigenous farmers; indeed, marked interest was shown in coffee planting by Land Dyaks in the First Division and by Iban in the Second Division in the late 1950's and early 1960's.

Research on these and other potential cash crops continues, and occasionally interest develops in new possibilities; thus the Commonwealth Development Corporation is assisting experimental work on cocoa, and proposals have been made to plant sugar-cane. Under present conditions, however, none of these offers much hope of large-scale development and in the long run the economy will remain based on a few extremely important export crops.

Livestock

Livestock play a minor role in the Sarawak farm economy. Recently pig-keeping and poultry-farming have developed on a significant commercial scale, but, although domestic consumption of animal products is rising, little progress has been achieved in other forms of livestock husbandry. Local development in this sphere could help to increase the protein content of rural diets and also provide a new supplementary source of cash income. The capital cost of establishing herds of livestock is high and training and supervision would be required to ensure adequate management standards; on the other hand, although imports are rising continuously, most animal feeding-stuffs can be produced locally.

Pigs

The pig is the most important farm animal in Sarawak. Pigs were kept by more than half the holdings enumerated in the 1960 Census of Agriculture, but pig-keeping falls into two distinct types. On the one hand, a small hardy local breed is kept widely as scavengers by the non-Muslim indigenous peoples. Usually these are not penned and live under and around longhouses; they are important as a source of protein in the diet of these peoples and occasional sales provide a useful cash supplement. In sharp contrast are the commercial piggeries operated by Chinese near the larger towns, most of which rear stock comprising crosses between the local Chinese breed and imported breeds such as Berkshires, Middle Whites and Tamworths. Standards of housing and management are usually good and the typical herd averages five to ten animals, although near centres of heavy population operations are on a larger scale and herds of fifty to a hundred pigs are common. The supply of foodstuffs forms the heaviest single item of expenditure in commercial pig-keeping. Imported protein-rich foods are used only on a limited scale, and the swill and kitchen waste emanating from coffee shops provides an important source of pig food; copra cake, rasped sago and other locally-produced foodstuffs are also used.

As an important segment of the economy, both as a commercial operation and for the supply of protein to interior peoples, pig-keeping has attracted much official attention. A decade ago local production of pork was totally inadequate to meet domestic requirements and 17,700 pigs were imported in 1956. There was a clear need to improve the quality of stock and to augment the total pig population. At this time Divisional piggeries existed to supply high-quality stock to the more progressive Chinese pig-keepers. Demand from these for improved stock was consistently heavy, exceeding supplies available from official sources, and in 1962 a scheme was introduced whereby selected operators were supplied with pure breeding stock to produce weaners for sale to the public at controlled prices. Subsequently the Sarawak

Development Finance Corporation initiated a loan scheme to help in the establishment of modern piggeries; by the end of 1964 a total of $250,000 had been advanced, largely to Chinese pig-keepers in the lower Rejang, Kuching and Miri areas.

Attempts are also being made to raise standards among Land Dyak and Iban pig-keepers. This entails two major changes: the local breed must be replaced by improved cross-bred stock and the animals must be penned and properly fed. Much progress has been made in the last half decade and pig-rearing in pens in association with fish ponds is becoming a feature of many interior settlements. To stimulate pork production in these remoter areas a pig-subsidy scheme was introduced in 1964 whereby farmers receive aid to construct a pigsty and to buy feed and stock. Five hundred and eighty-four units had been established under this scheme by the end of 1965, over two-thirds of which were in the First and Second Divisions.

Table 13   Imports and Exports of Pigs, 1960-1965

	Imports	Exports
1960	13,227	748
1961	16,585	558
1962	10,530	895
1963	10,974	616
1964	10,992	769
1965	8,029	1,647

(Source: *Sarawak: A Digest of Agricultural Statistics, 1966*,
Tables 36 and 37, pp. 62 and 63.)

Figures for the pig population of interior areas are confessedly inaccurate, but there are probably now over 300,000 pigs in Sarawak; this represents a large increase over the estimated total of 177,600 in 1960. The number of local pigs slaughtered doubled between 1962 and 1965 and the success of the various schemes is further indicated by the drop in pig imports. Moreover, some animals are now exported, chiefly from Miri to Brunei, and an internal trade in live pigs from Sibu to Kuching, reflecting marked local price differences, has developed[39] (Table 13). The main concentrations of improved stock remain in the vicinity of the larger towns and are predominantly in Chinese hands; yet about half the total pig population, mainly the local

[39] The average price for first quality pigs in Kuching in 1965 was $120.75 per *pikul* as against a price of $105.75 in Sibu (*Sarawak: A Digest of Agricultural Statistics, 1966*, Table 32, p. 59.)

breed, is in the Third Division. There is still, therefore, considerable scope for the improvement of this branch of agriculture.

Poultry

The total poultry population exceeds $1\frac{1}{4}$ million birds, the bulk of which are fowls with very much smaller numbers of ducks and geese. As with pig-keeping, a sharp distinction exists between the relatively highly organized commercial units that characterize the large urban centres and the keeping of poultry to satisfy family needs in rural areas. There is a substantial local demand for both table birds and eggs, and imports have been considerable. Commercial poultry-farming began to develop on an important scale in the late 1950's. Day-old chicks were imported from Australia and semi-intensive and intensive systems of management rapidly gained favour; of the latter the battery system is now widely used. Commercial poultry-farming is largely in Chinese hands. Today it represents considerable capital investment and flocks of up to 5,000 birds are not uncommon, feeding-stuffs consisting of rations either mixed locally or imported, with imported proprietary foods increasing in popularity. Efficiently-run commercial hatcheries now exist in Kuching, Sibu and Miri to supply hatching-eggs and day-old chicks to local farmers, although substantial numbers of both are still imported.

Table 14   Imports and Exports of Live Poultry and Eggs, 1957-1965

| | Imports | | Exports | |
	Live poultry	Eggs	Live poultry	Eggs
1957	34,592	9,034,200	56,402	4,979
1958	36,264	8,838,000	67,160	35,197
1959	61,798	10,501,300	46,519	48,054
1960	57,120	17,674,100	48,243	403,000
1961	35,298	16,510,800	38,689	473,600
1962	34,866	17,252,900	50,745	498,000
1963	35,019	22,539,800	62,871	659,300
1964	833	31,401,258	74,714	387,500
1965	16	23,841,864	81,464	27,032

(Source: *Sarawak: A Digest of Agricultural Statistics, 1965,* Tables 44, 45 and 53, pp. 55, 56 and 64, and *Sarawak: A Digest of Agricultural Statistics, 1966,* Tables 36, 37 and 38, pp. 62-64.)

The growth of the industry has resulted in a very marked decline in imports of live birds coupled with a noticeable increase in exports, and Sarawak is now almost self-sufficient in poultry production. In contrast, however, imports of eggs have risen steadily, and recently exports, which were important for a time from Miri to Brunei, have fallen sharply (Table 14). Considerable expansion and improvement remains possible, particularly among interior peoples whose standards of maintenance are poor. Modern systems of poultry-keeping are demonstrated by Department of Agriculture staff and groups of indigenous farmers are being taught to build small hen-houses from local materials.

Buffaloes, cattle and goats
Buffaloes, cattle and goats are also kept but they play an insignificant part in the local economy. In 1965 there were 8,200 goats in Sarawak. These roam freely around Malay and interior indigenous settlements where they supply meat for special occasions. Three-quarters of the total of 7,900 buffaloes are located in the Fifth Division. They are reared here as a source of meat, although their chief significance is as an indication of social standing; they are also used to some extent in wet-*padi* farming, a use which is currently receiving official encouragement. Elsewhere buffaloes are regarded mainly as an investment 'to be realized in times of financial stress'.[40]

The total cattle population numbered 7,000 in 1965. Small milking herds are stall-fed near the main towns by Indians and Chinese, but yields are low and the milk is often produced under poor, unhygienic conditions. Small herds of beef cattle occur on the drier sandy coastal stretches and there is a notable concentration in the Kalaka District of the Second Division. Indigenous peoples also keep cattle in limited numbers in the First, Second and Third Divisions, often on a communal basis. Standards of management are very low. Stock grazes on free range with a minimum of attention; no supplementary food is provided, in-breeding is common and there is a high proportion of males to females; indeed, it has been claimed that 'the aim of most owners appears to be to maintain their animals in a living condition with the minimum of trouble'.[41] The existing demand for beef and dairy products is largely satisfied by imports of frozen supplies. Undoubtedly rising living standards will bring increased consumption of these foods,

[40] *Sarawak: Annual Report of the Department of Agriculture, 1960*, p. 20.
[41] Ibid., p. 12.

However, although considerable scope exists for improvements in stock and in management methods, ignorance and the lack of capital are major impediments to development.

Fishing

The general absence of livestock means that fish provide the main source of animal protein for much of the population. Large quantities of fish—salted, dried and tinned—are imported annually; demand is rising steadily and since fish can be produced at much lower cost than other animal protein foodstuffs, the opportunity exists for expansion and improvement in both marine and freshwater fishing.

Marine fishing

Marine fishing concentrates in the shallow coastal waters and estuaries between Tanjong Datu and Tanjong Sirik. Almost entirely a product of the last hundred years, the industry is in the hands of Malays, Melanaus and Henghua Chinese who use a diversity of methods varying from traditional to modern, depending on nets, lines and traps.

Although catches comprise a wide variety of species, the seas adjoining Sarawak are relatively poor in fish. A survey in 1948 revealed that Sarawak waters contain too small a concentration of fish to justify large-scale operations; nor were there indications of 'any large fish concentrations worth serious attention in the deeper waters farther off shore'.[42] The fishing season usually lasts about ten months with the main period of activity between May and September; operations are severely restricted during the *landas* season when local supplies become scarce and irregular.

No large fishing organizations exist and the industry is characterized by small syndicates or individual boat owners and operators. Data on the quantity of fish landed are unavailable, but productivity is low; in 1949 it was estimated that the total annual catch averaged one ton per fisherman as compared with the average for Malaya of $2\frac{1}{2}$ tons in 1960.[43] Almost all the fish landed is either consumed locally or sold

[42] F. W. Roe, *The Natural Resources of Sarawak*, Kuching, Government Printer, 1952, p. 13.
[43] B. A. St. J. Hepburn, *The Handbook of Sarawak*, Singapore, Malaya Publishing House, 1949, p. 122; Ooi Jin-Bee, *Land, People and Economy in Malaya*, London, Longmans, Green & Co., 1963, p. 285.

in the fish markets of the main towns. Transport to market remains a major problem and marketing is dominated by Chinese middlemen. Dealers take fish from south-west Sarawak to Kuching and that from the Rejang delta goes to Sibu in special launches with ice boxes. Attempts to develop co-operatives to market members' fish have met with little success.

Table 15   Number of Fishermen, 1960

	Number	Percentage of total
Malay	2,402	54·4
Melanau	1,280	29·0
Chinese	681	15·4
Others	50	1·1
Total	4,413	100·0

(Source: *Sarawak: Census of Population, 1960*, Table 21, pp. 260-261.)

A total of 4,400 fishermen were recorded in the 1960 Population Census but 'because many people do fishing as a secondary occupation, dependent to some extent on the seasons and the weather, this figure may give little indication of the total amount of labour put into fishing'.[44] Over half the fishermen are Malays located on the coasts of the First and Second Divisions. Their small boats are usually equipped with outboard motors and operations are restricted mainly to in-shore fishing; recently, however, the Sarawak Development Finance Corporation has provided larger, more modern boats to selected Malay fishermen which permit them to fish farther afield. Along the shore and in river mouths they use a wide range of nets, basket traps and stake traps; some of these are operated only seasonally, others all year round. Few Malay fishermen engage solely in fishing; many are part-time fishermen and their village economy also includes *padi*, coconut and rubber cultivation and the collection of swamp and jungle produce. Samples taken of the Malay communities of south-west Sarawak in 1958 indicate that 42 per cent. of all man-days that year were spent mainly in fishing, while 34 per cent. were spent in agriculture or the collection of swamp and jungle produce. In fact these communities reveal a diversity of activity and do not depend entirely on fishing. Their integrated economy permits

[44] L. W. Jones, op. cit., p. 110.

substitution of activities according to climatic conditions, prices and personal need for ready cash.[45] Marine fishing is also an important activity among coastal Melanaus, particularly in the Rejang delta; it is characterized by large fishing craft, known as *barongs*, very different from those used elsewhere in Sarawak.

Chinese fishing is centred on the large Henghua village of Sungei Apong on the eastern outskirts of Kuching and differs markedly from that of the Malays. Fishing is almost the sole activity of this community which uses larger boats, known as *kotaks*, powered by diesel engines and with the traditional Henghua 'eye' painted on their prows (Plate V). In contrast to the Malays, the Chinese operate almost entirely outside the 10-fathom line using drift nets in the off-shore area between the mouths of the Sarawak and Rejang Rivers. There were about 350 *kotaks* here in 1966. Each carries a crew of two or three and goes to sea for up to three weeks, using ice for refrigeration purposes. Recently these fishermen have introduced imported nylon fishing nets. Although these are costly and the average *kotak* requires about fifty, they have increased the time available for fishing by eliminating the periodical drying and treatment with preservatives required by the old type of net. Chinese marine fishing entails a much larger capital outlay on boats, nets, fuel and ice than does that undertaken by Malays. Most boats are owner-operated, but the industry is organized on a community basis through the *Kotak* and Henghua Associations.

Extended production of molluscs and crustaceans is a likely future development. Cockles are already farmed at various points on the coasts of the First and Second Divisions. Success in this venture depends on the availability of seed cockles from suitable local beaches. These are bought and sown in prepared, fenced beds in the mud of the mangrove fringe which is rapidly falling under individual ownership. Yields are good and the produce is sold to Chinese middlemen. There are distinct possibilities that cockle-farming will extend in the future. Prawns and shrimps are also caught along the coasts of western Sarawak. Although failure attended an American attempt to establish a shrimp export industry at Sarikei in the early 1960's, the prospects for development of this type appear sound. Prawn culture is already a commercial success in Singapore and a brackish-water fish station is to be established in Kuching and sites for prawn ponds will be selected. Oyster culture is another possibility.

Before the Occupation, fishing attracted little official attention.

[45] T. Harrisson, op. cit., p. 358.

The report on the fisheries survey in 1948 did not encourage optimism regarding developmental potential. Government interest remained minimal and, although a loan scheme to provide inboard engines for non-Chinese fishing craft was operated in the later 1950's, the Marine Fisheries Division of the Department of Agriculture closed in 1958. For the last decade interest has centred on the development of inland fisheries. Nevertheless, fish remains a basic item of diet and output could be greatly increased if local methods of marine fishing were improved. There are now proposals to re-establish a Fisheries Department, to build a marine fisheries school, to subsidize co-operatives and to establish Fishermen's Associations. A total of $4 million has been allocated for fisheries development in the period 1966 to 1970; this will permit the introduction of more efficient gear and fishing methods and the improvement of processing and marketing.

Freshwater fisheries

Until the mid-1950's freshwater fish culture was restricted to a few small-scale Chinese ponds stocked with imported Chinese carp near the larger towns. Marine fishing then accounted for the bulk of output, but this was insufficient to meet local requirements. Thus the extension of freshwater fish-pond culture was looked to as a means of improving the protein-deficient diet of interior peoples and of providing a new source of cash income for farmers near towns. A survey of existing fish ponds was completed in 1957 and the Agriculture Department expanded its rearing ponds in the First Division to provide free supplies of fry for distribution to farmers; subsequently, breeding stations were established in all Divisions. Active extension work elicited a good response. During the early years this came mainly from Land Dyaks in the First Division, but since 1960, Iban, mainly in the Second Division, have shown most interest in the scheme. The ponds occupy land that otherwise would be unproductive; they provide the community with its chief source of protein; and the integration of fish culture with pig-rearing in pens overhanging the ponds to provide fertilizer, together with cheap fish-meal available for the pigs, offers tremendous prospects as a new complement to existing farm activities in interior areas.

Apart from free fry, this Freshwater Fisheries Development Scheme provides other forms of aid, including a cash grant for the construction of ponds over a certain size. By the end of 1965 9,420 ponds had been constructed, three-quarters of which lie in the First and Second

Divisions (Table 16). There has been a growing tendency to build larger ponds for mixed stocking, and the construction of communal ponds in excess of one acre is increasingly common. Starting with only two species in 1957, fry of ten species are now available to farmers. Two-fifths of the total fry distributed by the end of 1965 comprised *Tilapia mossambica*, one-fifth *Cyprinus carpio* (or *Lee Koh*) and one-eighth *Trichogaster pectoralis* (or *sepat siam*). For some years now rough releases have been made of some species in reservoirs, lakes, mining pools and *padi* fields to provide fishing opportunities for the local communities and the development of fish culture in wet-*padi* fields is a distinct future possibility.

Table 16   Freshwater Fish Ponds constructed, 1957-1965

Division	Number
First	4,271
Second	2,816
Third	1,038
Fourth	920
Fifth	375
Total	9,420

(Source: *Sarawak: A Digest of Agricultural Statistics, 1966*, Table 39, p. 65.)

The scheme has not only benefited interior, indigenous communities. Many new Chinese-owned ponds have also been established, largely for the culture of carp which finds a ready sale among the Chinese. Until 1960, mixed carp fry for these ponds were imported from Hong Kong by dealers in Kuching, the number imported rising from 41,000 in 1956 to 72,300 in 1959. Local Chinese farmers then began to breed carp fry and imports have now virtually ceased.

Although freshwater fish—dried and salted—is still imported in comparatively large amounts, the scheme has considerably augmented local fish production and increased the relative contribution of fresh-water fish to total output. Its most important effect, naturally, is on the economy and diet of many interior communities. Most freshwater fish is still raised for home consumption, but farmers are encouraged to send their fish to market for sale alive, and storage tanks for this purpose exist in Kuching. Yields are difficult to gauge, because harvesting tends to be piecemeal; moreover, they vary greatly with the experience and management methods of the farmers concerned. The average yield from freshwater fish ponds is estimated to be about $\frac{1}{4}$ ton per acre per year, but experienced urban Chinese farmers obtain yields of $1\frac{1}{4}$ tons and the more skilled indigenous farmers achieve $\frac{3}{4}$ tons.[46] Freshwater fish culture is to be greatly extended under the current Development Plan and an increasing number of training courses on pond construction and fish culture will be run for local farmers.

[46] *Sarawak: Annual Report of the Department of Agriculture, 1962*, p. 93.

4 Forest Products Industries

The forests are a traditional source of many jungle products for the indigenous peoples of Sarawak and it was largely to obtain some of these that foreign traders visited the area in the pre-Brooke era. The extraction of timber for export, however, is a relatively recent innovation and was begun by Chinese in the late nineteenth century. For long it remained a minor activity and its development into a large-scale industry dates entirely from the 1950's and 1960's. Forest products now comprise about two-fifths of the total value of Sarawak's exports, excluding petroleum, and timber has been the leading export product since 1964. In addition increasing amounts of timber and other forest products are consumed locally so that forest-product industries now play a significant role in the State's economy.

Timber and Veneer Industry

Until the late 1940's the timber industry was small and its produce was sold almost entirely on a restricted and rather erratic local market. Rapid development began in 1948 after the value of *ramin* as a timber export had been established in Sarikei District by the Colonial Timber Company Ltd formed at the end of the war by a group of enterprising Australians who had served with the forces in Sarawak.

Ramin is frequently the most abundant large tree in the mixed swamp forests, and good forest usually carries four or five trees per acre; exceptionally there may be ten or even more per acre over considerable areas. Moreover, it proved to be easily worked and generally easily accessible from the larger rivers and the existence of a suitable export point at Tanjong Mani on the Rejang was an additional favourable factor. *Ramin* is a clean-looking, light, whitish hardwood, usually very free from natural defects, and which floats in water. It can be sawn without difficulty but must be passed through a dipping tank immediately it comes off the saw to guard against insect attack, fungi and staining, and it also requires special care in seasoning. *Ramin* is not very durable under local conditions but in the post-war years a considerable demand arose for it, particularly in the United Kingdom, chiefly for furniture making, but also for mouldings, shop-fittings and similar purposes.

Exports of *ramin* increased almost tenfold between 1947 and 1951 and until the early 1960's it remained the backbone of the timber industry which was therefore largely concentrated in the coastal swamps. Sarawak has almost a monopoly of the *ramin* trade and until recently this single timber made up over three-quarters of the State's timber exports, almost all of it going to the United Kingdom. Nevertheless, development was by no means smooth. In the early 1950's expansion was limited by restricted shipping, port and labour facilities, and the industry was severely affected by alarming fluctuations in price in the United Kingdom between 1955 and 1958. The depression in the *ramin* trade was at its worst at the end of 1956 and in August that year export restrictions were imposed at the request of a substantial majority of the producers and were not lifted until the end of 1959. The timber industry in general enjoyed a boom in 1960 and *ramin* reached the highest price ever recorded in the United Kingdom. Thereafter it suffered a further recession until prices began to improve again at the end of 1962 and for the last three years there has been an increased demand for sawn *ramin*. However, considerable interest has now been awakened in other types of swamp timber and in the dipterocarp forests farther inland, particularly those of northern Sarawak; moreover, it is expected that the output of *ramin* will decline in the next few years.

During this same period several other light hardwoods were produced for export, particularly *jongkong* and *meranti*. Since 1959, when Japan made a strong entry into the local market for mixed light hardwood logs, production of these has increased rapidly and this has permitted a more thorough and more economical exploitation of the swamp forests than the concentration on *ramin* allowed. Partly as a result, total timber exports more than quadrupled between 1958 and 1965; moreover, the industry became less dependent on the single timber *ramin*, and therefore much less dependent upon the United Kingdom market (Table 17). Japan has risen to prominence as the main buyer of Sarawak timber and takes almost all the production of *jongkong* and *meranti* logs. The peat swamp forests, which have now all been surveyed, have been allocated to various sawmills on a long-term basis and there is little scope for new entrants into the industry in these areas.

Table 17   Timber Exports by Destination, 1958 and 1965

Exported to	Round timber (Tons)		Sawn timber (Tons)	
	1958	1965	1958	1965
United Kingdom	169	—	56,412	64,048
Japan	11,114	397,452	—	564
Hong Kong	44,358	136,355	2,023	14,921
Australia	10,859	12,869	22,299	27,167
Germany (Federal Republic)	904	233	5,317	23,629
Italy	14,520	42,935	2,781	2,992
Others	1,823	82,868	17,050	58,131
Total	83,747	672,712	105,882	191,452

(Source: *Sarawak Annual Report, 1958*, p. 53, and *Sarawak Government Gazette*, Part V, Vol. XXI, No. 11, 11th March 1966, p. 202.)

The softwood *bindang* is exported in small quantities and when prices were high in Australia in 1958 exports rose temporarily. Supplies are scattered and rather limited, however, and none of the accessible forests contains stands sufficiently extensive for management on the basis of sustained yield.

About one-fifth of Sarawak's total timber output is not exported, and in recent years government and private building has tended to absorb an increasing amount of locally-produced timber. Generally the timber produced commercially for domestic consumption differs from that produced for export. Exports comprise mainly the less durable or light hardwoods whereas timbers consumed locally comprise the naturally durable or primary hardwoods such as *belian, selangan batu* and *chengal. Belian,* the famed 'ironwood' of Borneo, is by far the most important of these, for it has a very wide range of uses under local conditions including the construction of houses and bridges, telephone and electricity poles and as supports for pepper vines. The rapid expansion of building and construction has led to a constantly growing demand for *belian* and despite increased production the local market price continues to rise, not least because this valuable timber is becoming scarce in accessible places and cannot be replaced easily; the export of this timber is, in fact, closely restricted. The other primary hardwoods are used chiefly in building coastal ships and fishing boats.

Four fundamental changes have occurred in the Sarawak timber industry since the late 1950's: the scene of logging interest has tended to shift from the coastal swamps of central Sarawak to the lowland dipterocarp forests of northern Sarawak, mechanization has been introduced into logging, the sawmills have been modernized and their efficiency greatly increased and several processing plants have been established.

Very little interest was shown in the lowland dipterocarp forests until the early 1960's. As late as 1958 it was felt that these would not be worked to any extent until a large market for miscellaneous timber developed, because stands are typically mixed and, it was argued, stands of the chief high-quality timbers were not heavy enough to justify the capital outlay in equipment that would be necessary.[1] In 1961 various plans to exploit these forests to the north and south of the Rejang River were abandoned because the stands investigated proved disappointing in quality. Nevertheless, 1961 witnessed the real beginning of successful exploitation of these forests when several companies, some with the backing of Sabah capital, started to extract timber, chiefly *seraya*, or red *meranti*, in the Fourth and Fifth Divisions.

The following year there was an invasion of timber businessmen mainly from Sabah but also from the Philippines and even from Korea in search of concessions in northern Sarawak. The basic causes of this sudden interest were the growing demand for *seraya* logs from Japan and the fact that some of the annual licensees in Sabah were running out of forest. As a result in August 1962 the Government decided that in future all uncommitted hill forest areas of importance involving the use of tractors would be advertised and that licences for felling would be granted only to those replying to such official advertisements. The government was faced with other problems because of this sudden awakening of interest in the commercial potentialities of these forests, for it had to arrange for the safeguarding of native interests and it hoped to ensure the maximum participation of indigenous Sarawakians in the expanding timber industry. With this in view, a committee was appointed to make recommendations on the granting of felling licences for these forests. The committee was unable to meet until 1963 and in

---

[1] *Sarawak: Annual Report of the Forest Department, 1958*, Kuching, Government Printer, 1959, p. 12.

the meantime the issue of new licences was frozen temporarily. Subsequently it became policy to invite applications from companies registered in Sarawak to work the timber in suitable areas of these hill forests. Several new companies have been formed for this purpose, some purely indigenous and others joint Chinese-indigenous enterprises, and recently there has been a rapid increase in hill forest logging operations, particularly in the Fourth Division from which total timber exports were almost 90 per cent higher in 1965 than in 1964. This Division now produces almost two-fifths of the round timber exported from Sarawak.

This growth of interest in the lowland dipterocarp forests was accompanied by the introduction of mechanical means of extraction. Until the late 1950's, logging and extraction methods in the inland forests were usually primitive and no mechanical means had been attempted, although one firm had used elephants in the Rejang. Tractors were first successfully introduced in 1961 on concessions in the Lubai valley and near Nanga Medamit in the Fifth Division. Before the end of the year they had also been introduced to start logging to the west of Gunong Bugoh up the Lawas Damit River, and a Chinese company, with Sabah-capital backing, had begun tractor logging between Niah and Suai in Miri District. Many tractors were imported during 1962 and by the beginning of 1963 there were 42 in operation in the Miri and Limbang areas. Although some of these were new, the majority were surplus machines from Sabah. This development of new methods was not restricted to the introduction of tractors. The Chinese sawmills in the Niah-Sibuti area began to use rail for haulage through the forests and mobile cranes for loading, and large Scammell trucks for haulage were introduced on a concession on the slopes of Gunong Bugoh. Although still on a smaller scale, in the last few years the Sarawak timber industry has begun to resemble the large-scale, modern and highly productive industry of neighbouring Sabah. As a result exports of timber increased by about 30 per cent between 1962 and 1965.

Today sawmilling is an extremely important industrial activity in Sarawak. Many sawmill owners are involved in both logging and sawmilling and although their operations therefore overlap the forestry and industrial sectors of some classifications of economic activities they are, in effect, the largest employers of industrial labour in the State. Directly or indirectly they provide employment for a total of about 15,000 workers; more than a third of these comprise the managers, office staff and labourers actually employed at the sawmills, another 6,000 loggers are employed directly by the sawmills and the remainder are loggers employed through contractors. Almost all the sawmills are Chinese-owned; over half the labourers employed in them are Malays and nearly a quarter are Chinese. Most of the loggers are Melanaus or Malays.

With the rapid development of the timber industry in the post-war era the number of licensed sawmills in operation increased more than fourfold between 1947 and 1962 (Table 18); of the eighty in operation in 1962, fifteen were in the First Division, twenty-four in the Third Division and twenty-eight in the Fourth Division.

Table 18   Number of Licensed Sawmills in Operation, 1947-1965

1947	18
1951	46
1956	63
1959	70
1962	80
1965	79

For long, however, most of the sawmills remained small and not very efficiently equipped; as late as 1958 less than a third had more than four sawbenches and all used circular saws. In August 1961 an FAO sawmill engineer arrived to advise local sawmill owners on the introduction of modern equipment and efficient sawmill layout. By the end of 1961 some had installed vertical band saws to replace the wasteful circular saws. The success they achieved in terms of increased recovery and more accurate sawing which made the timber more acceptable in high-grade markets persuaded others to follow their example, and by the beginning of 1963 most of the leading sawmills were in the process of converting to band saws of a type suited to the comparatively small mills of Sarawak. Significantly, by the end of 1962, 45 per cent of all the mills had more than four saw benches.

Until recently the Sarawak timber industry was based on exporting the better logs and sawing the remainder into lumber. Processing did not begin until the end of the 1950's; indeed plans for processing factories were first suggested by commercial companies in 1958. The following year the Sarawak Company (1959) Ltd established a factory at Selalang on the boundary of the Second and Third Divisions in

Plate I End view of an Iban longhouse near Sibu, Third Division, containing twelve 'doors' and housing about seventy people. Over 200 feet long and 70 feet wide it is supported by hardwood posts about 15 feet high.

Plate II A Malay village at the foot of Gunong Santubong (2,900 feet) on the coast north of Kuching. The villagers have an economy in which fishing and rubber production are combined with the collection of swamp and jungle produce.

Plate III   Henghua fisherman at Sungei Apong, Kuching, loading his *kotak* with ice prior to departure for off-shore fishing grounds.   Note the traditional Henghua 'eye' on the prow.   In the background is the Malay village of Sungei Tabuan.

Plate IV   The *umai* or farm clearings of Iban shifting cultivators in the ridge and valley country of the middle of Rejang basin.

Sarikei District to manufacture veneers chiefly from the *alan bunga* in their licensed area of forest in Saribas District. This factory was declared a pioneer manufacturer of veneers under the *Pioneer Industries (Encouragement) Ordinance* of 1957 (see Chapter 5). Initially the company had to struggle to establish markets for their *alan bunga* veneers and as late as 1961 over half their exports comprised *ramin* veneers, most of their produce going to the American market. In 1962 the factory was taken over by the Jones Plywood Corporation, an American company. The total output of veneer sheets had risen from 891 tons in 1960 to 2,973 tons in 1962 by which time three-quarters of the exports consisted of *alan bunga* veneers.

In 1961 the Borneo Timber Company Limited opened a modern, well-equipped factory at Sungei Merah, Sibu, for the manufacture of *ramin* mouldings (Plate VI). This too was a new industry in Sarawak and the factory was accorded pioneer status. It began production in July 1961, concentrating on specially moulded slats for use as window blinds in Italy where they were known as Taporelle shutters. Marketing difficulties in Italy forced the company to abandon this project in 1962. The machines were converted for general moulding purposes and the company began to search for new markets for their product, achieving some success in the United Kingdom, the United States and Hong Kong. This company has a timber concession in the Second Division and the *ramin* logs are brought by boat to the factory which comprises a highly mechanized sawmill and a well-equipped processing section (Plate VI). The chief products are broom handles, which go mainly to the United States, and dowelling and mouldings destined for Britain. Currently the company has plans to expand its factory and to develop new lines of production. Several of the larger sawmills have started to produce dowels, mouldings and furniture parts; these find a ready market in the United States and have good potential in European and Far Eastern markets. Clearly if suitable markets can be found, there are good prospects for further expansion of the timber processing industry in Sarawak, and plans to encourage more processing, reduce exports of logs and increase the export of finished products must form part of any general industrialization programme.

Poles, Firewood and Charcoal

The main concentrations of mangrove forest in Sarawak occur on the coast near Kuching, in the Rejang delta and on the shores of Brunei

E

Bay in Lawas District. These forests are the principal source of poles, firewood and charcoal both for home consumption and for export.

Table 19   Production of Poles, Firewood and Charcoal, 1960-1964

	Poles (number)	Firewood (tons)	Charcoal (tons)
1960	165,069	26,772	5,146
1961	178,023	45,983	5,026
1962	220,108	31,431	4,897
1963	388,411	19,632	4,809
1964	195,293	14,472	4,892

(Source: *Annual Bulletin of Statistics, Malaysia, 1964*, p. 12.)

Poles are used chiefly for piling and scaffolding by local building contractors, and the rapid expansion of the building industry, particularly in the main urban centres, in the last half decade or so produced a continuously growing demand. Indeed, the number of poles produced more than doubled between 1960 and 1963; more recently, however, there has been a decline in production (Table 19).

The *bako* of the mangrove forests is the main source of firewood and charcoal but *ru ronang*, which grows on the podsolic *kerangas* soils, is an important source of these products in the First Division. *Ru ronang* was formerly planted as a fuel crop in the neighbourhood of Kuching. The plantations were expensive to establish and maintain but they made use of land that otherwise would be valueless, and the tree produces much that can be sold profitably, even the tops finding some market as Christmas trees. A large part of these plantations has since been cleared for other purposes, and although a section still remains, the expanding use of other types of fuel discourages further attempts of this nature. Nevertheless, *ru ronong* is an extremely good firewood and commands higher prices than mangrove for this purpose; it also produces a very high grade charcoal.

Nevertheless, most of the firewood produced in Sarawak originates from the mangrove forests. Production varies considerably from year to year but rose from 21,400 tons in 1958 to a peak of almost 46,000 tons in 1961 since when it has declined steadily (Table 19). Generally most of the firewood is consumed locally but an increasing amount has been exported to Hong Kong in recent years, chiefly from Lawas

District, and exports rose from 6,000 tons in 1960 to 15,000 tons in 1962. The Hong Kong market, however, is subject to violent fluctuations depending in part on the quantity of firewood available from mainland China and the severity of the Hong Kong winter, so that it is unlikely that this will develop into an important established trade.

Charcoal production is a long-established industry in Sarawak but almost all the produce is destined for local consumption, exports never amounting to more than a few hundred tons. The number of charcoal kilns has decreased in the last few years, there having been 329 in 1958 and only 235 in 1962. In fact many of the kilns are only operated sporadically to supply the local market but production has remained fairly steady at around 5,000 tons for some time past (Table 19). Most of the kilns are in Lundu and Kuching Districts and in the Rejang delta; indeed there were only eight kilns north of the Rejang River in 1962, seven on the coast in the Fourth Division and one at Punang in Lawas District.

Minor Forest Products

Jungle produce ranked as one of the major items of export from Sarawak throughout most of the nineteenth century. Covering a vast range of products collected from the forests by the indigenous peoples, these export items declined rapidly in relative importance with the expansion of pepper, gold and rubber production in the closing years of last century and the opening decades of the present century. Usually in recent years these minor forest products have comprised less than 2 per cent of the total value of Sarawak's exports excluding petroleum; nevertheless, considerable quantities are still collected and consumed locally. The importance of the collection of these forest products lies more in the fact that it represents an integral part of the way of life of most of the State's subsistence farmers than in the contribution it makes to Sarawak's export earnings. For many it provides employment at slack periods of the farming year and, frequently, one of the few sources of cash income. The traditional uses that the indigenous peoples have made of the forests must be considered in any attempt to alter their patterns of living.

Jelutong Industry
Getah jelutong is one of the more important minor forest products exported from Sarawak. It is a milky latex obtained principally from

jelutong paya (*Dyera lowii*), a tree which is fairly evenly scattered throughout the mixed swamp forests. *Jelutong bukit* (*Dyera costulata*) which occurs as a widely distributed but very scattered and less abundant tree in most lowland forests, also yields latex but not so freely as *jelutong paya*.

The latex is tapped in much the same way as rubber. Licences or permits are granted for tapping which is done in the early dawn, the latex being caught in cloth bags. Yields vary widely but high-yielding trees can give about 8 lb. of refined latex per month. The latex is usually coagulated with phosphoric acid and coagulation is effected by either cold or hot treatment. In the former method 0·8 fluid ounces of 10 per cent acid are added to each gallon of latex and the mixture is allowed to stand for about three days; in the latter method 1 fluid ounce of 10 per cent acid is added to every 6 gallons of latex, the mixture is placed over a fire and stirred until it boils, the boiling continuing for about three minutes.

Bintulu is the main *jelutong* collecting centre. Until recently there was a refinery here which purchased raw *jelutong* from all parts of Sarawak and processed much of the State's production, although some was shipped raw to Singapore and processed there. Refining is a simple process aimed at cleaning the product and dissolving out all soluble impurities; it consists of boiling and kneading in frequent changes of water. Often this is followed by pressing into blocks which are then stored under water. *Getah jelutong* is exported in the raw, refined or pressed state and it almost all goes to the U.S.A. where it forms an important ingredient of chewing gum. The quantity exported varies annually, chiefly because tapping is a part-time occupation for indigenous subsistence farmers who respond to price changes and their personal needs for cash. Production was very high in the late 1940's and early 1950's. It then generally declined but showed signs of increasing again in the early 1960's and in 1962 Sarawak shipped 15 tons of raw, 296 tons of refined and 237 tons of pressed *jelutong* valued in total at more than 1¾ million dollars or 1 per cent of the State's total exports, excluding petroleum. Since then the refinery has closed. In 1965 exports totalled 148 tons of raw, 24 tons of refined and 399 tons of pressed *jelutong*.

The *jelutong* tree also yields an easily-worked special purpose timber used for pattern making, drawing boards, plane-tables and blackboards but because of the value of the latex there are restrictions on felling. Nevertheless, despite the licensing system for tapping, in parts of the peat swamps many trees have been tapped to death and often in the more accessible areas large trees are scarce. Moreover, on average there is one large *jelutong paya* tree per 2 to 3 acres of undisturbed forest so that collecting under natural conditions is time-consuming.

Jelutong has been tested on a small scale as a plantation crop but the results are disappointing. Seeds are very difficult to collect, germination is irregular and the trees take a considerable time to come into bearing, *jelutong bukit* taking nearly 60 years and *jelutong paya* 40 to 45 years to reach a tappable girth in their wild state. Even on the small experimental plantations established near Sibu, *jelutong paya* failed to reach a tappable size until 30 to 35 years old so that this does not appear an attractive commercial proposition. The collection of *getah jelutong* will therefore remain a matter of indigenous tappers working forest trees in their natural habitat.[2]

Nipah palm products

The main commercial product of the *nipah* palm is sugar. This is derived from the sap obtained from the fruit stalks by tapping. The tapping season lasts for about five or six months and is restricted to the months, usually from August onwards, when the flowers are formed and the fruit is developing. Sugar production from *nipah* palms concentrates heavily in the extensive areas of mud flats between the mouths of the Sarawak and Samarahan Rivers in the First Division. Here the palms are held under customary rights by individuals, almost invariably Malays. The palms do not flower very freely unless they have plenty of light and air so that all climbers and mangroves must be cleared and the palms themselves thinned out by removing at least half the fronds; even then, flowering is irregular and only about half the palms are in a tappable condition each year. They come into bearing when about five years old and may continue to yield sugar for as much as fifty years.

Each person generally does all the work of cleaning, tapping, collecting and processing himself. It is hard, time-consuming work and one man can tend up to 150 palms. Usually each man has a small evaporating plant in the middle of his tapping area. The sap is collected and brought here where it is put into large iron pans over clay fireplaces; in these it is boiled and stirred continuously for about five hours, by which time the product is solid. This is taken to market and sold

² F. G. Browne, *Forest Trees of Sarawak and Brunei, and Their Products*, Kuching, Government Printer, 1955, pp. 61-63.

E*

as *gula apong*, much of which is used locally as sugar. Until the mid-1950's some was also exported, but in recent years there has been a marked decline in exports. During the rest of the year the palm-owners are employed in cleaning their plantations or in making palm-thatch. There is, in fact, an important internal trade in *atap* roofing-thatch in Sarawak and, in areas where *nipah* palms are only used for this purpose, no special tending is necessary, although it is essential that no palm is completely stripped. *Nipah* palms also yield several other products, including vinegar and salt.[3]

Much of the locally-produced *gula apong* goes to Chinese-owned distilleries in Kuching, of which there are two, although it is probable that other, illicit, distilleries exist. Here the sugar is made into a strong solution with water, often with the addition of a little rice. Yeast is then added and after fermentation the solution is passed through a still and yields about 10 per cent proof spirit sold locally mainly in the form of 'brandy', 'whisky' and 'medicinal wine'.

Illipe nuts

Illipe nuts are the seeds of various species of *Shorea* and in Sarawak the recognized nut-bearing trees are known as *engkabang*. These grow wild on riverine alluvial flats and most of the crop comes from the Rejang basin. The seeds contain a high percentage of vegetable fat and are exported mainly to the United Kingdom where this is extracted and used principally in the manufacture of chocolate. Locally the fat is used to prepare cooking oil and is also eaten as a delicacy mixed with rice.

The fruits generally ripen in January and February and because germination is rapid they must be gathered as soon as they fall. They are collected from the ground by hand and by nets from the rivers. The fruits are shelled and the seeds dried either in the sun or over a fire to reduce their moisture content which should not exceed 6 per cent for export. The seeds are graded by size and colour; the larger nuts are prepared for export and the smaller ones retained for domestic consumption.

The illipe nut is a highly irregular and unpredictable export crop, really heavy seeding occurring once every two to six years. Flowering occurs at about the time of the onset of the north-east monsoon and often most of the flowers are destroyed by heavy downpours before the fruit has set. Since 1920, very heavy crops have been recorded in

[3] F. G. Browne, op. cit., pp. 284-286.

1923, 1929, 1931, 1935, 1947, 1954, 1959 and 1962. In some of the intermediate years no crop was harvested; in others a moderate return was achieved. The peak year in the last half-century was 1959 when the State exported 22,000 tons of illipe nuts valued at almost $20 million, representing 11 per cent of Sarawak's total export earnings, excluding petroleum; almost 20,000 tons, valued at $16 million, were exported in 1962. These peak years bring a considerable income to the Iban of the interior who collect, prepare and market the nuts; indeed, as Browne remarks, 'a good nut-year is a great event in Sarawak and provides a literal windfall for the native tribes'.[4] Nevertheless, a product as unpredictable as this can play little part in the long-term development of the State.

Other minor forest products
The collection of many other minor forest products provides a valuable part-time occupation for the indigenous peoples. Some of these products are exported, but many are sold and used locally so that the total output cannot be assessed. In terms of value of exports the most important is *damar*, the name applied to the resins produced chiefly by trees of the dipterocarp family. *Damar* is shipped to Europe where it is used in the manufacture of varnishes and in recent years an average of about $400,000-worth has been exported annually. Locally the product is used mainly for torches and for caulking boats.

Formerly two cutch factories extracted tannin from mangrove bark collected in the tidal swamp forests but the first, located in Brunei town, closed in 1952 and the second, at Selalang in the Third Division, closed in 1959 and exports have ceased; moreover, the extension of the use of nylon fishing nets has considerably reduced the local demand for this product as a net preservative. Other minor forest products which are exported in small quantities include *gaharu* wood—an incense wood shipped mainly to Singapore—canes, rattans and edible birds' nests. Large quantites of some of these are also consumed locally; thus logging companies use canes to make rafts for log-floating and rattan is used for furniture-making. Undoubtedly the collection of these minor forest products will remain a significant feature of the rural economy despite the extension of cash crop agriculture.

[4] F. G. Browne, op. cit., p. 91.

5 Mining and Manufacturing Industries

Mining and manufacturing industries play a relatively small part in the Sarawak economy. In the past, mining accounted for a substantial share of total export earnings, a share that has fallen progressively in the present century with the exhaustion of deposits and the rapid growth of export agriculture and, more recently, of timber production. Manufacturing industries have begun to grow in the last half decade but the problems facing industrialization are immense. Mining and manufacturing industries may increase in importance but there seems little doubt that economic development in Sarawak in the foreseeable future will hinge upon agricultural improvement and timber exploitation.

Mining Industries

At present, mining contributes less than 4 per cent of the value of Sarawak's total exports excluding re-exports of petroleum piped from Brunei; moreover, it provides employment for less than 2,000 people. Nevertheless, Sarawak has varied and widespread mineral deposits and during the century of Brooke rule these played an important part in development. Each of the five chief minerals reigned supreme at some time during this period (Fig. 25). Antimony was generally the leading mineral product until the mid-1880's, although it was supplanted by mercury for a short time in the 1870's; coal then took over the lead until 1898 when it was replaced by gold, which headed the list of mineral exports until the early 1920's when it gave way to petroleum. More recently bauxite has been the chief mineral product but this appears to have a limited future.

Significantly, with the exception of oil, mining has concentrated entirely in Sarawak west of the Batang Lupar; for long this has been the best-known, most densely-peopled and most developed part of the

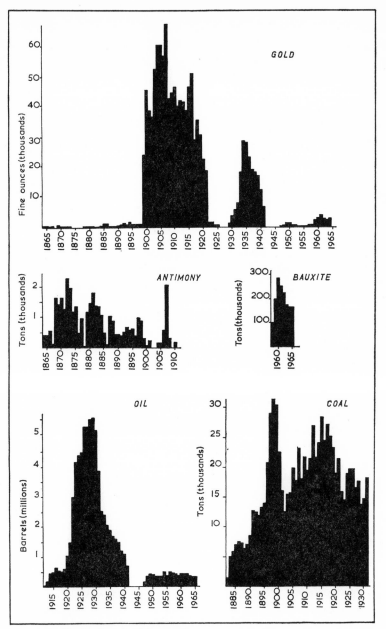

Figure 25 Production of chief minerals.
N.B.—Coal production from Sadong colliery only. Source of data: Annual Reports and Memoirs of Geological Survey, Borneo Region, Malaysia.

State, and, if further development of mining occurs, it is likely to concentrate in this area. On the basis of existing knowledge, however, there seems little hope that an expansion of mining can provide the extra employment opportunities and the economic diversification that Sarawak desperately needs.

Antimony

Exports of antimony ore were the main source of revenue for the first Rajah. Mining began in the Bau area in 1823 when it was discovered that there was a ready market for the ore in Singapore. It was stopped temporarily by the rebellion which Brooke helped to suppress, but in the twenty years after 1840, production averaged about 1,500 tons annually and Sarawak became the main source of supply for Europe. Output rose rapidly from 1868 to reach a peak in 1872 and, except for short periods, antimony remained the leading mineral exported from Sarawak until the mid-1880's. Throughout this period the principal mines were near Paku, Jambusan, Bidi and Buan Bidi in Bau District. The ore was worked by Chinese and Malays using primitive methods. A smelting plant was established in Kuching in the 1840's and in the 1860's the Borneo Company erected a smelter at Buso and built roads and tramways to the ore deposits. Production continued, fluctuating annually, until 1907; from then until 1941, small quantities were exported at irregular intervals, the industry losing all importance after 1916. Since 1823 a total of 83,000 tons of antimony ore has been produced in Sarawak and over four-fifths of this was mined before 1886.

A small amount of antimony ore was produced between 1948 and 1950 but no further activity occurred until 1963 when 6½ tons were produced. Mining continued in 1964 at the Kwei Fah Gold Mine and output totalled 155 tons, most of which was exported to Japan and Germany. Antimony mining may continue on a small scale for several years, but it seems highly unlikely that there will be a large-scale revival of what was once Sarawak's main mining industry.

Mercury

Mercury occurs as the sulphide cinnabar at Tegora and Gading to the south of Bau. The deposits at Tegora were discovered and proved to be of commercial value in 1867 by L. V. Helms, first manager of the Borneo Company. Mining began immediately and mercury was first exported in 1868; indeed, as Helms himself says, the discovery 'led very shortly to labours which made the jungle resound with the miner's blast and the engine's puff'.[1] Steam machinery was introduced, furnaces were built and two tramways were laid down on which waggons transported the ore from the steep mountainside to the work-sheds. The deposit at Gading was discovered slightly later and production rose rapidly to reach a peak in 1876 and 1877. Mercury was, in fact, the chief mineral produced in Sarawak for five of the six years between 1874 and 1879; output then declined, particularly after 1886, and by the late 1890's it was negligible. Apart from small quantities exported in 1908 and 1909 no mercury has been produced in the present century.

Enquiries about the possibilities of mercury mining were received in 1958 and some prospecting was done at Tegora in 1962. The results were promising and further prospecting was planned for 1964, but this was deferred because of the troubles on the Indonesian border. When sufficiently peaceful conditions return, the once-flourishing mercury mining and smelting industry may yet be revived.

Coal

Coal occurs at over thirty places in Sarawak and most of these have been known since the nineteenth century.[2] Nevertheless, the abandoned government-run Sadong colliery about three miles east of Simunjan on the Sungei Sadong in the First Division remains the only place at which mining has ever been undertaken (Fig. 26). The seams here are probably Eocene in age and yielded a fairly friable, sub-bituminous coal. They were first discovered in the 1840's and an abortive and costly attempt was made to work them the following decade. In 1872 the Government advertised the terms on which it would allow a company to work the coal but there was no response and two years later it was reported that the Government was 'working the Sadong Coal Mines and turning out sufficient to supply their own steamers'.[3]

Sales of coal produced here rose from 500 tons in 1874 to 2,600 tons in 1881, there being a steady demand from coastal steamers. Initially buffaloes were used for work in the mines and to haul the coal to the wharf on the Sungei Sadong; later a railway was built between the

[1] L. V. Helms, *Pioneering in the Far East*, London, W. H. Allen, 1882, pp. 243-244.
[2] T. Posewitz, *Borneo: Its Geology and Mineral Resources*, London, Edward Stanford, 1892, p. 287.
[3] *Sarawak Gazette*, May 1874, quoted by N. S. Haile, *The Geology and Mineral Resources of the Strap and Sadong Valleys, West Sarawak, including the Klingkang Range Coal*, Kuching, Government Printer, Geological Survey Department, British Territories in Borneo, Memoir 1, 1954, p. 85.

mines and the wharf, and was probably in operation by the mid-1890's. Production increased steadily up to 1898 when 31,390 tons were sold and coal was Sarawak's chief mineral product from 1889 to 1898. Thereafter coal gave way to gold as the leading mineral product and coal output declined slightly, averaging about 20,000 tons annually until the colliery was closed in 1931. In part the mines were closed because the demand for coal had fallen with the decline of the gold industry and the conversion of ships and power stations to oil; but closure was also desirable because much of the accessible coal had been extracted. Between 1874 and 1931 a total of about 1 million tons of coal was mined at Sadong, of which 876,345 tons were sold. From 1888 to 1924 the Sarawak Government also operated the Brooketon Colliery at Muara in Brunei.

Inaccessibility, the small local market and competition from coal

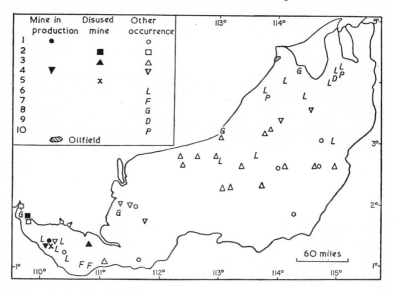

Figure 26   Mineral resources.

1	Gold	6	Limestone
2	Bauxite	7	Fireclay
3	Coal	8	Glass sand
4	Antimony	9	Dolomite
5	Mercury	10	Phosphate.

(Based on R. A. M. Wilson, *Annual Report of the Geological Survey, Borneo Region, Malaysia, 1964*, Fig. 3, p. 12, with the permission of the Acting Director, Geological Survey, Borneo Region, Malaysia.)

Plate V   Drying rice on the *tanju* or open verandah of an Iban longhouse in the middle Rejang basin.

Plate VI   Harvesting wet *padi* at Sungei Merah, Sibu, Third Division.   Animal-drawn implements are rarely used by *padi* farmers most of whom rely on simple hand methods.

Plate VII   Land cleared, terraced and holed ready for planting on the Sibintek Rubber Planting Scheme, Oya Road, Third Division.   Steep slopes, often over 40 degrees, characterize much of central Sarawak and make development difficult and costly.

Plate VIII   A Chinese pepper garden on the hills behind Miri, Fourth Division.   In the foreground recently-planted cuttings are shaded by bracken and the darker material on the terrace tops is burnt earth applied as fertilizer.

Plate IX   After transport by water, sago logs await processing outside a factory near Oya. The mudflats in the background have a covering of mangrove.

Plate X   Borneo Timber Company's factory at Sungei Merah, Sibu, Third Division. Logs brought by sea from the Second Division to this modern, well-equipped factory pass first through the sawmill section (above); after drying, the sawn timber enters the processing section which produces broom handles, dowelling and moulding for export.

Plate XI   Well Number 1, Miri, Fourth Division.   First drilled in 1910, this well continues to produce oil.   Although production from the Miri oilfield is declining steadily, over 170 wells are still in operation.

Plate XII   Bukit Young Gold Mine, Bau, First Division.   The mined ore is shovelled into bucket trucks which are winch-hauled up a light rail track to the plant for treatment by the cyanide process.

exported from other parts of the world have proved serious obstacles to the exploitation of Sarawak's other coal deposits, many of which are small and consist of thin or steeply dipping seams, chiefly of lignite. Currently interest centres on the deposits at Silantek in the Second Division. These were known as early as 1868 and they were examined in the 1870's and 1880's and again in the 1920's. They were examined once more in the late 1940's and early 1950's, and in 1954 it was estimated that measured and indicated reserves totalled 4·76 million tons. At that time, however, the area remained inaccessible and it was suggested that, if the deposit was worked, the best although most expensive method of transportation would be a railway from the field to a wharf to be built on the Batang Lupar or the Batang Lingga.[4]

A general prospecting licence was issued for the area in 1956 and a party of Japanese engineers and company directors visited the field the following year. Interest was intensified in the early 1960's by the growing demand for coking coal in Japan and the route of the new Kuching-Simanggang road which passed close to the field. A Japanese company undertook detailed prospecting and made studies of mining and transportation costs and in 1961 they prepared a preliminary plan for the development of the field which was discussed with the Government. Most of the coal was shown to have good coking properties although igneous intrusions had metamorphosed parts of the seam, raising the rank of the coal but destroying its coking properties, this latter being referred to as 'natural coke'. By 1964 the Silantek field had proved reserves of $7\frac{1}{4}$ million tons and indicated and inferred reserves of a further 50 million tons. The present development plan of the Japanese company provides for an annual production of 240,000 tons of coking coal and 60,000 tons of 'natural coke'. It is proposed that the coal and coke will be transported by road to Pending, about eighty-four miles away on the Sungei Sarawak, where the existing wharves can be reached by 10,000-ton ships. To a considerable extent economic factors will decide whether this plan ever becomes a reality. From the point of view of the company it has yet to be proved that coal and coke can be produced at a price competitive with existing Japanese imports from Australia and the United States; moreover, the Government must be convinced that the plan will provide sufficient return to Sarawak to finance the necessary reconstruction and maintenance of the Silantek-Kuching road. Recent troubles on the

[4] Haile, op. cit., pp. 51-83.

Indonesian border did little to encourage the immediate commencement of operations, because the field lies within two miles of the international boundary.

Gold

Gold-mining has the longest continuous history of any of Sarawak's mining industries although, like the others, it experienced a boom period. Chinese were mining gold in the Bau area in the 1820's. By the 1840's the production of gold was estimated to be 'at least 7,000 ounces' annually and the labour force numbered 700,[5] and the industry thrived until the Chinese insurrection of 1857. This almost ruined the gold mining industry and although some of the workers returned later and other immigrants joined them, Chinese mining never fully recovered. Nevertheless, panning and sluicing by Chinese, Malay and Dyak miners continued, the ore being crushed by hand. Streams were dammed and trenches dug to divert water to the working areas. Here the alluvial cover was removed and the ore-bearing layers were sluiced and the gold recovered by panning. Until 1885, however, the amount exported annually never exceeded 1,000 ounces and occasionally it fell below 100 ounces. During the 1870's the Borneo Company assisted the local miners with equipment and in 1882 erected a mill at Bau to crush the ore. Two years later it loaned pumping engines to the miners to enable them to work deposits below the water-table. Exports increased temporarily in 1885 and 1886 and by the 1890's were considerably higher than they had been for over three decades (Fig. 25).

Most of the deposits accessible to the crude Chinese methods of panning and sluicing had been worked out by the late 1890's. Much gold remained but it was in such fine particles that sluicing was unsuitable. Consequently in 1896 the Borneo Company began to experiment with the most modern methods of extraction, including the recently-discovered cyanide process. Technical difficulties in the use of this process with local ores were overcome by the Company's engineers and in 1898 a mine was opened at Bau. Further modifications to the original plant proved necessary but the new process was so successful that in 1900 a second plant was opened at Bidi to treat the ore found nearby. Exports of gold from Sarawak jumped suddenly from 984 ounces in 1898 to 24,192 ounces the following year, and, from then until 1921,

---

[5] H. Low, *Sarawak: Its Inhabitants and Productions*, London, Richard Bentley, 1848, p. 26.

gold remained the major mineral export. During this period Sarawak exported nearly 1 million fine ounces valued at almost $26 million.

By 1908, known eluvial ore deposits in the vicinity of Bau were almost exhausted and the Company began to mine the underlying and more refractory primary ore in the Tai Parit area. The Bau mill was modified to treat the new type of ore and the recovery rate was raised considerably. Rich deposits of eluvial ore had been discovered at Tai Ton by 1910 and these were conveyed to the Bau mill by rail. The plant at Bidi was closed in June 1911 but by the following year experiments on the treatment of tailings had proved successful at Bau and a concentrator was added to the plant there. Meanwhile the Tai Parit mine developed into a large opencast working which by 1920 was almost 2,000 feet long and 200 feet deep at one point. By this date about 3 million tons of overburden had been removed from this mine and the amount of overburden that had to be removed for each ounce of gold recovered was rising. Increased depth brought greater dangers of the walls slumping, and flooding greatly increased the already high costs of pumping. Consequently the Tai Parit mine was closed in August 1921 and the Borneo Company withdrew from gold mining. Production fell immediately (Fig. 25).

Subsequently mining was undertaken by numerous Chinese concerns, mostly comprising people formerly employed on the Company mines, who used the cyanide process on the smaller remaining deposits. Others acquired mining leases at Bau and Bidi over areas on which the Company had dumped tailings and these were re-worked successfully. Production began to increase again in 1930 and rose to over 28,000 ounces a year in 1934 and 1935; thereafter it declined until the Japanese Occupation because many of the deposits had been worked out.

Recovery was slow in the post-war period. Machinery had been removed during the Occupation, replacements were costly, and rubber, pepper and the building industry provided serious competition for the available labour. Production exceeded 1,000 ounces in 1949 and 1950 but then remained below this figure until 1959 when output rose suddenly to 2,450 ounces. To help the industry, in 1958 the payment of royalty was waived and the regulations governing the sale of gold were altered, making it possible to sell to local goldsmiths at a price of about $122 per ounce as compared with the price of about $102 that was obtained for gold exported to Singapore. This aroused considerable interest in mining gold, all of which is now sold locally.[6]

[6] *Annual Report, Sarawak, 1959*, Kuching, Government Printer, 1960, p. 82.

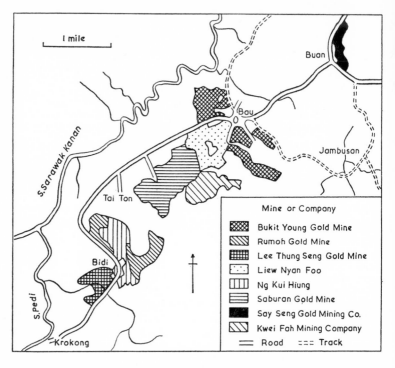

Figure 27   Gold mines in production, 1964. (Redrawn from R. A. M. Wilson, *Annual Report of the Geological Survey, Borneo Region, Malaysia, 1964*, Fig. 6, p. 25, with the permission of the Acting Director, Geological Survey, Borneo Region, Malaysia.)

Output rose to over 4,100 ounces in 1961, declined slightly in the next two years, but in 1964 stood at 3,113 ounces. Mining is entirely in Chinese hands. Eight mines were in operation in the Bau-Bidi area in 1964, employing a total of about 200 workers. By far the most productive of these mines was the Bukit Young Gold Mining Company's mine close by Bau town (Fig. 27 and Plate VII). Despite the long history of the industry and the fact that 1,235,000 ounces of gold were produced between 1864 and 1964, Tai Parit remains the deepest mine ever worked and most have been either surface workings or shallow adits. A prodigious area of land has been worked over in the past and today abandoned and existing workings dominate the landscape around Bau. Currently tests are in progress to explore the possibility of deeper deposits as yet untouched.

Petroleum

Petroleum was the leading mineral produced in Sarawak from the early 1920's until 1959, when it was supplanted by bauxite. It remains the State's most valuable export but most now comes from the Seria field in Brunei and appears in Sarawak's trade returns because it is shipped from Lutong in either the crude or refined state.

The sole oilfield in Sarawak is that at Miri in the Fourth Division; this small field is only about five miles long and half a mile wide. The oil occurs in Upper Miocene to Lower Pliocene sandstones, the accumulations being trapped by faults on the down-thrown north-western flank of a narrow anticlinal structure. Oil seepages here were referred to as early as the 1870's and some drilling was done by the Borneo Company between 1888 and 1907. However, the initial development of the field owes much to Charles Hose, a former Resident of the Fourth Division. After personal exploration in the area, Hose suggested in 1907 that the Rajah might grant a concession to a company to work the deposit. Two years later the Anglo-Saxon Petroleum Company obtained an oil exploration and development licence. The first well was put down in 1910 and is still in operation today (Plate VIII). Production rose from 260 tons in 1911 to 26,067 tons in 1913 when the first crude oil was exported. Development of the field was relatively slow and by 1920 only about 70 wells had been completed; nevertheless, by 1923 production had reached 558,224 tons. Rotary drilling was introduced in 1925 and by the following year most of the oil accumulations had already been discovered.[7] Production continued to increase and reached a peak of over $\frac{3}{4}$ million tons in 1929; thereafter it declined steadily until the Japanese Occupation, by which time a total of 597 wells had been drilled.

In 1941, before the Japanese invasion, the field was closed down and some of the equipment taken to Singapore. Wartime damage was severe; rehabilitation was undertaken in the late 1940's but output has remained small and is decreasing annually (Table 20). Over 170 wells, with depths ranging from 57 to 3,355 feet, are still in operation but the future of the Miri oilfield is limited and Sarawak Shell Oilfields are plugging and abandoning wells, thus releasing the land for other forms of development.

The shallow coastal waters prevent large vessels from reaching the

[7] C. Hose, *Fifty Years of Romance and Research, or a Jungle-Wallah at Large*, London, Hutchinson, 1927, pp. 233-237.

Table 20   Output from Miri Oilfield, 1956-1965

(in long tons)

1956	70,616
1957	65,906
1958	56,902
1959	54,708
1960	59,442
1961	59,498
1962	57,274
1963	51,126
1964	48,243
1965	48,125

shore here and initially the crude oil was taken in drums by lighters to tankers lying a few miles out to sea, but production increased quickly and this method of export soon became impracticable. In 1914 the first submarine pipeline, two and a half miles long, was launched from Tanjong Lobang to the south of Miri town to connect the shore directly with a loading point at sea. This was not entirely satisfactory and three years later a new 'sea-line' was laid from Lutong, some seven miles to the north of Miri. Designed to accommodate larger more modern tankers, this new line was two and three-quarter miles in length and at that time was the longest submarine pipeline in the world. Considerable improvements have since been made to shipping facilities at Lutong and by 1960 there were four loading berths, each equipped with two sea-lines, with terminals between three and four miles off-shore capable of handling tankers up to 32,000 tons.[8]

The siting of the new pipeline at Lutong determined the location of the small refinery built to treat Miri oil in 1917. Despite the discovery of the larger Seria oilfield in Brunei in 1929 and the subsequent decline of production from the Miri field, this has remained the sole refinery in north-western Borneo. A small and somewhat primitive affair at first, it was gradually improved and enlarged, and by 1941 it was processing about $1\frac{1}{4}$ million tons of oil per year. The refinery was severely damaged during the Occupation; rebuilding began in 1945 and two years later the output again exceeded 1 million tons a year.

[8] *Sarawak Annual Report, 1960*, Kuching, Government Printer, p. 81.

Today Lutong has a large and modern refinery consisting of two distillation units, a deisobutaniser tower and a gasoline stabilizing tower. With the decline of the Miri field most of the crude oil passing through Lutong is now piped from Brunei Shell's Seria oilfield. Roughly half the crude oil arriving at Lutong is processed at the refinery. In 1964 output totalled $2\frac{1}{2}$ million tons comprising 1·1 million tons of diesel fuel, 682,000 tons of a waxy residue known as 'Lutong residue', 401,000 tons of gasoline, 139,600 tons of gas oil, 135,500 tons of kerosene and 31,000 tons of isobutane concentrate. The remainder of the crude oil from Brunei is exported as such through the ocean-loading facilities at Lutong to refineries in Australia, Japan, Holland and the United Kingdom; the refined products go mainly to Singapore, Japan and Europe. In 1964 total oil exports, including re-exports from Brunei, were valued at over $205 million; of this, oil produced on the Miri field contributed a mere $2·2 million.[9]

The Miri field shows signs of imminent exhaustion and the Seria field cannot last indefinitely. Since 1909 the companies of the Royal Dutch-Shell Group have drilled exploration wells in many parts of Sarawak in an attempt to discover a new, commercially-exploitable field. Exploration work on land has proved extremely costly and, although forty-nine wells had been drilled by 1960, it has not met with success (Fig. 28). As a result, in 1956 Sarawak Shell Oilfields began marine exploration in neighbouring off-shore areas and two exploration wells were drilled from a fixed platform built at Siwa to the south-west of Miri. These were completely unsuccessful and were abandoned in late 1957; moreover, drilling from fixed platforms proved very expensive.

Nevertheless, in 1960 the company announced that future prospecting would concentrate on off-shore areas and the following year they introduced a mobile drilling barge known as *Orient Explorer*. Between mid-1961 and early 1963 nine wells were drilled from this outfit off the coast at Bintulu, and non-commercial oil and gas showings in several of these provided considerable encouragement. In 1962 a floating platform, known as *Sidewinder*, was hired from the United States. This began work off the mouth of the Baram in late 1963. Four wells were drilled but were abandoned when no significant commercial shows were encountered (Fig. 28). Difficulties were experienced with both these drilling outfits and both had left the

[9] R. A. M. Wilson, *Annual Report of the Geological Survey, Borneo Region, Malaysia, 1964*, Kuching, Government Printer, 1965, pp. 10 and 29.

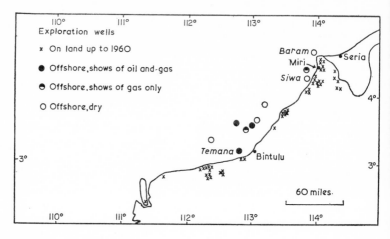

Figure 28   Oil exploration.

N.B.—Off-shore wells drilled between June 1956 and November 1964. These wells were drilled at both Baram and Temana and two at Siwa.

(Based on R. A. M. Wilson, *Annual Report of the Geological Survey, Borneo Region, Malaysia, 1964*, Fig. 7, p. 31 and *Sarawak Annual Report, 1960*, p. 82 with permission.)

area by the end of 1964. They are to be replaced by new outfits better suited to local conditions, and it is to be hoped that these achieve the success that the company has long awaited by revealing a new off-shore field because, if they do not, it is difficult to see a prolonged future for the oil industry of northern Sarawak.

Bauxite

Bauxite was discovered at Sematan in western Sarawak in 1949. The main deposits occur at Munggu Belian, where the bauxite is derived from andesite by weathering, and at Bukit Gebong, with smaller deposits at Tanjong Serabang and in several less accessible areas. From late 1949 until 1952 these deposits were prospected by geologists and mining engineers of the British Aluminium Company Ltd but although over 5½ million tons of ore were proved, the company decided not to mine.

In 1955 a local company, Sematan Bauxite Ltd, was formed to work the deposits. Two years later they obtained a 21-year lease over 480 acres at Munggu Belian and imported mining equipment and built a washing plant and wharf. Mining began in early 1958 and by the end of the year 99,930 tons of washed bauxite had been exported, mainly to Japan and Taiwan. In 1959 a new washing plant was completed and the wharf extended and since then bauxite has been the leading mineral produced in Sarawak. In 1961 the company obtained an extension to their lease at Munggu Belian and exports reached a peak in that year (Fig. 25).

The bauxite forms a 10-foot bed under a thin cover of soil and it also extends under the surrounding alluvium. Mining, which began on the hills, consisted of the removal of the overburden by bulldozer and the extraction of the ore by excavators which loaded it into trucks. In 1961 a drag-line was imported to work the bauxite beneath the alluvium. The ore was taken to a central plant for washing and screening, and the washed bauxite, which represented about a quarter of the bulk of the ore mined, was then ready for export. The company employed a total of about 200 workers at Munggu Belian. The heavy swells characteristic of the north-east monsoon restricted export to the period March to October. The washed bauxite was loaded mechanically into lighters in the Sematan River and transferred to ocean freighters anchored about three miles offshore.

By the end of 1965 a total of 1·6 million long tons had been exported and with the exhaustion of the existing reserves at Munggu Belian mining ceased. This deposit was of excellent quality, containing about 56 per cent aluminium oxide in the form of gibbsite. That at nearby Bukit Gebong is believed to contain 1½ to 2 million tons of washed bauxite, but the grade is poorer, giving a lower recovery rate, and it seems unlikely at the moment that it will be worked; moreover, the deposit at Tanjong Serabang is too high in iron and low in alumina to justify development at present, so that the short-lived bauxite boom appears to have petered out.

Other minerals

Sarawak possesses several other mineral deposits, including dolomite, fireclay, glass sand and phosphate, but as yet only the latter has been worked commercially. As valuable fertilizers, guano and rock phosphate are important resources in Sarawak and have long been worked on a small scale at several places for local use. The largest deposits occur in the Niah Caves in the Fourth Division; these are estimated to total 29,000 tons and production here is supervised by the Museum, itself involved in archaeological work in the caves. Dolomite is another important source of fertilizers and is also used to reduce soil acidity, particularly in pepper gardens. Currently most of the dolomite used in Sarawak is imported from Malaya. Early in 1962 a relatively accessible deposit sufficient to supply the demands of Sarawak's farmers for many years was discovered near the Benar River, a tributary of the Melinau, in the Fourth Division. Exploitation has been discouraged by the fact that transport costs may prove prohibitive and it has been suggested that Sarawak's proposed main trunk road should be re-routed to run closer to the deposit.

Kaolinitic clays have been found near Balai Ringin and Silantek on the Kuching-Simanggang road and near the bauxite mines at Sematan. These are of variable quality but are suitable for the manufacture of ceramics and refractory bricks and for use in paper manufacture. In 1964 a Japanese company was negotiating with the Government to exploit the Balai Ringin and Silantek deposits, while Sematan Bauxite Ltd hope that the clay near their mine may form the basis for a cottage industry, producing pottery, now that bauxite mining has ceased.

Deposits of sand suitable for glass manufacture have been discovered near Bintulu, near Sematan and near Roban in the Second Division. Interest in these deposits has been evinced by the Japanese, who are concerned about the future of their existing sources of supply in South Vietnam. The Bintulu deposits were prospected in 1964 and reserves of sand suitable for sheet and bottle-glass manufacture were estimated to total at least 2 million tons. However, these deposits will be worked only if the sand can be produced at a competitive price.

Constructional Materials

The growth of the building industry and the extension of road development in post-war Sarawak have been matched by an expansion in the local production of the requisite constructional materials (Table 21).

Table 21   Production of Constructional Materials,
1951-1964

	1951	1957	1960	1964
Bricks (pieces)	2,215,500	3,240,000	1,911,000	6,918,711
Tiles (pieces)	375,000	120,000	20,000	Nil
Lime (long tons)	1,113	253	15	222
Stone (cu. yards)	40,100	110,849	218,352	318,245
Gravel (cu. yards)	n.a.	16,789	71,326	46,362

(Source: Roe, *The Natural Resources of Sarawak*, p. 27; *Sarawak Annual Report*, 1957 and 1960; Wilson, *Annual Report of the Geological Survey, Borneo Region, Malaysia, 1964*, p. 10.)

The brick, tile and lime manufacturing industries are dominated by the Chinese. Most of the brickworks are situated in the First and Third Divisions, serving the needs of building contractors in Kuching and Sibu respectively and in general operations are on a small scale. Production of bricks rose steadily until 1957 but then declined markedly in the late 1950's when output in the Kuching area fell sharply; however, between 1961 and 1964, production more than trebled and the Kuching area now accounts for over two-thirds of the total output. As a result of the growing demand, some of the brickworks have been mechanized and the quality of the bricks produced has improved considerably. Significantly local prices for bricks vary noticeably in the different parts of the State, thus influencing building costs. Prices are lowest in Kuching and the average price in Miri is 75 per cent higher than that in the capital. A small amount of lime is produced by four brickworks in the First Division; no tiles were produced in 1964.

By 1960 it was felt that the local demand for cement was sufficient to justify the establishment of a factory. It was pointed out that the main raw materials were available in large amounts in western and northern Sarawak and only gypsum need be imported.[10] An application to establish a cement factory from the Borneo Cement Manufacturing Corporation (a subsidiary of Asian Flour Mills Ltd) was approved in 1963 and a site was chosen for the factory near Gunong Pangga, Bau.

Stone and gravel find their chief use in road construction and repair. Accessible supplies of both are of first importance in the planning of new roads and have proved a major factor in determining their cost and the speed of their construction. Officers of the Geological Survey are engaged in locating potential quarry sites and frequently new roads have been routed to take advantage of possible sources of road-stone. Sand and gravel are obtained from the beds of the larger rivers, particularly from the Sarawak and Rejang.

The output of stone has increased steadily in the last decade and a half, in tune with rising demand and the opening of new quarries, and production in 1964 was nearly eight times that in 1951 (Table 21). There were fifteen quarries in operation in 1964 of which six were in the First Division and four in the Second Division. The First Division produces over three-fifths of the total output. Plans for greatly increased road construction will cause a further marked increase in quarrying and, in this connection, limestone, which occurs at about fifty widely scattered localities in Sarawak, will prove an important

[10] *Sarawak Annual Report, 1960*, p. 86.

resource (Fig. 26). Currently quarried only in the Bau and Penrissen areas of the First Division, limestone will be used in increasing quantities for road construction in the future.

Manufacturing Industries

It has been estimated that manufacturing in Sarawak employs about 4 per cent of the total labour force and produces about 8 per cent of the gross domestic product.[11] This includes, however, the processing of primary produce for export. Rubber and pepper processing, sago and copra milling, sawmilling and oil refining have been covered already in the relevant sections and manufacturing industry here refers to the small industrial concerns which manufacture goods for the domestic market. Almost invariably these produce consumer goods, in the main using local raw materials and relatively simple production methods, although there are a few more capital-intensive industries using imported materials. Manufacturing industry thus defined contributed a mere $2\frac{1}{2}$ per cent to Sarawak's gross national product in 1961.[12] Thus, although there has been a steady expansion in recent years, manufacturing industry is still on a very small scale: the range of products is narrow, there is a very heavy concentration in Kuching and, to a lesser extent, in Sibu, and producing units are small, most of them employing less than fifty workers.

Industrial development
As part of a long-term effort to diversify the economy and to provide employment opportunities for the rapidly-growing population, the Government has taken various steps to encourage industrial development. But the problems are enormous and the prospects of success limited. Indeed, the Government recognizes that Sarawak lacks the basis for successful rapid industrialization. There is a deficiency of capital and much of that available among the Chinese is channelled into the traditional investment in commerce and retail trade. There is a shortage of skilled and semi-skilled labour and trained technical and

[11] *Sarawak Development Plan, 1964-1968*, Kuching, Government Printer, 1963, p. 4.
[12] *Report on the Economic Aspects of Malaysia by a Mission of the International Bank for Reconstruction and Development*, Kuala Lumpur, Government Printer, 1963, p. 25 (hereafter referred to as the *Rueff Report*).

Plate XIII Mukah, a typical riverside 'bazaar', in which the brick-built Chinese shop-house core is surrounded by more dispersed detached residences.

Plate XIV   Industry in Sarawak is usually small-scale.   This modern cigarette factory on Lanang Road, Sibu, Third Division, is one of the few exceptions.   Using a mixture of imported and Sarawak tobaccos it produces cigarettes sold locally under brand names.

Plate XV   Coastal and river craft remain the chief means of transport in many parts of Sarawak.   Launches and speedboats, such as these at Sibu, provide regular passenger and goods services on the main rivers.

managerial personnel. Electricity and water are relatively expensive in Sarawak. Transport presents immense difficulties, internally because roads are few and population densities low, and externally in the form of high freight rates. There is a small local market and inadequate marketing arrangements. Most important of all, however, is the fact that Sarawak has such a large agricultural population barely above subsistence level and largely on the fringes of the money economy. The agricultural base must be improved before a vigorous industrialization plan can be effective.[13]

Thus far the measures taken to offset these difficulties include the development of communications and other basic facilities, and the granting of guarantees in respect of foreign investments. Credit facilities are available from the Borneo Development Corporation Ltd (a subsidiary of the Commonwealth Development Corporation) in which the Government holds shares. In an attempt to encourage local industry by enlarging the potential market, the Borneo Free Trade Area was established by the Governments of Sarawak and North Borneo (now Sabah) on 1st January 1962. With the advent of Malaysia this has been supplemented by a common market (now termed 'customs area'). It was suggested that in the long run this should enlarge substantially the opportunities for industrial production, although initially several existing firms would have to make adjustments to the new Malaysian competition.[14] Indeed in early 1964 the manager of the Borneo Development Corporation stated that he did not see Malaysia as a stimulus to further development and, in fact, he regarded the flow of goods from Malaya as 'to the detriment of any policy of industrialisation here'.[15]

The most effective government measure has been the *Pioneer Industries (Encouragement) Ordinance* introduced in 1957. Under this Ordinance, manufacturers may be granted 'pioneer status' if the industry they propose to establish does not exist in Sarawak and there are insufficient manufacturing facilities already available to enable it to be conducted on a commercial scale, or if there is a favourable prospect of further development of the industry. Those industries which are granted pioneer status receive certain valuable privileges. For a period of five years they may import free from customs duty

[13] Shim Kah Foo, 'Problems of Industrialization in Sarawak and Sabah' in Commonwealth Development Corporation, *Development Seminar*, Kuching, April 1964 (mimeographed).
[14] *Rueff Report*, pp. 42-43.   [15] Shim Kah Foo, op. cit., p. 6.

F

anything required for the construction, alteration, reconstruction or extension of their pioneer factory; they are also entitled, for purposes of income tax, to set off one-fifth of the permitted capital expenditure against income derived from manufacturing the pioneer product in each of any five years during a period of eight years beginning on the first production day. Since the introduction of the Ordinance, thirteen industries have been granted pioneer status, eleven of which were still in operation at the end of 1965. Many of these, such as the production of metal containers, textiles, biscuits and footwear, represent consumer goods for the local market but others, notably the manufacture of veneers and *ramin* mouldings, represent the beginnings of new export industries. The Ordinance has clearly stimulated some growth of industry but it provides incentives chiefly for relatively small-scale operations that are not highly capitalised and produce quick profits. In the future new legislation may provide incentives for increased investment in operations that take longer to produce profits. In the words of the Malaysian Minister of Finance more industrial investment would be channelled to areas such as Sarawak 'if incentives were directly related to the quantum of investment instead of being tied to profits'.[16]

In addition to granting pioneer status the Government has taken the initiative in the development of small industrial sites. The small industrial estate appears to be a practical answer to many of Sarawak's problems, for land, roads and other basic facilities can be provided at minimum cost and industry can be directed to sites chosen by Government. The ideal would be a 'package deal' of loan, land and ready-built factory on a developed site, but this requires very careful planning. The only industrial site sponsored by the government so far is that at Padungan, Kuching. This scheme began in June 1959 and was designed to aid those wishing to build small factories. Land was alienated at an economic rent and premium and finance was provided by the Sarawak Development Finance Corporation and the Borneo Development Corporation Ltd, the latter administering the scheme. Government spent about $270,000 on the construction of internal roads and by 1963 thirty-two factory sites had been provided, of which twenty-six had been taken up.[17]

[16] Tan Siew Sin, Budget Speech, 17th November 1965, *Straits Times*, 18th November 1965, p. 14.
[17] *Sarawak Annual Report, 1962*, p. 131; *Sarawak Development Plan, 1964-1968*, p. 12.

Existing manufacturing industries

Apart from the processing of primary products for export, existing industrial activity in Sarawak comprises the cottage and small industries common throughout South-East Asia, such as furniture-making, pottery, boat-building, brick-making and printing, car and bicycle-repairing and other service industries, together with several more recently developed and larger plants manufacturing a limited range of consumer goods for local sale. Many of the latter have been granted pioneer status.

The textile industry, for instance, owes its development to the granting of pioneer status to the manufacture of knitted products and printed *batek* cloth. A textile factory was established in Kuching in late 1959 to produce singlets, underwear, towels and pullovers for the local market and employs a regular work-force of over fifty, mostly female. A new factory to produce printed *batek* cloth was opened in Kuching in mid-1963.

The manufacture of biscuits is not new to Sarawak but the product is of poor quality because the machinery used in existing factories is locally made and somewhat primitive. To encourage local producers to modernize their production methods, the manufacture of biscuits by mechanical processes was declared a pioneer industry in 1961 and a new modern biscuit factory was opened at Tanah Puteh in 1963.

The bulk importation of kerosene oil, increased production of coconut oil and the manufacture of biscuits have all increased the local demand for metal containers, the manufacture of which was accorded pioneer status in 1959. By 1962 three factories had been established and in that year these produced about three million metal containers of various types.

The production of rubber footwear is also a pioneer industry. This began in 1959 and by 1962 there were three factories, two in Kuching and one in Binatang, producing slippers, sports and house shoes for the domestic market.

Several other manufacturing industries exist which have not been accorded pioneer status. Thus in 1962 there were nine factories producing non-alcoholic beverages, of which six were located in Kuching, two in Sibu and one in Miri. Six soap factories existed in 1962, five in Kuching and one in Sibu, and these produce mainly washing soap for domestic use.[18] The cigarette industry began in 1959 when the Ireland Tobacco Company Ltd opened a modern factory at Sibu: this uses a

[18] *Sarawak Annual Report, 1962*, pp. 136-138.

mixture of imported and local tobaccos to produce cigarettes sold locally under various brand names (Plate IX). It is possible that some of the existing cottage and small industries may be improved, re-organized and expanded to enter the export trade.

Clearly there has been a growth of manufacturing industry in Sarawak since 1959 and to a large extent this has resulted from the granting of pioneer status to the manufacture of specific products. There has been substantial foreign investment in several of these new industries, (e.g. biscuits and rubber footwear), but it is officially believed that local capital is responsible for much of the industrial investment. Thus far, however, industrial growth has had scant effect on Sarawak's economic or occupational structure and the growth that has occurred represents little more than 'a start in changing the pattern of production'.[19] Although factory organization is beginning, operations remain on a small scale; moreover, development con-centrates heavily in Kuching and, to a smaller degree, Sibu.

Perhaps the most important development in the last half decade has been the appearance of the small to medium manufacturer 'making use of relatively modern techniques and tending to avoid the under-capitalization and the tight-knit family structure of the past.'[20] This represents the beginnings of the organizational change necessary, particularly among the Chinese who dominate the urban, commercial and financial scenes, before industrialization can proceed much further; it will provide a training ground for the acquisition of the technical and managerial skills and the outlook essential for larger-scale operations.

Nevertheless, while giving encouragement to industrial expansion the Government has conceded that 'the prospects of substantial industrialization in Sarawak are small . . . [and that] . . . it is probable that the proportion of people gaining their living from the countryside will remain at about 80 per cent of the total.'[21] Indeed, it is expected that in the period 1964 to 1968, mining will provide only 600 extra jobs and manufacturing industry about another 2,700.[22]

[19] *Sarawak Annual Report, 1962*, p. 139.   [20] *Sarawak Annual Report, 1961*, p. 84.
[21] *Sarawak Development Plan, 1964-1968*, p. 17.   [22] Ibid., pp. 23-24.

6 Transport

As a factor influencing social and economic development, transport is crucial and, in a sparsely peopled land of tropical forest and swamp whose economy depends so heavily on foreign trade, it assumes immense importance. Devoid of railways, save a short line formerly used to transport stone from quarries south of Kuching and now abandoned, and still lacking a fully developed road system, inland waterways retain much of their significance as the traditional routeways of Sarawak, and the main areas of development and population concentration remain closely linked to the coast and the major rivers.

The last decade has witnessed a considerable public investment programme in the improvement of transport facilities and total public development expenditure on transport amounted to $90·6 million in the period 1961 to 1965. Extension and improvement of transport facilities remains necessarily a key feature of government development policy and a total outlay of $111.9 million is provided for under the First Malaysia Plan.[1] Here, as elsewhere, an adequate road system will provide the foundation for rural economic and social progress, and road development absorbs over three-quarters of this expenditure. It is recognized, however, that to achieve maximum effectiveness and efficiency, planning must aim at the over-all co-ordination of road, inland water, coastal and air transport. Thus, the new inter-Division trunk road will run parallel to the coast, leaving the Rejang River as the highway for much of central Sarawak, and internal air services will remain the basic link between the outside world and the small communities of the mountainous interior of northern Sarawak, where river transport is slow and often difficult and road building is precluded by distance and the nature of the terrain.

[1] *First Malaysia Plan, 1966-1970*, Kuala Lumpur, Government Printer, 1965, pp. 151-152.

River and Coastal Transport

Transport has always focused on water in Sarawak and it is only in the recent past that other forms of communication have began to appear. Despite the expanding road network and the development of an internal air service, coastal and river craft remain the chief means of transport for much of the population, providing a relatively cheap method of moving passengers and goods.

The rivers provide an immense mileage of inland waterways penetrating deeply into the interior; almost all settlements are located on or close to their banks and so are accessible from the coast by river. Rivers have an advantage over roads in that maintenance costs are low except for the provision and upkeep of wharves, and transport charges on the fleets of Chinese launches that ply along them are moderate. Most of the rivers, however, have bars at their mouths which restrict the size of vessel entering, and the lower courses of many rivers have frequent shallows, mud flats and swift currents; moreover, river transport is sometimes hampered by lack of water during the dry season. Some rivers have dangerous bores and, on others, rapids hinder movement farther inland. Attempts have been made to overcome this latter problem by blasting rocks and other obstructions.

In 1961 almost eight hundred river and coastal launches were in operation. Built locally, mainly of wood and powered by diesel engines, these are largely Chinese owned; most are small, over three-quarters being less than 20 net registered tons and on average they have a crew of six. The Rejang River is the main highway for river launch traffic and over two-fifths of the launches in use in 1961 were in the Third Division; over one-quarter operated on the First and Second Division rivers. These vessels include cargo and passenger launches serving their own particular rivers and tributaries as well as others providing links between the major coastal settlements, some of the latter being over 100 net registered tons in size. On the Rejang some are engaged in the timber trade and deliver their cargo direct alongside timber loaders at Tanjong Mani. The passenger launches are relatively slow and do not provide a high degree of comfort so that, particularly on the Rejang, a host of privately-owned small, outboard, motor-driven craft act as river buses (Plate X). In the interior, where rapids prevent the use of even small launches, these give way to small outboard boats and on the shallow stretches of the far interior slow transport is maintained by longboats or rafts. The Government has its own fleet for

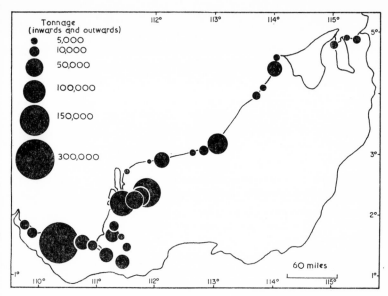

Figure 29 Coastwise tonnage, 1960. (Source of data: *Sarawak Annual Report, 1960*, p. 156.)

coastal and river communication. Most of these are passenger launches used for conveying administrative personnel but there are also several specialized vessels such as stone carriers, a water barge and craft to carry heavy machinery, bulldozers and trucks.

Coastal trade and communication depends upon small vessels plying regularly between Kuching and the main coastal and river ports. Most of these local coasters act as feeders to ocean-going vessels calling at Kuching and Sibu. They bring to these ports a variety of export products, some of which originated far inland, and usually return with cargoes of imported consumer goods. Thus a pattern of internal water transport has developed which involves expensive transhipment and extra handling of cargo, often more than once, before the destination is reached; moreover, the coastal vessels are generally of a local design 'which does not lend itself to economical running or fast cargo handling'.[2]

Kuching and the Rejang ports of Tanjong Mani, Sarikei, Binatang and Sibu dominate this coastwise traffic. The deep inlets of the Batang Lupar and the Batang Saribas have fostered the growth of half a dozen small river ports based on coastal trade in the Second Division; else-

[2] *Sarawak Annual Report, 1960*, Kuching, Government Printer, p. 154.

where small ports are scattered along the coast, the largest of which are Bintulu, Mukah and Miri. Isolated by Brunei, the Fifth Division is generally neglected by this internal coastal traffic (Fig. 29).

Economic and social development brought a marked increase in this coastal movement in the last decade and a half, and the total volume of coastwise trade doubled between 1953 and 1960; there was, however, little change in the general nature of the traffic. Although competition in this traffic is fierce, it cannot provide rapid and economic cargo-handling, and crew and passenger accommodation is poor. It has already lost some passengers to the new internal air services and as roads are extended it will lose an increasing amount of business to the new bus and lorry services which these bring. Nevertheless, efforts are being made to improve inland water transport which is of paramount importance to the rural development programme in many parts of Sarawak.

Ports and Ocean-going Transport

All the ports of Sarawak are located on rivers. The economy rests heavily on overseas trade, yet ocean-going transport is inhibited by shallow coastal waters, the paucity of good harbours and the bars at the entrance to most rivers. Few sites exist at which deep-water ports might be established and those that do, such as Gunong Ayer on the lower Rejang, would involve very great expense. Neither of the two largest port towns, Kuching and Sibu, is directly accessible by other than medium-sized ocean vessels, and, until recently, entrance to both was restricted to vessels of a maximum draught of 16 feet. The new port at Tanah Puteh, opened in 1961, has permitted a slight increase in the size of vessel approaching Kuching but most normal European traders are still precluded. The discovery of the new deep-water Kuala Paloh channel to Sibu has also enabled the successful handling of larger vessels at this port. Excluding the large tonnage calling to load oil off-shore at Lutong and the shipment of bauxite from Sematan, ocean-going transport focuses on Kuching and the Rejang ports.

Until the early 1950's direct services to overseas ports were limited to Singapore and Bangkok. Since then there has been a marked increase in direct services to other parts of the world and by 1965 Hong Kong, Japan, Taiwan, Australia, Europe and the United Kingdom were all included in regular schedules. To a large extent this was a reflection of local economic development: the rapid growth of the timber trade produced an increase in the number of ocean vessels calling at Tanjong Mani, from 17 in 1948 to 334 in 1962, and increasing bulk imports of oil to Biawak (Kuching) and Sibu, and exports of bauxite from Sematan, have had similar effects. In turn the development of direct services to consumer countries has aided the economy by avoiding transhipment at Singapore and by providing more favourable freight rates.

Port development schemes were devised for Kuching and Sibu in the early 1950's and have resulted in vastly improved facilities at both. The volume of traffic using these ports has increased annually, however, and despite the improvements the facilities are generally inadequate for existing traffic; in fact the overseas cargo handled at both Kuching and Sibu increased by about 30 per cent between 1959 and 1962 and the regular use of Tanah Puteh and the Kuala Paloh channel has attracted further shipping to these ports. At both Kuching and Sibu ships now frequently have to wait for a berth and there is a lack of warehouse space. The congestion at Sibu is alarming and that at Tanah Puteh increased with the military operations resulting from 'confrontation'. The new channel means that larger ships now have access to Sibu than to Kuching and this may result in an increased concentration of overseas trade on the Rejang River. To meet expected requirements over the next five years wharf capacity is to be extended at both Kuching and Sibu at a total cost of $21 million. The possibility of developing Tanjong Baram for the export of palm-oil is also under consideration.[3]

Roads and Land Transport

Prior to the Second World War communication between the main settlements was entirely dependent upon river and sea transport. Only a few short, poorly surfaced or unsurfaced earth roads existed in the immediate vicinity of the larger towns and the only properly constructed and surfaced road outside Kuching was that from Miri to Lutong. In addition there were rough roads, usable by motor vehicles, around Kuching and from Lutong to Brunei, and tracks connecting Kuching and Serian, Sarikei and Saratok, Oya and Mukah and Lawas and Trusan. In 1928 it was proposed to construct a trunk road from Kuching to Simanggang, headquarters of the Second Division, but

[3] *First Malaysia Plan, 1966-1970*, p. 147.

F*

only the 40-mile stretch to Serian had been completed by the time of the Japanese invasion.

These roads and tracks were not maintained during the Occupation and in 1945 they were generally in an impassable condition. Thus, the immediate post-war years were devoted mainly to reconstruction and improvement of the existing road system. As late as 1953 there were only 95 miles of all-weather bitumen or concrete surfaced road in Sarawak; in addition there were 65 miles of gravel or stone-surfaced road and a further 115 miles of earth road suitable for motor traffic under favourable weather conditions but causing considerable wear to motor vehicles. Such roads as existed at this date were heavily concentrated in western Sarawak; elsewhere there were incipient local networks radiating from the larger towns. The whole interior of the State was devoid of roads, and movement between Sarawak and the neighbouring areas of Indonesian Borneo and North Borneo was restricted to a few well-defined jungle paths (Fig. 30A).

Problems of road construction
This lack of an adequate land transport system acted as a major brake on social and economic progress in the post-war era. Vast areas remained isolated from the effects of government development policy and the costs of providing and maintaining administrative and social services were excessive. Road development and improvement has been therefore a basic feature of all development planning in the last two decades and has ranked as the largest single item of development expenditure in the field of transport and communications. Road construction in Sarawak is hampered, however, by severe difficulties.

One of the greatest needs is for inter-Division land communication. Dependence upon water transport for communication between the major centres of population entails lengthy journeys by river in a general east-west direction followed by coastwise movement and often further river travel. To replace this by speedier motor transport involves the construction of roads roughly parallel to the coast and the provision of these is complicated by the swampy nature of much of the coastal plain where the deep peat entails considerable filling. Moreover, these roads must run almost at right angles to the major rivers and also cross a multitude of smaller rivers and streams so that much bridging must be undertaken; in addition, particularly in central Sarawak, the necessary south-west—north-east routes are aligned transverse to the ridge and valley grain of the terrain inland of the coastal plain.

The very heavy rainfall that characterizes Sarawak introduces further problems. It hinders construction work and makes it imperative that roads be stoutly built and well surfaced if they are to stand up to permanent motor traffic; simple earth-surfaced minor roads are unsatisfactory under Sarawak conditions and flash floods can have disastrous effects. The provision of adequate surfacing is hampered by the great shortage of roadstone over most of the State. Suitable outcrops are most frequent in western Sarawak; east of the Batang Lupar it is generally necessary to rely on scattered outcrops and inferior gravel deposits and indeed here, wherever possible, new roads are routed to take advantage of such deposits as occur, for the alternative is to transport roadstone by water over considerable distances. Continued dependence on water transport, even during an era of road expansion, often entails the transportation of labour, equipment and materials by boat to the more isolated construction sites. To these physical difficulties must be added the problems of road planning and survey in areas still largely uncovered by adequate and detailed topographic maps, the lack of suitably trained personnel and the fact that most new roads necessarily pass through large tracts with a thinly scattered population, often of shifting cultivators, thus making the mileage of new road per person served very high in much of central and northern Sarawak.

In total these problems make road construction extremely expensive. On average the 438 miles of road built under the 1959-1963 Development Plan cost $123,000 per mile and the average cost per mile for the Serian-Simanggang trunk road was $228,000.[4] Indeed in 1960 it was estimated that about $200 million would be required to meet the capital cost of linking Kuching and Miri with a trunk road and that many millions more would be needed for its annual maintenance.[5] An expansion of the road network has long been recognized as a prerequisite for the economic and social development of the State but construction costs per mile and per person served are exceedingly high; moreover, every new road requires regular maintenance which is also expensive under Sarawak conditions. Although desirable, rapid growth of the road network has been limited by the amount of capital available.

[4] *Sarawak Development Plan, 1964-1968*, Kuching, Government Printer, 1963, p. 9.
[5] Sarawak Information Service, *Information on Sarawak*, Kuching, Borneo Literature Bureau, 1960, p. 64.

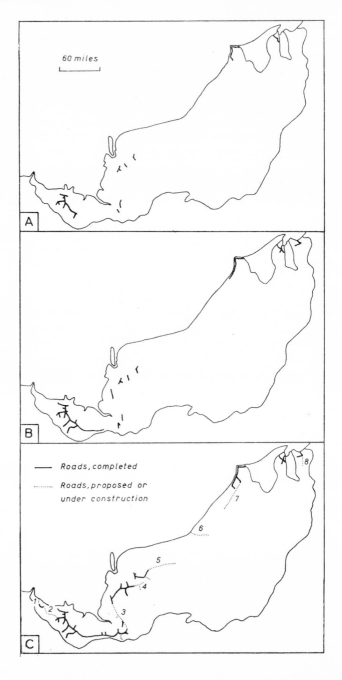

Road construction programme

Until the late 1950's effort was directed towards reconstruction of existing roads and the Road Construction Programme did not become fully operative until 1958, although plans had been prepared for the Serian-Simanggang trunk road several years earlier. Under this programme a large proportion of public development expenditure was devoted to the construction of trunk, secondary and feeder roads. Designed to run from 1958 to 1963, the programme provided for the construction of a total of 504 miles of roads; this included the 81-mile Serian-Simanggang trunk road, completed in mid-1962, plus some 232 miles of secondary and 190 miles of feeder roads.

The principal aim was to provide a main line of road communication to link Sematan in the First Division with Durin on the Rejang River. This road would pass through the most densely settled rural areas and thereby permit their development by means of subsidiary networks; it could also be used to open up new land for development (Fig. 30c). It became the government's explicit policy to build the maximum mileage of road with the money available; thus, only a nine-foot wide running surface was provided on roads other than trunk roads and emphasis was placed on the building of suitable feeder roads, some of which were designed to simplify their eventual upgrading to secondary road status. In the present decade the growing concentration on agricultural improvement and the planned settlement of newly-opened land under the 'Development Area' concept made it increasingly necessary to select secondary and feeder road routes carefully in order

Figure 30   Roads. (A) 1949; (B) 1960; (C) 1964.

1 Lundu-Serian-Sematan	5 Sibu-Oya Extension
2 Bau-Lundu	6 Bintulu-Pandan
3 Simanggang-Engkilili-Saratok	7 Lambir-Subis
4 Kelupu-Julau-Durin	8 Lawas-Lawas Damit.

(Based on 'Sarawak' (1:1,000,000), Sarawak Series No. 7, 1st edition, 1949; 'Sarawak' (1:1,500,000), Sarawak Series No. 12, 1960 and 'Road Map of Sarawak' facing p. 252 in *Sarawak Annual Report, 1962* with the permission of the Director of Lands and Surveys, Sarawak. Fig. 30c is based in part on Directorate of Overseas Survey's map D.O.S. 979, 'Sarawak and Brunei', 2nd edition, 1964, with permission.)

to achieve maximum rural economic and social development at reasonable cost. Highest priority was accorded to areas where land settlement or agricultural improvement schemes existed, for roads are expensive in Sarawak and 'it is common sense to ensure that the maximum use is made of the land alongside'.[6]

Despite the difficulties of road construction, considerable success was achieved under this programme. The total mileage of all types of road increased from 557 in 1958 to 847 in 1962 and during the same period the mileage of completed bitumen or concrete-surfaced roads over eight feet wide increased by two-thirds and that of gravel or stone-surfaced roads over eight feet wide more than doubled. By 1965 there were about one thousand miles of roads of all types and work was planned or in progress on several important extensions to the rapidly growing road system (Fig. 30c).

Under the Sarawak Development Plan for 1964 to 1968 almost two-fifths of the total allocation for road development was earmarked for the construction of feeder roads. The idea of constructing the maximum mileage with the capital available remained strong and it was intended to build approximately 500 miles of feeder roads at an average cost of $80,000 per mile, chiefly in connection with agricultural development schemes, during the plan period. A further $41 million were allotted to the construction or completion of several other approved road schemes, including one to link Miri and Bintulu to foster the establishment of an oil-palm industry on the large area of good agricultural land indicated by recent soil surveys in this region[7] (Fig. 30c).

This Development Plan has since been absorbed into the First Malaysia Plan, 1966-1970, and has undergone notable changes. It is now proposed to spend $35 million of the $75 million allocated for road construction and development on the building of trunk roads. As now outlined, the programme will provide by 1970 a through trunk road for Sarawak running parallel to the coast which will be complete except for a hundred-mile gap between Sibu and Bintulu and another in the Fourth and Fifth Divisions. This programme aims at the completion of trunk roads between Kuching and Lundu, Kuching and Sibu, and Miri and Bintulu. Early in 1967 it was possible for the first time to travel by road from Kuching to Sibu. A further $26 million has been allocated to the extension of feeder roads to meet the requirements of agricultural development and land settlement schemes, and

[6] *Sarawak Development Plan, 1964-1968*, pp. 28-29.
[7] Ibid., pp. 33-34 and 40.

$12 million is set aside for road improvement so that existing roads may be given a bituminous surface wherever traffic is sufficient to justify such improvement. Under the new plan it is expected that the road system of Sarawak will be extended by over 400 miles by 1970, bringing it to a total of over 1,400 miles.[8]

Road transport

This rapid growth of the road network is producing a transport revolution in Sarawak. Motor transport services for passengers and freight follow closely on the heels of the road construction units continuously fingering their way ever farther out from the major centres of population. For the last decade the number of registered motor vehicles has increased steadily, and the bicycle, the motor-cycle and the motor-scooter are inducing the type of local social revolution that they have brought already to many parts of Malaya. Road transport is bringing greater personal mobility and a greater degree of national cohesion. It brings obvious social and economic advantages by facilitating the movement of goods and the provision of social and welfare services. One of the more important long-term geographical effects of road transport, however, is a complete reorientation of internal transport lines, for in general the new roads run transverse to the old river routeways.

Ten years ago, before road expansion began, road transport services were largely confined to the Kuching area and the economical use of motor vehicles was extremely limited. In 1956 about seven-tenths of the licensed motor vehicles in Sarawak were located in Kuching and there was, even then, a high density of traffic in the Municipal Area. In the surrounding area fifty-five buses provided services under franchise on defined routes. Work had just begun on the introduction of bus services to the Sibu and Miri areas.[9]

The bus operators in the Kuching area in the mid-1950's faced severe difficulties. Their vehicles were in poor condition because of the lack of proper garage and maintenance facilities; the carrying of passengers in goods vehicles provided competition as did the growing fleet of taxis and, among operators, largely Chinese, competition was cutthroat. Moreover, the bus services provided were poor. Rural areas were neglected, there were no authorized timetables and the services were totally unreliable.

[8] *First Malaysia Plan, 1966-1970*, pp. 144-145.
[9] *Sarawak Annual Report, 1956*, p. 117.

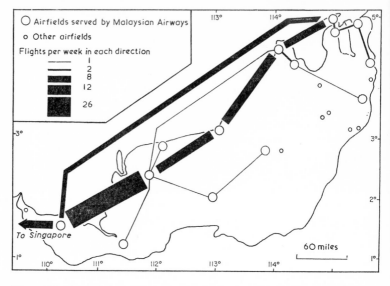

Figure 31   Internal air services. The service in the Fifth Division connects with flights to the remainder of Sarawak at Brunei which is therefore included in the above map.

Steps were taken to co-ordinate the public transport system in 1954 when it was proposed to grant route monopolies to properly constituted limited liability companies. Reorganization progressed slowly, partly because individual owners were loath to join companies and partly because the companies that were formed lacked qualified managerial and technical staff and faced high maintenance costs and continued competition from taxis, private cars and goods vehicles. In 1957 steps were taken to prevent goods vehicles carrying passengers and three years later the government imposed conditions to prevent direct rivalry between buses and taxis. In 1961 changes were introduced into the system of control of commercial transport 'to provide and maintain a sound economic road transport structure throughout the whole country.' It was hoped to eliminate wasteful competition and provide improved services, and the desired effect was achieved.[10] Thirty-four new buses were brought into operation in Sarawak in 1961 and larger capacity, modern diesel buses are now in use throughout the State. Generally the new roads built in the last half decade are an extension of the existing network, and it has been the policy to allow established

[10] *Sarawak Annual Report, 1962*, p. 256.

companies to extend their services along newly-opened roads rather than permit the entry of newcomers into the industry. The number of buses operating in Sarawak increased from 160 in 1960 to 268 in 1965. Simultaneously there has been a marked increase in the number of private cars, taxis and motor-cycles and motor scooters (Table 22).

As with buses, so motor goods vehicles were generally in a poor condition and greatly overworked and overloaded in the mid-1950's. Very considerable improvements have occurred in the last few years. Almost 600 new lorries and vans were introduced between 1960 and 1965 and most of these are of the more economical diesel-powered type. Clearly, increased road-building operations have stimulated the provision of wider transport services and have encouraged local investment in the introduction of new vehicles. As the road construction programme proceeds, motor transport will play an increasingly important role in the social and economic development of Sarawak.

Table 22   Registered Motor Vehicles, 1960-1965

	Private cars	Motor-cycles and scooters	Taxis and hired cars	Buses	Lorries and vans	Government vehicles	Total
1960	2,807	2,081	200	160	854	759	6,861
1961	3,304	2,617	199	176	1,015	1,006	8,317
1962	3,573	3,577	202	206	1,083	1,340	9,981
1963	4,167	4,590	241	224	1,182	1,434	11,838
1964	5,179	6,047	249	243	1,335	1,501	14,554
1965	6,288	7,387	264	268	1,419	1,608	17,225

(Source: *Annual Bulletin of Statistics, Malaysia, 1964,* p. 32, and *Sarawak in Brief,* Government Printer, Kuching, 1966, p. 4.)

Air Transport

Civil aviation is a post-war development in Sarawak. It has become, nevertheless, a significant means of internal transport for both passengers and freight in this jungle-covered, sparsely-peopled land, and the administration and the economy are heavily dependent upon the maintenance of daily air communication with the Malaysian mainland, Singapore, Brunei and Sabah.

A twice-weekly Malayan Airways service from Singapore through Kuching to North Borneo began in 1949. Initially a landing ground built before the war about seven miles south of the capital was used, but work was already in progress on a new airfield for Kuching, and this was officially opened in September 1950. Civil aviation developed steadily: by the end of 1952 there were five flights weekly on the Singapore-Kuching-North Borneo route into which a new airport at Sibu had been introduced to provide the first internal air link. The value of air transport was quickly appreciated and successive development programmes provided for the construction of new airfields and the purchase of aircraft. By 1956 Malayan Airways ran a daily service to Singapore and North Borneo; since then, Kuching airfield has been improved sufficiently to enable *Comets* to land, and the terminal building has been extended, and this daily service, now operated by Malaysian Airways, provides a fundamental link with mainland Malaysia. A service from Kuching to Hong Kong, via Labuan, was introduced by Cathay Pacific in 1958.

An internal air transport system began in 1955 when the North Borneo Feeder Service was extended on a twice-weekly basis to Miri, Bintulu and Sibu (Fig. 31). The importance attached to the new internal link was reflected in a continual upsurge of traffic. For the first few years services were confined to routes over the coastal lowlands, but the need to provide more remote communities, still dependent on rivers and jungle paths, with the speedy communication necessary for modern commercial activity led to the construction of airfields and airstrips in the interior. By 1957 an airstrip had been constructed at Long Akah on the upper Baram and the Government proposed to develop some of the seven small airstrips built by the Borneo Evangelical Mission in interior northern Sarawak to cater for its projected hinterland services. In that year the Borneo internal air service unit of Malayan Airways was formed into a private company known as Borneo Airways Ltd in which the Governments of Sarawak, Brunei and North Borneo and BOAC and Malayan Airways all held shares. Recently this company has become part of Malaysian Airways.

The small trading communities of interior Sarawak are separated by vast stretches of roadless and sparsely-peopled jungle, and, to provide these with efficient transport services, the internal air communications network was expanded. The introduction of *Twin Pioneer* aircraft in 1958 marked an important step forward, for the very short runway that these require increased the possibility of communication with remote mountainous areas. By the end of 1958 internal services operated to seven airstrips. Three years later, twenty-two airfields of varying sizes and standards were in use. The extension of these internal services has had important social and economic effects on some remote communities. Thus when the service to Long Akah was extended to Bareo in 1961 it enabled the formation of a co-operative society among the Kelabits to handle and distribute freight and this formerly isolated community now imports consumer goods and exports its produce by air.[11] Light aircraft are available for charter to the small interior airfields not served by Malaysian Airways.

The main population concentrations occur on the coastal lowlands where the construction of airfields suitable for larger aircraft was relatively easy. Development in the mountainous interior presented many serious problems. The nature of the relief is such that areas of land suitable as airstrip sites is extremely limited. 'Almost invariably the communities to be served were centred upon riverside villages surrounded by mountainous terrain and thick jungle, and aerodrome site-surveys were carried out entirely relying on the local advice available since accurate maps were and still are virtually non-existent'.[12] In addition it was often exceedingly difficult to move equipment and labour to sites where only river transport was available. In some cases the necessary equipment had to be flown to interior construction sites; work on many has taken the form of hand labour by the local people. All the interior airstrips have grass runways suitable for *Twin Pioneers* or light aircraft, and services now operate to the most important population centres of interior central and northern Sarawak (Fig. 31). The heavy rainfall received by these areas has caused some difficulties in the use of even the *Twin Pioneers*. In order to make all these small grass-surfaced airstrips fully serviceable throughout the year runways must either be lengthened, for which there is often little space available, or they must be surfaced with gravel or bitumen, which is costly. A total of $6.5 million has been allocated for the development of civil aviation in Sarawak in the period 1966 to 1970 and it is proposed to improve and increase these interior services.[13]

Passenger traffic, particularly on main line services, increased rapidly in the late 1950's and the number of passengers using Kuching airport rose by 120 per cent between 1955 and 1960. Since then, greatly im-

---

[11] *Sarawak Annual Report, 1961*, p. 148.
[12] *Sarawak Annual Report, 1962*, pp. 245-246.
[13] *First Malaysia Plan, 1966-1970*, p. 147.

proved internal and international services, the formation of Malaysia, and 'confrontation' have all promoted an even more marked growth of air passenger traffic which for Sarawak as a whole doubled between 1960 and 1964. The movement of freight by air is also becoming increasingly important (Table 23).

Table 23   Air Traffic, 1960-1964

	Passengers*		Freight† (in kilos)	
	Incoming	Outgoing	Incoming	Outgoing
1960	32,533	32,946	241,000	121,000
1961	34,357	34,893	296,000	156,000
1962	37,216	37,765	379,000	214,000
1963	43,378	44,488	406,000	316,000
1964‡	63,397	64,333	627,000	398,000

   * Internal and international, excluding those in transit.
   † Internal and international.
   ‡ Subject to revision.

(Source: *Annual Bulletin of Statistics, Malaysia, 1964*, p. 34.)

7 Trade and Commerce

The trade and commerce of Sarawak centres on the collection of primary products for export and the local distribution of imported consumer and capital goods. The national income is largely derived from the export of a few primary products and in 1965 over four-fifths of Sarawak's total export earnings, excluding re-exports of petroleum, came from timber, rubber and pepper. Over the last century, development has been increasingly in the direction of a narrowly-based export economy and, despite measures to promote increased rice production and some degree of industrialization, production for the domestic market remains relatively insignificant. The State continues to import a large proportion of its foodstuffs, including rice, and almost all the other consumer and capital goods that it requires (Fig. 32). There has been a marked rise in the level of imports in the last half decade and for some time the visible balance of trade has been generally unfavourable, although this is probably largely offset at present by the export of services in connection with the military operations resulting from 'confrontation' and by grants received from the central Malaysian Government and from the Commonwealth Development and Welfare Fund.

The economy is therefore very heavily dependent on the export trade and is extremely vulnerable to fluctuations in the prices of the major export commodities in world markets; declining rubber prices have meant that the total value of Sarawak's exports in 1965 was only a little higher than five years earlier. This has aggravated problems of economic development and focused attention on the desirability of greater economic diversification because, to a considerable extent, an improvement in living standards depends upon raising levels of export earnings.

Growth of Trade

Overseas traders, mainly in search of jungle produce, visited Sarawak long before the beginning of the nineteenth century, but it is only in the last century and a half that external trade has become the key to the State's economic well-being. This development is related closely to the foundation in 1819 and subsequent rapid growth of the entrepôt of Singapore which opened the markets of the West to the products of this north-west Bornean State.

The export of antimony ore to Singapore had begun shortly before the arrival of James Brooke but, to a large extent, the growth of trade in the nineteenth century sprang from the efforts of the first 'White Rajah'. Soon after becoming Rajah, Brooke promulgated a series of simple laws for his newly-acquired territory and decreed that, except for the export of antimony ore, which was to remain a government monopoly, all other branches of trade should be free. He then visited Singapore and interested some Chinese merchants there in trade with Sarawak, thus establishing a link that strengthened as the century progressed and the State developed. Moreover, at this time, trade on the Bornean coast was severely hampered by piracy, and during the 1840's Brooke did much to remove this menace. The combined effect of these measures was immediately apparent. Before Brooke arrived, the small-scale local trade was carried on entirely by native *prahus*. By 1850 merchant vessels were calling at Kuching to load sago, antimony ore and jungle produce, and the town already contained a small but growing Chinese trading community. Indeed one observer remarked in that year that

> 'A few, a very few years ago, no European merchant vessel ventured on the north-west coast of Borneo; now they are numerous and safe'.[1]

The growth of trade was interrupted temporarily during the 1850's by the Chinese insurrection and by other internal disturbances, but the extension of Brooke rule over the Second Division in 1853 and over the whole of central Sarawak in 1861 signified a new upsurge of trading activities, for it brought control of the sago-producing areas and of the rivers draining a huge area yielding various jungle products. In consequence, the value of Sarawak's total external trade trebled

[1] S. Baring-Gould and C. A. Bampfylde, *A History of Sarawak under its Two White Rajahs, 1839-1908*, London, Henry Sotheran and Co., 1909, p. 150.

between 1858 and 1864. Chinese traders moved into these new lands east of the Lupar to barter with the indigenous peoples and already by the early 1860's Spencer St. John could remark that they 'abound at every place where profit can be obtained'.[2] Kuching remained the centre at which local products were collected, and in some cases partially processed, before being exported to Singapore, but certain coastal stations, notably Mukah and Bintulu, rose to prominence with the new-found peace. A century ago the basic pattern of small-scale Chinese traders in the interior selling to Chinese merchants in Kuching who in turn exported Sarawak's produce to Singapore had already emerged.

For the remainder of the century the value of Sarawak's external trade rose steadily, changing little in character or direction, although first mercury and later gambier and pepper replaced antimony ore behind the top-ranking sago and jungle produce. By the turn of the century Chinese shopkeepers had appeared in even the remoter settlements, which were now being drawn into a modern commercial economy. A rising population, growing largely through immigration from China, and the introduction of rubber now laid the basis for further growth and the confirmation of existing patterns of trade. By 1908 trade was mainly in the hands of Chinese merchants, 'mostly country born (i.e. in Sarawak), who are successfully carrying on thriving businesses of which the foundations were laid by their fathers in the early days of the raj'; moreover, 'practically Singapore has the benefit of the whole of the Sarawak trade', although there was now a small trade in timber with Hong Kong and a few junks arrived annually from Siam and Cochin China.[3]

Sago and jungle produce had lost their dominant position in the export trade by the second decade of the present century; pepper, rubber and gold had now risen to prominence. It was, however, the development of the Miri oilfield and the maturation of considerable areas of rubber that caused a remarkably sudden upswing of Sarawak's export trade in the 1920's, an upswing followed by an equally spectacular decline precipitated by the world depression of the early 1930's. In these two decades the vulnerability to world market conditions of the Sarawak economy, now very heavily dependent on exporting primary produce, was first clearly demonstrated. Trade was

[2] S. St. John, *Life in the Forests of the Far East*, London, Smith, Elder and Co., 1862, Vol. II, p. 288.
[3] Baring-Gould and Bampfylde, op. cit., pp. 426 and 429.

still recovering from this heavy blow when Japanese forces invaded Sarawak.

Locally-produced oil was the main Sarawak export for only a short period in the 1920's. Since then, agricultural products, rubber, pepper and sago, and, recently, timber, have provided most of the State's export earnings. Imports, as always, comprise mainly foodstuffs and manufactured goods so that in the post-war era Sarawak's external trade has reflected very closely world prices for her primary products. Thus the peak prices for rubber during the Korean War brought a marked rise in total exports and imports in 1951. If re-exports of oil imported from Brunei are excluded, however, in every year for the last decade, except 1959, the visible balance of trade has been unfavourable (Table 24). This has acted as a brake on developmental progress. Rising levels of imports and the declining price of natural rubber offer scant hope of a change in the situation in the immediate future.

Table 24   External Trade, 1955-1965

	Exports*	Imports†	Visible trade balance
1955	$159,797,145	$148,891,946	+ $10,905,199
1956	$134,054,507	$150,147,126	— $16,092,619
1957	$126,202,648	$143,858,961	— $17,656,313
1958	$119,399,005	$132,600,108	— $13,201,103
1959	$182,208,114	$160,872,881	+ $21,335,233
1960	$203,035,575	$204,856,926	— $1,821,351
1961	$178,027,915	$221,826,882	— $43,798,967
1962	$183,525,489	$206,152,233	— $22,626,744
1963	$168,838,943	$222,934,695	— $54,095,752
1964	$196,775,816	$270,509,644	— $73,733,828
1965	$213,135,924	$295,372,287	— $82,236,363

* Excluding petroleum exports and re-exports.
† Excluding crude oil imports.

Characteristics of Trade

The trade and commerce of Sarawak lies almost entirely in the hands of two groups of merchants. Branches of a few large European 'Agency Houses', well known throughout South-East Asia, control

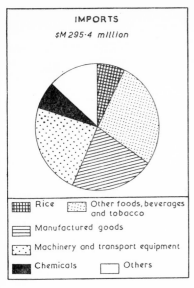
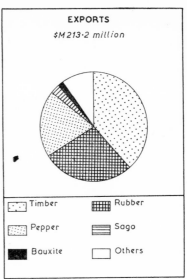

Figure 32   Composition of foreign trade, 1965.

N.B.—Imports exclude crude oil from Brunei, exports exclude petroleum exports and re-exports.

much of the wholesale importation of branded consumer goods for which they usually act as sole local distributors. Each of these firms has branch offices in the larger towns and some conduct business direct with agents in small and remote bazaars. In general, however, these European wholesalers sell to the Chinese merchants who control the retail trade. To a much smaller extent these same European firms buy and export local produce.

In contrast, although some Chinese firms are also engaged in this wholesale import trade on a relatively large scale, it is in the retail and distributive trade and in the export of Sarawak's primary produce that the Chinese merchants and traders hold an impregnable position. Virtually the whole of the trade of Sarawak passes through their hands at some stage and the commercial life of the State still hinges on a trading-cum-credit hierarchy extending from the large-scale merchants of Singapore to the small-scale Chinese traders in the isolated settlements of interior Sarawak.

Almost all retail traders in the coastal and up-river bazaars combine the sale of miscellaneous consumer goods with the purchase of local produce; they are therefore last in the line of retail distribution and first in the line of collection of local produce for export. They are, however, more than just traders, because the Chinese shopkeeper also plays a fundamental role as a source of credit for the rural population. He provides financial backing to those opening new holdings or those in need of cash in the pre-harvest period, usually providing credit in the form of goods in return for future produce. Occasionally he himself borrows from banks or from wealthier Chinese merchants to lend to the rural population at enhanced interest rates. Thus in rural areas Chinese shopkeepers act as both traders and bankers; in effect, at the village level, buying, selling and the provision of credit are inseparable parts of a single process.

Through this system the peasant, whether Chinese or indigene, becomes indebted to the local Chinese shopkeeper and, once established, the creditor-debtor relationship is seldom broken. Superficially it would appear that the rural population is in economic bondage to grasping Chinese middlemen and that much might be gained by introducing some form of co-operative system to provide these trading and credit facilities. However, in providing essential services, the rural shopkeeper is himself caught in the system, for he must lend to sell and he must sell to survive. In the small bazaar economy, the peasant and the shopkeeper are thus interdependent. Moreover, the system does not end with the shopkeeper, for he himself is associated with Chinese merchants in the larger towns who receive from him the produce he has collected and supply him with goods for retail sale. In turn, the most important of these larger town merchants are usually linked with firms in Singapore to whom much of the general produce is despatched and from whom some of the imported goods are acquired.

Basically, internal trade in Sarawak involves a type of 'transmission belt' process, with the Chinese dominant at each stage. Agricultural and jungle produce is acquired by the small rural trader who passes it to local merchants and agencies in the larger towns who in turn arrange export, usually to Singapore. Consumer goods are imported either by European 'Agency Houses' or by Chinese merchants and in general these pass down the line to the rural trader, special credit relationships existing at each stage. This internal trading system whereby goods pass through several hands, is the direct outcome of the particular economic and environmental circumstances of rural Sarawak: population is sparse and scattered, transportation is difficult and capital is in short supply.

The stages in this internal trade are clearly revealed in the case of rubber. Rubber sheet is collected from smallholders by the small rural shopkeepers who distribute groceries in return. These shopkeepers do not deal direct with exporters but pass the rubber to larger bazaar and town shopkeepers who act as middlemen between them and the exporting firms. The latter, located principally in Kuching, have no direct dealings with either the producers or the rural shopkeepers and they ship the rubber to Singapore firms with which many of them have close connections. There are relatively few really large rubber exporters in Sarawak and several of these are, in fact, branches of Singapore firms.[4] A similar situation exists in the case of pepper exporters.

In the last decade large Chinese timber exporters have also emerged, particularly in the Rejang ports and Kuching. Timber, of course, is basically different from agricultural products, because it is mostly shipped direct to consumer countries, chiefly from Tanjong Mani, and it does not involve collection from a multiplicity of small peasant producers. In the case of this newly-developed trade, producers are frequently also exporters.

In 1961 there were approximately 2,400 retail businesses in Sarawak of which about 640 were located in Kuching and 320 in Sibu.[5] These are mainly family concerns and, indeed, two-thirds of the Chinese shops in Kuching are separately owned by single individual owners.[6] Some Indians are engaged in the textile trade in the larger towns and there are also occasional Malay-owned shops, but over four-fifths of those engaged in commerce are Chinese. This large Chinese trading community is marked by significant dialect concentrations. Large-scale trade is chiefly a Hokkien and Tiechiu preserve and the latter dominate the importation of groceries. At the rural shopkeeper level, on the other hand, there is a close relationship with the dominant dialect group in each locality, although even in the smaller bazaars there will be a shop owned by a member of a minority dialect group if there are sufficient of his clansmen in the immediate area. It is partly for this reason that often shops side by side sell identical goods for, as elsewhere in South-East Asia, clan association plays a basic role in Chinese trading at all levels.

[4] T'ien Ju-K'ang, *The Chinese of Sarawak: A Study of Social Structure*, London School of Economics and Political Science, Monographs on Social Anthropology, No. 12, second impression, 1956, pp. 55-56.
[5] *Sarawak: Report on Gross Domestic Product and Gross Capital Formation, 1961*, Kuching, Government Printer, 1963, p. 32.
[6] T'ien, op. cit., p. 46.

Changing Patterns of External Trade

Historically, Singapore has been Sarawak's major trading partner, serving as the clearing house for her exports and the source of her imports of consumer goods. Singapore still remains the immediate destination for a large proportion of the agricultural exports, particularly rubber and pepper, and still sorts, grades, bulks and re-exports many of them. Sago flour, on the other hand, tends to go direct to consumer countries, chiefly Japan, the United Kingdom and Taiwan.

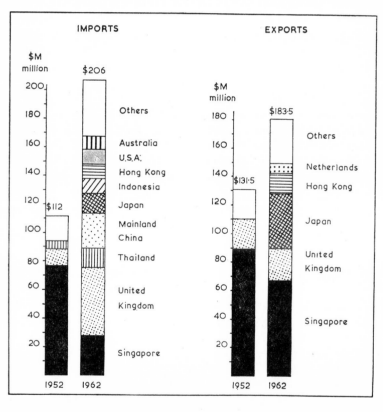

Figure 33   Direction of foreign trade, 1952 and 1962. (Source of data: Colonial Office, *An Economic Survey of the Colonial Territories*, Vol. V, The Far Eastern Territories, London, H.M.S.O., 1955, p. 149 and *Sarawak: Statistics of External Trade, 1962*, Kuching, Government Printer, 1963.)

However, the rapid development of the timber industry as Sarawak's main export earner has hastened the relative diminution of the role played by Singapore in the State's export trade, a change that has been greatly facilitated by the development of direct shipping contacts between Sarawak ports and some of the more significant customers. Thus, whereas in 1948 three-quarters of Sarawak's exports, excluding petroleum, were bound for Singapore, a decade and a half later less than two-fifths went to this entrepôt. In the recent past there has been a marked geographic dispersal of Sarawak's export trade with the rise of Japan and Hong Kong as important buyers and the development of direct trading with Australia and several west European countries (Fig. 33).

The decline of Singapore in Sarawak's import trade is even more startling. In 1948 seven-tenths of Sarawak's imports, excluding Brunei oil, were drawn from bulk supplies held by Singapore merchants or from large Singapore distribution depots. Nearly one-tenth came direct from the United Kingdom, and smaller, but significant quantities, chiefly rice, came from Thailand and Burma. By 1964 the situation had altered markedly; over 22 per cent of the imports came direct from the United Kingdom and less than one-sixth from Singapore. Mainland China and Thailand are prominent, chiefly as sources of rice, and as local traders begin to import direct instead of through Singapore intermediaries, Japan, the United States and Australia have become increasingly important in Sarawak's import trade (Fig. 33).

In the past neither Malaya nor Sabah has figured prominently in Sarawak's external trade. The establishment of the Borneo Free Trade Area in January 1962 did result in a doubling of Sarawak's trade with neighbouring Sabah in that year and the new Malaysian 'customs area' will undoubtedly stimulate an increase in trade with fellow members of the Federation. It seems, however, that Sarawak's long-standing trade dependence on Singapore will continue to give way to direct consignment of exports to consumer countries and direct import from producer countries.

8 Public Utilities and Social Services

The process of development is as much social as economic; to improve living standards in both these intimately-related spheres is essential and the 'revolution of rising expectations' applies as much to schools, hospitals and electric lighting as it does to the material features of developed countries. Public utilities and social services have come to most settlements in Sarawak only recently and many people remain on or beyond the fringes of the areas served. To provide and maintain these facilities requires heavy capital outlay and the chief difficulty of the development planner is 'to establish a balance between the demand for social services, and the need for economic development'.[1]

Electricity

The main towns are supplied with electricity by the Sarawak Electricity Supply Corporation or SESCO. The provision of public electricity supplies to Kuching and Sibu began in the mid-1920's and these were taken over by the newly-formed, partly government-owned Sarawak Electricity Supply Co. Ltd. in 1932. To satisfy the increasing public demand, small stations were also opened at Mukah, Sarikei, Binatang, Bintulu and Simanggang during the 1930's. With the partial exception of the Kuching station, these all provided direct current supplies; they comprised isolated diesel stations and it is unlikely that the total generating capacity exceeded 1,250 kW in 1941.[2]

Plant and equipment were neglected during the Occupation and, although new stations were opened at Miri and Betong, the immediate post-war years were devoted to rehabilitation. It was soon apparent, however, that rapid expansion was necessary to cater for the needs of

[1] *Sarawak Development Plan, 1964-1968*, Kuching, Government Printer, 1963, p. 48.
[2] 'A Brief History of the Development of Public Electricity Supplies in Sarawak' in ECAFE, *Proceedings of the Regional Seminar on Energy Resources and Electric Power Development*, New York, United Nations, 1962, pp. 42-43.

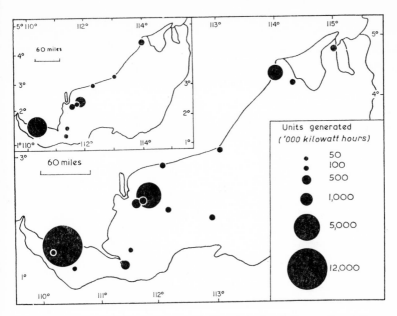

Figure 34 Electricity generated by Sarawak Electricity Supply Corporation stations, 1960-1961. Inset: 1950-1951.

the growing population and to provide for higher standards of living, and in 1952 wide powers governing the generation, transmission and supply of electricity were granted to the Government which became the sole owner of SESCO the following year. Starting with Sibu in 1950, work proceeded on the conversion of existing stations to alternating current supplies and a much greater coverage was provided in the areas served by these stations; moreover, by 1960 several new small stations had been opened to provide supplies in areas previously unserved (Fig. 34). Installed generating capacity totalled 9,814 kW at the end of 1960. The number of consumers had almost doubled since 1955 and SESCO generated twice as many units as it had five years earlier. Nevertheless, only nine of these stations provided continuous supplies and the rural population remained almost entirely outside the scope of the electricity network.

It was observed in 1961 that public electricity supplies in Sarawak were still at a stage 'where a large amount of capital is required for development and reconstruction, not all of which will be economic in the first instance but which is essential if the country is to meet the demand for power emanating from rising standards of living, light industrialization and an increasing population'.[3] Between 1961 and 1965 a total of $16.4 million was invested in the improvement and extension of public electricity supplies. Large new power stations have been erected at Sungei Priok, Kuching and Sungei Merah, Sibu. Most of the larger population centres now have continuous supplies and efforts have been made to extend rural electrification. SESCO now operates seventeen stations with an installed generating capacity of 18,620 kW in 1965 and the number of consumers has risen by over 50 per cent since 1960. Nevertheless, four-fifths of the installed capacity lies in the western third of Sarawak and roughly half the consumers served are in Kuching. Elsewhere, with the exception of Miri, very small, isolated stations supply power in the larger bazaars but virtually the whole of the rural population remains unserved.

Rapid development is hindered by severe problems which greatly enhance electricity charges in Sarawak. Stations are not interconnected and are developed as separate, isolated units with their own distribution and transmission systems, and the lack of communications, low population densities and low load and consumption potential make extension in rural areas very expensive. Because of the relatively small size, isolation and lack of interconnection between stations, all the generating stations are diesel-powered. In the limited areas served, transmission is mainly by overhead networks, although underground systems are used in Kuching and Sibu. It is estimated that by 1975 annual consumption will be about 100 million units, or nearly treble 1965 consumption, and a total of $24.3 million is provided under the First Malaysian Plan for the expansion of the Corporation's diesel generation, distribution and transmission facilities. An important aim of the development programme is to extend rural electrification and $1.2 million of this sum will be used for this purpose.[4]

The supplies provided by SESCO are used largely for domestic and commercial purposes. Industrial demand is as yet small but there are, nevertheless, several industrial consumers not covered by the Corporation's network, the most important of whom are Sarawak Shell Oilfields Ltd, together with a growing number of sawmills which, by virtue of their location, cannot be supplied from existing stations. To

---

[3] 'A Brief History of the Development of Public Electricity Supplies in Sarawak', p. 44.
[4] *Sarawak Development Plan, 1964-1968*, p. 24; *First Malaysia Plan, 1966-1970*, Kuala Lumpur, Government Printer, 1965, p. 159.

provide electricity for these, and for domestic use in small settlements outside the Corporation's network, private licensees operate minor supply schemes, most of which are financed by individuals or small partnerships, although co-operative schemes are appearing. The totalled installed capacity of these schemes rose from 211 kW in 1958 to 8,500 kW at the end of 1963; at that time they accounted for two-fifths of the total installed generating capacity in Sarawak and as demand increases, more of these minor private schemes will be opened.

Sarawak is a land of many rivers, and although electricity generation currently depends entirely on diesel-powered stations there is vast potential for the development of hydro-electric power. A recent survey indicated that the catchments of the Rejang and Baram Rivers offer substantial prospects for such development. Here the three most promising areas are the Pelagus Rapids on the Rejang, a point immediately below the confluence of the Baram and Pateh Rivers and a site on the Ulu Baram above Lio Matoh. Development here could provide abundant cheap power for electro-chemical, forest products and other industries, as well as for extended domestic supplies; however, the sites are isolated in difficult, forested country with very low population densities and exploitation would involve heavy capital outlay. Water power is one of Sarawak's major natural resources but the report emphasizes that 'the nature of the rivers is such that economic development will only be feasible in conjunction with a major increase in demand for electricity'.[5]

Water Supply

The bulk of the rural population relies on stream and river water for washing and drinking purposes and in some interior areas stream water is transported to settlements by means of split-bamboo pipes. Often rain water is also stored against possible shortages. Despite the heavy rainfall and the multitude of rivers and streams, water is in short supply in many coastal areas, for on the coastal plains where rivers flow sluggishly, silt and peat cause deep staining and, in the tidal

---

[5] *Sarawak Annual Report, 1962*, Kuching, Government Printer, p. 229. In 1966 the Sarawak Government requested technical and financial assistance from the FAO Special Fund for a comprehensive survey of a vast area of virgin forest in interior central Sarawak. Included will be investigations of the hydro-electric power potential of the Pelagus Rapids.

G

reaches, river water is brackish. Wells, which usually draw water from alluvial sands, are therefore characteristic of most coastal settlements. However, the risk of contamination by run-off is high in the case of wells and, apart from spreading intestinal complaints, this can cause cholera outbreaks such as the one that began in Kampong Sourabaya, Kuching, in July 1961. In the far interior where rivers flow swiftly, often over rapids, and where population is sparse, there is little danger of pollution affecting water supplies. In the lower reaches, however, where riverine settlement is more frequent, the dangers are proportionately greater.

The extension of piped water supplies to rural areas would enable adequate control of quality. It would also prove a boon to most communities by eliminating the need to fetch and carry water for domestic uses which often requires much time. However, the scattered nature of the small rural communities makes the provision of piped water supplies prohibitively expensive. Existing supplies to smaller settlements are already highly subsidized and 'the smaller and more scattered the communities the more the subsidy required'.[6] Nevertheless, a sum of $3.6 million is allocated to provide new supplies in rural areas between 1966 and 1970. These will be developed in coastal settlements and in the new villages on land development schemes. Where communities are too small to warrant an individual piped supply, treated water will be made available through stand-pipes and the Government will assist in the provision of well and unpolluted river supplies for individual longhouses.[7]

Piped water supplies for domestic use serve about one-fifth of the population. These are provided by Water Boards in Kuching and Sibu and by a Water Authority under the immediate control of the Public Works Department in sixteen smaller settlements. Over four-fifths of the total supplies provided by these schemes serve the three major towns of Kuching, Sibu and Miri and, with the exception of small installations at Kanowit, Song and Kapit, which draw water from the Rejang River, virtually the whole of interior Sarawak is unserved. Topographic and geological conditions generally preclude the construction of large storage reservoirs, because structure and lithography are often unsuitable and the frequent steep-sided narrow valleys limit the size of catchment areas. Most schemes therefore depend on water either pumped direct from the major rivers to purification plants, as at Sibu, or collected behind small dams as at Bintulu and diverted

[6] *Sarawak Development Plan, 1964-1968*, p. 45.   [7] *First Malaysia Plan*, p. 162.

to purification plants. Elsewhere, tube wells tap underground supplies for local distribution but the high iron content of water acquired by this means makes it unpalatable unless passed through treatment plants.

Until 1957 Kuching relied on its pre-war water supply system. This was based on diversion dams and a small impounding reservoir in the valleys of streams draining the sandstone Matang Range to the west of the town. In 1948 consumption in Kuching averaged 1.26 million gallons per day and five years later had risen to nearly 1.5 million gallons daily. The town was growing rapidly, however, and potential demand far exceeded supplies; moreover, periodical shortages were not uncommon. The catchment area in the Matang Range was small and local topography made the construction of large storage reservoirs impracticable. Plans were therefore completed for a new scheme at Batu Kitang to draw water from the Sarawak River. This was to be chemically treated, filtered and pumped to Kuching to make available an additional 3 million gallons per day. This scheme came into operation in 1957 and average daily consumption had risen to 2.4 million gallons by 1962; subsequently, it was planned to increase the capacity of the Batu Kitang waterworks. Improved supplies have been provided to cross-river settlements, mains renewal has been undertaken, and the area served by the Kuching Water Board has been extended.

Sibu is served by water pumped from the Rejang River to a purification plant whence it passes to high-level storage tanks. In 1948 supplies available averaged about 300,000 gallons daily. The town grew rapidly during the 1950's and storage capacity was greatly increased, new distribution mains were laid, and supplies were extended to Sungei Merah. Average daily consumption had risen to 824,000 gallons by 1962. A growing population, rising living standards and small-scale industrial development have all increased the potential demand in Kuching and Sibu and two-thirds of the total public expenditure on water supplies in the period 1959 to 1963 was spent on these towns.

Miri is supplied with water purchased from Sarawak Shell Oilfields Ltd, an arrangement that dates from before the Occupation. Small-scale installations existed in several other townships in the early 1950's: Mukah, for example, received filtered supplies from the Sungei Petanak; Bintulu was served by a dam on the Sungei Nyabau; and unfiltered water for Bau was drawn from the Tai Parit mine-workings flooded and then dammed some three decades earlier. Work on the provision of new supplies in smaller towns and bazaars progressed steadily during the 1950's. Many of these provided untreated water which, at least initially, was often available only from public stand-pipes. Subsequently, all supplies were chlorinated or fully treated, and as the older supply systems became inadequate extensive, new works were constructed. Since 1961 completely new schemes have come into operation at Serian, Kanowit, Song, Kapit and Marudi. It is estimated that over $16 million were invested in the provision of water supplies between 1952 and 1963.[8] Whilst it is desirable to provide pure drinking water supplies to as large a proportion of the population as possible, the investment per person supplied in terms of capital equipment and maintenance necessarily increases as supplies are provided in these smaller townships. Moreover, demand continues to rise in the main urban centres and three-fifths of the total allocation of $9 million for development in this sphere in the period 1966 to 1970 will be used to provide extended supplies in the larger towns.

Medical and Health Services

There have been resident medical officers in Sarawak for over a century. For long, however, such facilities as existed were restricted to the Kuching area. Elsewhere the population was regularly decimated by disease until well into the twentieth century and modern medical services have reached many communities only recently; indeed only twenty years ago the facilities available were 'inadequate for the health and medical problems of the area'.[9] A Medical and Health Department under a Director was instituted in 1947 and today a Divisional Medical Officer supervises the services in each Division.

The improvement of public health is one of the most outstanding achievements of the post-war era. The range of diseases prevalent was extremely wide, the largely illiterate population used primitive methods of sewage disposal, was totally unaware of the relationship between bad sanitation and disease, and remained ignorant of modern medicine, relying instead on traditional procedures. Moreover, progress was hampered by lack of communications and the shortage of trained

[8] *Sarawak Development Plan, 1964-1968*, p. 45.
[9] J. S. Simmons *et al.*, *Global Epidemiology: A Geography of Disease and Sanitation*, Philadelphia, J. B. Lippincott Co., 1944, Vol. I, p. 392.

personnel. Almost all temperate disorders are present in Sarawak, together with many others caused by poor standards of hygiene and low nutritional levels; to these must be added the specifically tropical diseases to indicate the complete gamut of health risks facing the population. In total these accounted for the high death-rates which severely limited population growth, despite immigration, until recently; in many cases they were also responsible for reducing the efficiency of the survivors. Most of these diseases are preventible and efforts have therefore focused on preventive medicine.

Widespread in the humid tropics, malaria is a disease complex involving a microbe, an insect vector and a human host. The anopheline mosquito acts as vector, but the offending species vary throughout the tropics, as do their habits, and the principal vector in Sarawak, *Anopheles leucosphyrus*, breeds in hilly, jungle-covered country. Infection begins soon after a child is born and although partial immunity may be developed later, malaria seriously undermines energy, thus opening the door to secondary infection. Until recently malaria was the most important single cause of illness and death in Sarawak. During the Japanese Occupation it spread alarmingly and by the liberation had assumed 'epidemic proportions'.[10] After a preliminary survey, a pilot eradication project using domestic residual spraying began in Baram District in 1953 under the auspices of the World Health Organization. This proved successful and three years later it was converted into a country-wide eradication scheme. Many localities were heavily infected, but by 1959 every known malarious area had been sprayed at least once. Within Sarawak the incidence of malaria is now of small proportions, but the prevention of infection spreading from over the Indonesian border remains a difficult problem; constant vigilance is necessary to control what was once Sarawak's major killer.

The virtual eradication of malaria left tuberculosis as perhaps the most widely prevalent disease. Poor living conditions and low nutritional levels had induced infection in much of the rural population in addition to the high incidence in crowded urban areas, and by 1958 tuberculosis was 'in a very acute, almost epidemic, phase'.[11] There was very little provision for treatment until 1950, when a Chest Clinic Service started in Kuching. During the 1950's the voluntary Anti-Tuberculosis Association of Sarawak did much to foster public interest and provided a small convalescent home in Kuching and a small

[10] *Sarawak Annual Report, 1962,* p. 160.   [11] *Sarawak Annual Report, 1958,* p. 73.

hospital at Miri. Beds were made available in government hospitals and X-ray examinations were made in schools around Kuching. A scheme for mass control was launched in Kuching in 1961 with Colombo Plan assistance and financial aid from the Colonial Development and Welfare Fund. The following year the campaign extended to Sibu, and then to Miri and other smaller towns. It has now spread to rural areas and work is in progress in all Divisions. Anti-tuberculosis campaigns always face problems arising from the failure to report for further investigations of those whose initial investigations arouse doubt. To ignorance of the need for treatment and therefore lack of desire to enter hospital must be added, in the case of Sarawak, the financial inability of many of those infected to forego income for the necessary hospitalization period. To encourage indigenous patients to accept treatment the Anti-Tuberculosis Association opened longhouse sanatoria at Marudi and Bintulu in the Fourth Division. It now plans to open another at Sungei Poyan near Limbang to serve the Fifth Division.

In 1947 yaws was described as probably 'one of the most important diseases' in Sarawak.[12] A mass campaign launched against this easily communicable disease a decade ago has now reduced its occurrence to sporadic cases. For long, cases of endemic goitre were frequent in the interior, particularly in the Second and Third Divisions, and the cause was discovered to be iodine deficiency in the imported salt used in these areas. Plant was installed at Sibu in 1959 to iodize salt supplies imported into the Third Division. The scheme is being extended and cases are becoming increasingly uncommon. Trachoma, which has serious effects on eyesight, remains fairly widespread, however, and the problem of this disease is to be investigated. Skin complaints are also common.

Leprosy is prevalent, as in all tropical, developing countries. A leper settlement existed near Kuching in 1947, but treatment with drugs did not begin until the following year. Since then this settlement, now known as the Rajah Charles Brooke Memorial Hospital, has been transformed into a modern leprosarium and the disease will probably be eradicated in the not-too-distant future. Mental diseases, which are not infrequent, are treated at a modern hospital near Kuching. Today the commonest diseases result from intestinal infections caused by contaminated water supplies and in many places intestinal parasites are present in virtually the whole population.[13] Nutritional standards are generally low with lack of protein as the main cause of diet deficiency.

[12] *Sarawak Annual Report, 1962*, p. 160.   [13] *Sarawak Annual Report, 1959*, p. 100.

Work on nutritional problems is in progress, but the promotion of health education and improved methods of sanitation remain a basic aspect of preventive medicine of no less significance than the control or eradication of communicable diseases. All school-children are taught simple rules of hygiene and a rural health improvement scheme is extending rapidly.

These advances have accompanied a marked extension of general medical facilities. In 1949 there were two government hospitals with a total of 430 beds. There were also twenty-four rural dispensaries which dealt with simple cases, forwarding others to the hospitals for treatment, and a small hospital at Miri, run by the oil company, also served the public. Much of the population was far-removed from any form of medical service and there was an average of only one qualified doctor for every 23,000 people. To extend medical services in rural areas, a scheme for travelling dispensaries was quickly introduced. Because of the lack of roads and the river-bank location of settlements, boats were used which followed fixed timetables on particular stretches of river. By 1953 there were sixteen travelling dispensaries; fourteen still operated in 1965.

One of the chief difficulties in extending rural medical services was shortage of staff, caused not so much by lack of training facilities as by the dearth of people with a sufficient educational background. It was not possible to post fully-trained personnel to all parts of the country, and for several years suitable young men were selected from rural areas and given rudimentary training before returning home as '*ulu* dressers'. In the last ten years, however, an increasing number of suitably-qualified local girls have presented themselves for training as nurses or midwives. This permitted the opening of many more rural dispensaries equipped with rest-beds; 38 were in operation in 1965 and very few people are not now within reach of some form of medical aid. It also facilitated the extension of maternity and child health services. In 1947 these were virtually non-existent outside Kuching and Sibu; subsequently clinics were opened elsewhere and by 1965 64 maternity and child health centres were operated by the various Local Authorities.

The hospital at Miri was taken over by the Government in 1960. The much-improved Kuching and Sibu hospitals were supplemented by a small government hospital at Simanggang and another was built by the Methodist Mission at Kapit. Several more small hospitals have been opened since 1960, bringing the total number of government general hospitals to eight in 1965. The Missions now operate six hospitals. Nevertheless, the total accommodation in all these hospitals provides an average of only one bed to 685 people, and as more people accept medical treatment and population grows, pressure on accommodation increases. To meet this growing demand, six new small local hospitals will be built before 1970, but the most outstanding addition will be the new general hospital now under construction in Kuching. The serious shortage of doctors has been partly remedied but the ratio of one doctor per 14,000 people in 1964 compared very unfavourably with the ratio of 1:6,000 in Malaya the same year; neither ratio is satisfactory by the standards of developed countries.

As recently as 1956 there were only five fully-qualified dentists, of whom four were in government service; there were also many registered unqualified dentists. Subsequently, dental clinics were opened and a school dental service was initiated and the number of pre-school and school children treated rose from 27,000 in 1960 to 48,000 in 1965.[14]

Table 25   Crude Death-Rates, 1950-1964

	Chinese	Malay	Iban	Land Dyak	Melanau
1950	8·2	16·0	9·0	16·6	13·5
1955	6·4	11·4	4·2	12·2	9·7
1960	5·1	10·6	3·3	9·1	6·8
1964	4·2	8·0	3·4	7·6	8·1

(Source: Department of Statistics, Kuching.)

N.B.   The crude death-rate is calculated on the basis of registered deaths per 1,000 of estimated end-of-year population. There is considerable under-reporting of both births and deaths in rural areas. This seriously reduces the accuracy of figures for interior indigenous communities, and the figure for the Chinese is probably the closest to reality.

Much still remains to be done in the extension of medical and health services, particularly in rural areas, and a sum of $21 million has been allocated for this purpose for the period 1966 to 1970. The advances of the last decade and a half have produced a marked improvement in local health standards. The crude death-rates shown in Table 25 are by no means reliable, for there is considerable under-reporting of deaths in rural areas and this affects the *apparent* rates for indigenous peoples, especially the Iban; nevertheless, crude death-rates have fallen substantially and infant mortality rates are also improving. Little wonder

[14] *First Malaysia Plan*, p. 174.

then that the rate of population increase in Sarawak has risen so sharply in the post-war era.

Education

In all developing countries an expanded educational system is a prerequisite for economic and social advancement. In multi-lingual Sarawak, education acquires additional significance as the chief means of fostering greater national unity, and here the need is not only to make good the deficiencies but also to eliminate the serious divisive elements of the past system.

The Brookes left education largely in the hands of private bodies, the most important of which were the Christian Missions and the Chinese school boards established, financed and managed by local Chinese communities. An Education Department was created in 1924 but during the Depression the post of Director was abolished and was not revived until 1939. Chinese schools remained under the Chinese Affairs Department until 1946, when the Education Department was reconstituted. Total school enrolment was about 19,000 at the time of the Japanese invasion. Many schools were destroyed or damaged during the Occupation, the remainder were neglected, the teaching of English ceased and enrolment declined. However, rehabilitation was rapid and by 1948 over 33,000 pupils were attending 380 schools.

The situation in the immediate post-war years was, however, far from satisfactory. Over four-fifths of the population were illiterate and literacy rates were abysmally low among the indigenous peoples. Moreover, three-fifths of the enrolled pupils attended Chinese-medium schools in which the curriculum resembled that used in China. These schools had been established over the years in all settlements with a sufficiently large Chinese population and provided, in addition to primary classes, secondary education up to junior middle and senior middle standards. The Chinese-medium schools were attended almost exclusively by Chinese pupils. The Missions provided primary education in English in large urban schools and in central boarding schools and ran small rural schools based on a vernacular language with English as a subject. Secondary divisions were attached to the urban schools which provided most of the English language secondary education in Sarawak and were the chief source of potential government officers. Most of the pupils in Mission schools were Chinese. There were also

G*

government and local authority primary schools in which teaching was in a vernacular language with English as a subject, in addition to several private schools. The Chinese community was therefore fairly well served with schools, but facilities for indigenous peoples were totally inadequate; moreover, opportunities for secondary education were minimal.

In the late 1940's local authorities began to assume responsibility for primary education in their respective areas and with government assistance constructed primary schools mainly to serve the indigenous peoples. Concurrently, in response to a rapidly increasing population and a growing demand for education, the Missions and the Chinese management boards opened more schools so that by 1955 there were nearly 600 schools in Sarawak and the total number of enrolled pupils had risen to 59,500, nine-tenths of whom were at primary level. This rapid expansion continued in the second half of the decade and by 1960 the number of enrolled pupils had risen to 104,000.

Table 26   Illiteracy Rates, 1960

Ethnic group	Percentage illiterate (of population aged 10 years and over)
Chinese	47·0
Malays	75·5
Melanaus	82·2
Land Dyaks	89·2
Iban	92·9
Other indigenous	88·9
Total	74·7

(Source: *Sarawak: Census of Population, 1960*, pp. 77-80.)

Nevertheless, despite this tremendous post-war development, the basic problems remained. Three-quarters of the total population aged 10 years and over were illiterate in 1960 and apart from the Chinese each ethnic group showed very high illiteracy rates (Table 26). For census purposes literacy was defined as 'ability to read and write a letter' so that, in fact, many people were merely 'on the borders of literacy'.[15] Literacy was, however, very much more widespread in the

[15] L. W. Jones, *Sarawak: Report on the Census of Population, 1960*, Kuching, Government Printer, 1962, p. 75.

younger age-brackets, and literacy rates were markedly higher in urban areas where there were more schools, more educated parents and fewer children were required to help their parents earn a living. Almost three-fifths of the children aged between 6 and 11 years attended school in 1960, but a mere 9 per cent of the total school population was in secondary classes and the Chinese retained their near-monopoly of education at full secondary level. Moreover, the distinction between Chinese-language and other schools remained sharp; the former tended to accentuate divisive influences within the population and aroused suspicions regarding their political role as disseminators of communist ideology.

In the last decade educational policy has focused on three major aims: the development of a single national school system, the provision of more opportunities for secondary education and a rapid expansion of the educational facilities for indigenous peoples. The introduction of the Grant Code in 1956 whereby all aided non-government schools were placed on the same financial basis was the first step towards a unified school system and was followed by the introduction of common textbooks and examinations in both English and Chinese. This policy was designed 'to bring the different types of school into a uniform national system with the aim of developing among all people a sense of common citizenship, brotherhood and loyalty'.[16] It would also reduce tensions caused by the great difficulty that the purely Chinese educated persons experience in obtaining jobs. To this end it was deemed necessary to have a common medium of instruction and English was chosen for this purpose. In 1961 the managements of Chinese secondary schools were informed that in future government financial aid was conditional upon them agreeing to a programme of gradual conversion to English as the medium of instruction. This aroused a fierce controversy, but almost all the aided Chinese-medium secondary schools agreed. Meanwhile a Colombo Plan team from New Zealand gave advice on the preparation of a common curriculum for all secondary schools. The programme of extending the use of English has achieved considerable success and by mid-1965 about two-thirds of all pupils attended English-medium schools.

In 1961 only 34 per cent of the indigenous children of school age were receiving education. The policy of providing primary education for all children as soon as possible called for many new schools in rural areas. The building programme was accelerated and total enrolment

[16] *Sarawak Annual Report, 1960*, p. 95.

in primary schools rose by over 26,000 between 1960 and 1965 when it stood at 121,000. Over two-thirds of all school-age children now attend school and four-fifths of these are at primary level. Although this reflects the growing desire of most parents to educate their children, less progressive families still consider school attendance a drain on the family work-force and the drop-out rate in primary schools remained high. Ultimately it is hoped to make primary education compulsory and by 1970, when places should be available for all children at primary level, enrolment will exceed 158,000. The sum of $12.3 million has been provided to finance the necessary expansion.

A rapidly-growing primary school enrolment inevitably increased the demand for secondary education. In the mid-1950's Government took upon itself the function of satisfying this demand and by 1965 sixteen government secondary schools had been established, with at least one in each Division. Many private unaided English-medium secondary schools also appeared. It is now policy to provide secondary school places for about 30 per cent of those who complete the primary level and by 1965 about 18 per cent of the total school population was in secondary classes. Current plans provide for a marked increase in the number of government secondary schools before 1970 and a sum of $29.2 million has been allocated for this purpose under the First Malaysia Plan. Educational policy must take account of the fact that Sarawak will remain basically an agricultural country and that therefore those who receive secondary education must be adapted to rural life. For this reason secondary education is given a 'rural bias' to overcome the general belief that it provides an automatic *entrée* into urban employment. Commercial and technical training have not been neglected, however, for a Technical Institute and Trade School have been established in Kuching. Adult education classes are conducted in certain towns and adult literacy classes are held in rural areas.

Educational expansion is expensive because it faces many problems other than those arising from multi-lingualism. One of the most urgent of these concerns the provision of adequately-trained local staff for the new schools, and particularly indigenous teachers for the new primary schools. The shortage of qualified staff at secondary level is acute. Superficially at primary level it appears less severe, for there is an average of one teacher to about 30 pupils, but only two-fifths of these teachers are classified as 'trained' and many have a low standard of basic education. The English-medium teacher training college at Batu Lintang, Kuching, first established in 1948, has been greatly improved and enlarged to meet this demand for teachers. In 1957 a Chinese-medium training centre was opened at Sibu to produce teachers for Chinese schools and subsequently introduced English to cater for the new situation in Chinese schools. A third teacher training college is due to open near Binatang in 1966-67.

Sparsity of population and lack of communications impede the provision of schools for interior indigenous communities. Enrolment in many rural schools is only sufficient to justify the employment of one teacher and often it has proved necessary to establish centralized boarding schools, even at primary level; indeed about 12,000 children were boarders in 1964, of whom three-quarters were in primary classes. During the last five years a system of 'school mothers' who supervise the boarders and cook subsidized meals has been introduced, but this need to provide board raises the cost of education per pupil. In view of the problems involved and the work still required to provide an adequate educational system, almost 10 per cent of the total allocation for public development expenditure in the period 1966 to 1970 has been earmarked for education; only the agricultural and transport sectors have received larger allocations.

Telecommunications, Posts and Radio

In a land where settlements are separated by extensive and often roadless jungle, the provision of adequate telephone, telegraph and postal services is essential to the proper functioning of administration and commerce. There were eighteen telephone exchanges in Sarawak in 1949, of which six were in the immediate vicinity of Kuching, whilst there were only four in the Fourth and Fifth Divisions. Except where there were telephone extensions from telegraph offices, the whole telegraph system depended on radio telegraphy, a necessity in view of the cost of constructing and maintaining lines through densely forested country. The seriously neglected system was rehabilitated in the years following the liberation and by the early 1950's plans were afoot for its extension and improvement.

Physical difficulties resulted in a proposal to establish a VHF radio system to link all telephones. The VHF systems in the Kuching and Simanggang Zones were completed in 1956 and three years later almost every bazaar and government station was linked by VHF radio telephone to its Divisional capital.[17] A survey completed in 1956

[17] Sarawak Information Service, *Information on Sarawak*, Kuching, Borneo Literature Bureau, 1960, p. 66.

indicated that it was possible to provide a multi-channel trunk telephone system to link Kuching, Sibu and Miri by VHF radio. The ultimate aim was to connect the Divisional headquarters and by 1960 this had been achieved. In that year telephone services to Singapore, Malaya and the United Kingdom became available and now cover most foreign countries. During the 1950's the main towns were provided with automatic exchanges and an extensive programme of automating the smaller manual exchanges is now in progress. By 1965 the telephone network connected 60 stations throughout Sarawak, half of which were in the more densely-peopled First and Second Divisions. There is virtually no service for the sparsely-peopled interior of central and northern Sarawak, but a Radio Call Service links remoter villages with the telephone network. There has been heavy capital investment in buildings and equipment in the last decade and a half; services have expanded rapidly and the number of telephones rose from 720 in 1952 to 8,099 in 1965. Improvements, including the introduction of teleprinters, were also effected in the internal telegraph services but, in general, the use of these has been reduced with this spread of telephones. The telephone provides by far the easiest means of internal communication and a major programme of development is envisaged which will eventually include the establishment of a micro-wave trunk circuit.

High rates of illiteracy mean that the postal services have little effect on much of the population. They are important, however, for government and commercial purposes, and with the expansion of educational facilities the letter-writing population is growing rapidly. There were 37 post offices in 1949 located in the various government stations. The dearth of roads made delivery difficult and mail was carried by whatever means were available.[18] In the interim, new buildings have been erected in many places and several new post offices have been built to handle the increase in mail that has occurred. The opening of new roads has permitted the improvement of delivery services, for example the introduction of a daily mail service between Kuching and the Second Division in 1962. The first mobile post office was introduced in 1963 and the use of these will be expanded. In total a sum of $7 million was invested in the development of telecommunications and postal services between 1961 and 1965; $18.5 million will be spent on further development between 1966 and 1970.[19]

[18] B. A. St. J. Hepburn, *The Handbook of Sarawak*, Singapore, Malaya Publishing House, 1949, p. 166.   [19] *First Malaysia Plan*, p. 152.

Radio programmes are the chief means of keeping the largely-illiterate interior population in touch with developments in the outside world. Radio Sarawak, now a regional division of Radio Malaysia, was inaugurated in 1954 after the British Government had made available substantial grants for the construction of a transmitting and receiving station at Kuching. Further grants and aid from overseas have enabled continuous expansion and improvement of services, including the development of a Schools Broadcasting Service. Programmes in all the main languages are produced and these can be received on short wave transmission throughout the State. In 1954 there were less than 7,000 radio receivers in Sarawak. Annual licence fees were introduced in 1957 and over 51,000 were issued in 1965.

9　The Challenge of Development

It is easy to be pessimistic about the future development of Sarawak. The preceding chapters have indicated the innumerable difficulties that must be overcome before the social and economic aspirations of the population can be even partly satisfied. As Professor Silcock has observed, the problem of economic development appears more intractable in Sarawak than in Malaya.[1] Sarawak lacks the infrastructure that came to western Malaya in the train of the tin and rubber booms, and the possibility of rapid development occurring there now under conditions such as those that prevailed on the mainland at an earlier date is extremely remote. If economic development is to occur in modern Sarawak it must be on the basis of careful, overall, central planning financed largely by overseas aid.

The problems elaborated earlier fall into three basic groups: physical, socio-cultural and economic. Poor soils, steep slopes in the interior and extensive peat swamps on the coastal plains offer little prospect of agricultural development over wide areas and seriously enhance the cost of any scheme that is undertaken. Mean annual rainfall is exceedingly high, it shows significant monthly variations from year to year and it usually falls as short, intense showers that can cause serious soil erosion. Sarawak has a small population in relation to its vast area and much of the rural population relies on a bush-fallow agricultural system which precludes large settlements. The road network remains far from complete so that relative isolation characterizes most of the State, bringing with it a host of difficulties.

Illiteracy is widespread and nutritional levels are often low. At the present rate of increase the population will double in a quarter of a century. The economy must grow at least as quickly if living standards are to be maintained, and growth must be accelerated if they are to be raised. Moreover, the high proportion of young people constitutes a

---

[1] T. H. Silcock, *The Commonwealth Economy in Southeast Asia*, London, Cambridge University Press, 1959, p. 29.

burden on the economy which it is ill-equipped to bear. Many problems arise from the existence of a multi-racial population speaking a variety of languages and with differing social customs, religious beliefs and economic levels. Often these are political in nature and, as in other developing countries, the selection and siting of development projects is sometimes guided more by political expediency than by economic desirability.

Despite the recent rapid growth of the timber industry, the economy remains basically agricultural. In view of the difficulties confronting any programme of industrialization, development plans focus on agricultural improvement and rural development. Inefficient and primitive farming systems are largely responsible for the low per capita income which is probably below $700 as compared with an average of about $900 for Malaysia as a whole. Marked increases in agricultural productivity are possible and, indeed, long overdue, but the changes necessary to achieve them are not simply economic: social and cultural change must march in step with economic development; sentiment must not overshadow reason. The scattered rural communities must abandon their traditional farming patterns if they are to achieve social and economic progress. This is all the more necessary if the indigenous communities are to approach the levels already enjoyed by many of the Chinese. The economy depends heavily on a few export crops typified by price fluctuations: falling natural rubber prices have acted as a drag on development and have counterbalanced, to some extent, external financial aid. Yet, despite gloomy forecasts of the future of natural rubber, there are, at present, few alternative cash crops upon which the small-scale Sarawak farmer can rely for a regular income. Much high-yielding rubber has been planted under government subsidy, but shortage of labour leaves rubber in several areas untapped. Sarawak, in fact, faces a dearth of skilled and semi-skilled labour and high wage-rates further increase the cost of development projects.

The effects of these problems are highlighted by the marked concentration of development hitherto in that part of Sarawak lying west of longitude 112° East. Although this region comprises less than a quarter of the total land area, it contains about three-quarters of the total population, over two-thirds of the land devoted to settled cultivation and perhaps three-quarters of the acreage planted with wet-*padi* and rubber. The road network and the provision of public and social services have advanced furthest here; nevertheless, even western Sarawak is at a low level of development compared with western Malaya. The rest of the State remains largely under virgin jungle, and it is difficult to envisage any significant development occurring there except possibly an extension of timber exploitation. This marked regional imbalance of development is matched by the sharp contrast between urban and rural areas even in the west. A problem with political implications arises here because the better-served, more wealthy urban population is predominantly Chinese.

The pessimism induced by the size of these problems must be tempered by the progress achieved in the post-war era and more particularly by the tangible results of development in the last half decade. In all respects there was scant foundation upon which to build, but living standards have improved, new roads have been built and new land has been opened and planted.

Table 27   Allocation of Public Development Expenditure,
1966-1970
(targets in $ millions)

Sectors

Agriculture and rural development	131.4
Roads	79.8
Education	45.6
Defence	44.5
Ports	25.6
Electricity	24.3
Health	21.0
Social and community services	19.6
Internal security	19.0
Posts and telecommunications	18.5
General administration	11.6
Water supplies	9.0
Civil aviation	6.5
Broadcasting	4.8
Industrial development	2.5
Total	463.7

(Source: *First Malaysia Plan*, pp. 69-70.)

This progress resulted from the rehabilitation and development programmes instituted by the Colonial Government in the period 1947 to 1963. Essentially these were public investment programmes financed to a considerable extent from the Colonial Development and Welfare Fund and from Colombo Plan sources. They have now been replaced by the First Malaysia Plan which aims to accelerate the pace of development in the period 1966 to 1970. Table 27 indicates the priority accorded to the various sectors under this plan. Agriculture and rural development hold the key position because the income and living standards of the rural population lag far behind those of the urban dweller, and agriculture will remain the basis of the export economy. The relatively under-developed infra-structure has hindered social and economic progress, and the development of roads, ports, power and telecommunications receives a high priority; other public and social services will also be extended. A rapid expansion of educational facilities can alone combat the dearth of skilled labour, reduce illiteracy rates, increase the acceptance of improved agricultural methods and awaken the population to the demands and rewards of modern life. As is typical of developing states, however, the ultimate success of development programmes rests on the availability of substantial foreign aid.

Development on this scale under Sarawak conditions is extremely expensive. Planned development expenditure for the period 1966 to 1970 totals $463.7 million which is over 80 per cent greater than the estimated expenditure in the preceding five-year period. Funds from the central Malaysian Government will be supplemented by British grants for development projects in Sarawak and aid is forthcoming from other Commonwealth countries. It is clear, however, that much more assistance is needed to stimulate the rate of development required in Sarawak because in recent years the annual rate of growth of gross national product has been far below the rates recorded by western Malaya and Sabah. The economic prospects of Sarawak are not encouraging and it must be concluded that, without greater external aid, the rate of economic growth will fail to satisfy the aspirations of this newly-independent people.

Bibliography

'A Brief History of the Development of Public Electricity Supplies in Sarawak', ECAFE, *Proceedings of the Regional Seminar on Energy Resources and Electric Power Development*, New York, United Nations, 1962.

R. G. Aikman, *Episodes from Sarawak History*, typescript of talks broadcast over Radio Sarawak, c. 1955, and issued by the British Council, Kuching.

J. A. R. Anderson, 'The Structure and Development of the Peat Swamps of Sarawak and Brunei', *Journal of Tropical Geography*, Vol. 18, 1964, pp. 7-16.

Annual Bulletin of Statistics, Malaysia, 1964, Department of Statistics, Kuala Lumpur, 1965.

G. Arnold, *Longhouse and Jungle: An Expedition to Sarawak*, London, Chatto and Windus, 1959.

S. Baring-Gould and C. A. Bampfylde, *A History of Sarawak under its Two White Rajahs, 1839-1908*, London, Henry Sotheran and Co., 1909.

O. Beccari, *Wanderings in the Great Forests of Borneo* (trans. E. H. Giglioli), London, Constable, 1904.

P. H. T. Beckett and D. Hopkinson, 'Some Sarawak Soils, 1. Soils of the region centred on the Usun Apau Plateau', *Journal of Soil Science*, Vol. 12, 1961, pp. 41-51.

E. Belcher (Captain Sir), *Narrative of the Voyage of H.M.S. Samarang, during the years 1843-46; employed surveying the islands of the Eastern Archipelago; accompanied by a brief vocabulary of the principal languages*, London, Reeve, Benham and Reeve, 1848, 2 Vols.

J. S. Blacklock, 'A Short Study of Pepper Culture with Special Reference to Sarawak', *Tropical Agriculture*, Vol. XXXI, No. 1, 1954, pp. 40-56.

F. Boyle, *Adventures among the Dyaks of Borneo*, London, Hurst and Blackett, 1865.

C. Brooke, *Ten Years in Sarawak*, London, Tinsley Brothers, 1866, 2 Vols.

F. G. Browne, 'The Kerangas Lands of Sarawak', *Malayan Forester*, Vol. XV, No. 2, 1952, pp. 61-73.

F. G. Browne, *Forest Trees of Sarawak and Brunei and Their Products*, Kuching, Government Printer, 1955.

Chiang Liu, 'Chinese Pioneers, A.D. 1900: The New Foochow Settlement of Sarawak', *Sarawak Museum Journal*, Vol. VI, No. 6, 1955, pp. 536-548.

Colonial Office, *An Economic Survey of the Colonial Territories*, Vol. V, The Far Eastern Territories, London, H.M.S.O., 1955.

Commonwealth Development Corporation, *Development Seminar*, Kuching, April 1964 (mimeographed).

Country Survey Series, *North Borneo, Brunei, Sarawak (British Borneo)*, Human Relations Area Files, New Haven, 1956.

G. Dalton, 'Pepper Growing in Upper Sarawak', *Sarawak Museum Journal*, Vol. I, No. 2, 1912, pp. 53-61.

M. G. Dickson, *Sarawak and Its People*, Kuching, Government Printer, 1954.

G. R. Elliston, *The Marine Fishing Industry of Sarawak*, Department of Geography, University of Hull, *Miscellaneous Series in Geography*, No. 4, 1967.

First Malaysia Plan, 1966-1970, Kuala Lumpur, Government Printer, 1965.

C. P. FitzGerald, *The Third China: The Chinese Communities in South-East Asia*, Singapore, Donald Moore for the Australian Institute of International Affairs, 1965.

J. D. Freeman, *Iban Agriculture: A Report on the Shifting Cultivation of Hill Rice by the Iban of Sarawak*, London, H.M.S.O. (Colonial Research Studies No. 18), 1955.

W. R. Geddes, *The Land Dayaks of Sarawak*, London, H.M.S.O. (Colonial Research Studies No. 14), 1954.

W. R. Geddes, *Nine Dayak Nights*, London, Oxford University Press (Oxford Paperbacks), 1961.

Government of Sarawak, *Report on Gross Domestic Product and Gross Capital Formation for the Year 1961*, Kuching, Government Printer, 1963.

E. Hahn, *James Brooke of Sarawak*, London, Arthur Barker, 1953.

N. S. Haile, *The Geology and Mineral Resources of the Strap and Sadong Valleys, West Sarawak, including the Klingkang Range Coal,*

Kuching, Government Printer, Geological Survey Department, British Territories in Borneo, Memoir 1, 1954.

N. S. Haile, *The Geology and Mineral Resources of the Lupar and Saribas Valleys, West Sarawak*, Kuching, Government Printer, Geological Survey Department, British Territories in Borneo, Memoir 7, 1957.

T. Harrisson (Editor), *The Peoples of Sarawak*, Kuching, 1959.

T. Harrisson, 'The Malays of South-west Sarawak before Malaysia', *Sarawak Museum Journal*, Vol. XI, Nos. 23-24, 1964, pp. 341-511.

L. V. Helms, *Pioneering in the Far East*, London, W. H. Allen and Co., 1882.

B. A. St. J. Hepburn, *The Handbook of Sarawak*, Singapore, Malaya Publishing House for the Government of Sarawak, 1949.

N. Heyward, *Sarawak, Brunei and North Borneo*, Singapore, Eastern Universities Press, 1963.

B. W. Hodder, 'The Economic Development of Sarawak', *Geographical Studies*, Vol. 3, 1956, pp. 71-84.

C. Hose, 'The Metamorphosis of Miri', *British Malaya*, 11, 1927, pp. 41-46.

C. Hose, *Fifty Years of Romance and Research or a Jungle-Wallah at Large*, London, Hutchinson, 1927.

E. Hose, 'Notes from the Old Days', *Sarawak Museum Journal*, Vol. X, Nos. 17-18, 1961, pp. 108-111.

International Bank for Reconstruction and Development, *Report on the Economic Aspects of Malaysia by a Mission of the International Bank for Reconstruction and Development*, Kuala Lumpur, Government Printer, 1963.

A. Ireland, *The Far Eastern Tropics: Studies in the Administration of Tropical Dependencies*, London, Archibald Constable and Co., 1905.

L. W. Jones, *Sarawak: Report on the Census of Population, 1960*, Kuching, Government Printer, 1962.

L. W. Jones, *The Population of Borneo: A Study of the Peoples of Sarawak, Sabah and Brunei*, London, Athlone Press, 1966.

H. Keppel (Captain), *A Visit to the Indian Archipelago, in H.M. Ship Maeander. With portions of the private journal of Sir James Brooke*, London, Richard Bentley, 1853, 2 Vols.

E. R. Leach, *Social Science Research in Sarawak*, London, H.M.S.O., (Colonial Research Studies No. 1), 1950.

Y. L. Lee, 'Some Factors in the Development and Planning of Land

Use in British Borneo', *Journal of Tropical Geography*, Vol. 15, 1961, pp. 66-81.

Y. L. Lee, 'Historical Aspects of Settlement in British Borneo', *Pacific Viewpoint*, Vol. 2, September 1961, pp. 187-211.

Y. L. Lee, 'The Longhouse and Dayak Settlements in British Borneo,' *Oriental Geographer*, Vol. VI, No. 1, 1962, pp. 39-60.

Y. L. Lee, 'The Population of British Borneo', *Population Studies* Vol. XV, No. 3, 1962, pp. 226-243.

Y. L. Lee, 'The Port Towns of British Borneo', *The Australian Geographer*, Vol. VIII, No. 4, 1962, pp. 161-172.

Y. L. Lee, 'Rural Settlements in British Borneo', *Tijdscrift voor Economische en Sociale Geografie*, January 1963, pp. 12-22.

Y. L. Lee, 'Padi Production and further Settlement in Borneo', *World Crops*, December 1964.

Y. L. Lee, 'The Chinese in Sarawak (and Brunei)', *Sarawak Museum Journal*, Vol. XI, Nos. 23-24, 1964, pp. 516-532.

Y. L. Lee, 'The Population of Sarawak', *Geographical Journal*, Vol. CXXXI, 1965, pp. 344-356.

Y. L. Lee, 'Agriculture in Sarawak', *Journal of Tropical Geography*, Vol. 21, 1965, pp. 21-29.

Y. L. Lee, 'The Dayaks of Sarawak', *Journal of Tropical Geography*, Vol. 23, 1966, pp. 28-39.

M. B. Leigh, *The Chinese Community of Sarawak: A Study of Communal Relations*, Department of History, University of Singapore, Singapore Studies on Malaysia No. 6, 1964.

Liang Kim Bang, *Sarawak, 1941-1957* (including E. Lee, *Sarawak in the Early Sixties*), Department of History, University of Singapore, Singapore Studies on Borneo and Malaya No. 5, 1964.

P. Liechti *et al.*, *The Geology of Sarawak, Brunei and the Western Part of North Borneo*, Kuching, Government Printer, Geological Survey Department, British Territories in Borneo, Bulletin 3, 1960, 2 Vols.

H. Longhurst, *The Borneo Story: The History of the First 100 Years of Trading in the Far East by the Borneo Co. Ltd.*, London, Newman Neame, 1956.

H. Low, *Sarawak: Its Inhabitants and Productions*, London, Richard Bentley, 1848.

H. McDougall, *Sketches of Our Life at Sarawak*, London, Society for Promoting Christian Knowledge, n.d. (c. 1882).

Malaysian Information Department, Kuching, *Sarawak in Brief*, Kuching, Government Printer, 1966.

F. S. Marryat, *Borneo and the Indian Archipelago*, London, Longmans, 1848.

Ministry of Information and Broadcasting, Malaysia, *Some Facts about Sarawak*, Kuching, Government Printer, 1964.

H. S. Morris, *Report on a Melanau Sago Producing Community in Sarawak*, London, H.M.S.O., (Colonial Research Studies No. 9), 1953.

H. S. Morris, *A Report on the Sago Industry on the Oya and Mukah Rivers*, Department of Social Anthropology, London School of Economics and Political Science, University of London, June 1964 (mimeographed).

H. Morrison, *Sarawak*, London, MacGibbon and Kee, 1957.

A. H. Moy-Thomas, 'Economic Development under the Second Rajah' *Sarawak Museum Journal*, Vol. X, Nos. 17-18, 1961, pp. 50-58.

R. Mundy (Captain), *Narrative of Events in Borneo and Celebes, down to the Occupation of Labuan: from the Journals of James Brooke, Esq., Rajah of Sarawak, and Governor of Labuan. Together with a Narrative of the Operations of H.M.S. Iris*, London, John Murray, 1848, 2 Vols.

J. L. Noakes, *Sarawak: A Report on the 1947 Population Census*, Kuching, Government Printer, 1950.

Ooi Jin-Bee, *Land, People and Economy in Malaya*, London, Longmans, Green & Co. Ltd., 1963.

R. Payne, *The White Rajahs of Sarawak*, London, Robert Hale, 1960.

T. Posewitz, *Borneo: Its Geology and Mineral Resources*, London, Edward Stanford, 1892.

J. Rawlins, *Sarawak, 1839 to 1963*, London, Macmillan, 1965.

A. J. N. Richards, 'The Migration of the Ibans and their Poetry', *Sarawak Museum Journal*, Vol. V, No. 1, 1949, pp. 77-87.

A. J. N. Richards, *Land Committee Report*, Kuching, Government Printer, 1962.

A. J. N. Richards, *The Sea Dyaks and Other Races of Sarawak; contributions to the Sarawak Gazette between 1888 and 1930*, Kuching, Borneo Literature Bureau, 1963.

F. W. Roe, *The Natural Resources of Sarawak*, Kuching, Government Printer, 1952.

H. L. Roth, *The Natives of Sarawak and British North Borneo*, London, Truslove and Hanson, 1896, 2 Vols.

'Rubber in Sabah and Sarawak', *Rubber Trends*, No. 26, June 1965, pp. 19-24.

S. Runciman, *The White Rajahs: A History of Sarawak from 1841-1946*, Cambridge, Cambridge University Press, 1960.

Sarawak Annual Report, Kuching, Government Printer, 1956-1962.

Sarawak: Annual Report of the Department of Agriculture, Kuching, Government Printer, 1956-1962.

Sarawak: Annual Report of the Forest Department, Kuching, Government Printer, 1956-1962.

Sarawak: Census of Agriculture, 1960, Kuching, n.d. (mimeographed).

Sarawak Chamber of Commerce, *Annual Report, 1964*, Kuching, 1965.

Sarawak Development Finance Corporation, *Annual Report and Statement of Accounts, 1964*, Kuching, 1965.

Sarawak Development Plan, 1964-1968, Kuching Government Printer, 1963.

Sarawak: A Digest of Agricultural Statistics, Kuching, Agricultural Economics Section, Department of Agriculture, Sarawak, December, 1965 (mimeographed).

Sarawak: A Digest of Agricultural Statistics, 1966, Kuching, Agricultural Economics Section, Department of Agriculture, Sarawak, March, 1966 (mimeographed).

Sarawak Forest Department, *Common Sarawak Timbers*, Kuching, Borneo Literature Bureau, 1961.

Sarawak Information Service, *Information on Sarawak*, Kuching, Borneo Literature Bureau, 1960

Sarawak Information Service, *The Danger Within: A History of the Clandestine Communist Organization in Sarawak*, Kuching, Government Printer, 1963.

Sarawak: Statistics of External Trade for the year 1962, Kuching, Government Printer, 1963.

J. Seal, 'Rainfall and Sunshine in Sarawak', *Sarawak Museum Journal*, Vol. VIII, No. 11, 1958, pp. 500-544.

Sendut, Hamzah, 'Resettlement Villages in Malaya', *Geography*, Vol. XLVII, 1962, 41-46.

T. H. Silcock, *Fiscal Survey Report of Sarawak*, Kuching, Government Printer, 1956.

T. H. Silcock, *The Commonwealth Economy in Southeast Asia*, London, Cambridge University Press, 1959.

J. S. Simmons *et al.*, *Global Epidemiology: A Geography of Disease and Sanitation*, Philadelphia, J. B. Lippincott Co., 1944, 2 Vols.

B. J. C. Spurway, 'Shifting Cultivation in Sarawak', *Malayan Forester*, Vol. VI, April 1937, pp. 124-128.

H. St. John, *The Indian Archipelago: Its History and Present State*, London, Longman, Brown, Green and Longmans, 1853, 2 Vols.

S. St. John, *Life in the Forests of the Far East*, London, Smith, Elder and Co., 1862, 2 Vols.

S. St. John, *The Life of Sir James Brooke, Raja of Sarawak, from his Personal Papers and Correspondence*, Edinburgh, Blackwood, 1879.

S. St. John, *Rajah Brooke: The Englishman as Ruler of an Eastern State*, London, T. Fisher Unwin, 1899.

T'ien Ju-K'ang, *The Chinese of Sarawak: A Study of Social Structure*, London School of Economics and Political Science, Monographs on Social Anthropology No. 12, Second impression, 1956.

R. O. Tilman, 'The Sarawak Political Scene', *Pacific Affairs*, Vol. XXXVII, No. 4, 1964-65, pp. 412-425.

W. H. Treacher, 'British Borneo: Sketches of Brunai, Sarawak, Labuan and North Borneo', *Journal of the Straits Branch, Royal Asiatic Society*, No. 21, 1890, pp. 19-121.

United Chambers of Commerce of Malaysia, *Malaysian Trade Review, 1964*, Kuala Lumpur, 1965.

P. W. F. de Waard, 'Pepper Cultivation in Sarawak', *World Crops*, September 1964.

J. R. D. Wall, 'Topography-Soil Relationships in Lowland Sarawak', *Journal of Tropical Geography*, Vol. 18, 1964, pp. 192-199.

Wang Gungwu (Editor), *Malaysia: A Survey*, London and New York, Pall Mall Press and Frederick Praeger, 1964.

G. E. Wilford, *The Geology and Mineral Resources of the Kuching-Lundu Area, West Sarawak, including the Bau Mining District*, Kuching, Government Printer, Geological Survey Department, British Territories in Borneo Memoir 3, 1955.

G. E. Wilford, *The Geology and Mineral Resources of Brunei and adjacent parts of Sarawak with descriptions of Seria and Miri Oilfields*, Brunei, Government Printer, Geological Survey Department, British Territories in Borneo Memoir 10, 1961.

G. E. Wilford and J. R. D. Wall, 'Karst Topography in Sarawak', *Journal of Tropical Geography*, Vol. 21, 1965, pp. 44-70.

R. A. M. Wilson, *Annual Report of the Geological Survey, Borneo Region Malaysia, 1964*, Kuching, Government Printer, 1965.

Wong Yew Ming (Editor), *Commercial and Industrial Directory of Sarawak, Sabah and Brunei*, Sibu, 1965.

T. W. W. Wood, and P. H. T. Beckett, 'Some Sarawak soils, 2. Soils of the Bintulu coastal area', *Journal of Soil Science*, Vol. 12, 1961, pp. 218-233.

Index